yellowtail snapper barramundi h
trout tuna spearfish t
ish perch rainbow run
bonito bream cobia cod
uda jewfish saratoga wahoo yellowt
ish queenfish pike dart coral trout
permit mackerel sailfish perch r
oga flathead emperor bonito bream
amberjack barracuda jewfish sar
ing marlin kingfish queenfish pike
a squid trevally scad permit macke
pon jewfish salmon saratoga flathe
mark samson fish spearfish amber
il snapper barramundi herring ma
tuna spearfish mulloway tuna squ
ch rainbow runner tailor tarpon jeu
ream cobia cod bass fingermark sa
ish saratoga wahoo yellowtail snapp
fish pike dart coral trout tuna spe
mackerel sailfish perch rainbow ri

THE BOOK OF *Lures*

Ron Calcutt and Tim Simpson

SIMON & SCHUSTER
AUSTRALIA

THE BOOK OF LURES
First published in Australia in 2004
by Simon & Schuster (Australia) Pty Ltd
Suite 2, Lower Ground Floor
14–16 Suakin Street, Pymble NSW 2073

A Viacom Company
Sydney New York London Toronto Singapore

Visit our website at www.simonsaysaustralia.com.au

National Library of Australia
Cataloguing-in-Publication data

Calcutt, Ron.
    The book of lures.

    Bibliography.
    Includes index.
    ISBN 0 7318 1208 5

    1. Fishing lures – Australia – Handbooks, manuals, etc. 2. Lure fishing –
    Australia – Handbooks, manuals, etc. I. Simpson, Tim. II. Title.

    799.10994

Cover and internal design by Avril Makula
Typeset in 11 pt on 15.5 pt Birka

Printed in China through Colorcraft Ltd, Hong Kong

10 9 8 7 6 5 4 3 2 1

To the many anglers, guides, manufacturers
and writers who over several decades have willingly
shared their knowledge and secrets with us

Contents

Prologue

The man had been fishing for hours without a sign of a fish. He wasn't worried though; he knew the poor results were due to his impatience more than anything else. He'd grown tired of sitting around the house waiting for the sun to start its final slide towards the horizon, which was when the fish would become active. Instead, he'd gone down to the narrow section of the river and started walking the bank, looking for deep bank-side undercuts, rock outcrops and areas in deep shade where fish might be laying up, waiting for the sun to go off the water before they ventured out in search of food.

The man was far from bored, even though the fishing had been quiet. To him, casting lures was an end in itself. Getting the lure to land exactly where he wanted it was a highly developed skill in which he took great pride. There was also the pleasure of reading the stream – thinking like a bass to understand which structural elements would appeal to, and offer shelter for, his quarry.

He was fishing with a lure shaped like a big fat tadpole. It had a large plastic shovel-like piece attached to the chin. Called a bib, this large plastic disc caused the lure to dive sharply, wriggling as it went. If he stopped the retrieve, the lure would float straight back to the top. This was a good choice: the fish would be in tight against the cover so he needed a lure that would dive straight down, giving the fish a chance to spot it before it moved out of range. The floating body was also a great help as it allowed him to work the lure over submerged timber without snagging. Fishing from the bank, a snag would mean either a swim or a lost lure.

He was briefly distracted by three spectacular adult brahminy kites gliding from a thick stand of trees and soaring away across the treetops; their snow-white and deep chestnut plumage was magnificent. The birds were just one more reason for being where he was.

He made a final retrieve from a section of uninteresting water where he had made a few casts, not really expecting to raise a strike where the stream was exposed to full sunlight.

He walked the bank again and came to the stand of trees from which the kites had been keeping an eye on the immediate countryside. Thick undergrowth and a dense mat of vines forced him away from the bank. He worked his way around the undergrowth and managed to get back to the water's edge while still amongst the trees. He surveyed the scene in front of him and his pulse quickened.

He had regained access to the stream at a point where it had taken a hard turn, and he was on the inside bank of that turn. The run of water always scours the outside bank on a river bend, and this was an acute turn in the stream where countless floods over the years had cut a deep channel. Making things even more interesting, the same water movement had eroded the bank so severely that a huge tree had been undercut until its roots had finally let go, bringing the tree down into the stream. With big trees on both banks, the branches had interlocked above, cutting out light to the extent that this bend was in deep, constant shade. It was always evening in this place – it was a bass paradise!

The man studied the tangled mess of branches and picked one clean opening. Even in this dark water, the fish would probably be lying under some substantial piece of timber and the small clearing in the tangle offered the opportunity to put a cast well back into the cover to fall alongside one of the bigger branches. With a tight network of twigs over the opening and all around it, the cast would have to go in close to the water in a hard flat trajectory. To get the lure in and take a fish out of there would demand a high level of expertise.

He removed the diving lure from the line and from his backpack selected a popper: a cigar-shaped lure with one end cut off and hollowed out to form a concave face. When moved with a short hard stab of the rod tip, the little lure would emit a loud 'bloop' noise that could be heard very clearly underwater. The lure had the advantages of being easy to cast with a sonic effect that would call fish in from some distance, and would remain effective when left sitting in the one place for some time. In short, one good cast would result in a lot of fishing time in the prime fish-holding zone.

The man moved slightly to his left so he was looking directly into the opening in the branches, then he lowered the rod tip and punched away a hard flat cast. A quick catch of breath as the lure flew towards the branches, then went straight through the opening, hit the water and bounced once before slamming against the main branch and flopping back into the water. The man smiled, delighted with the sheer perfection of the cast.

Below the target log, under the main trunk of the tree, a big bass was stationed close to the bottom and hard up against the timber, using a slight eddy to keep itself exactly where it was – facing upstream and in a position to see anything coming downstream into the tangle of snags. The fish heard the whack of the lure hitting the timber and the subsequent splash as it bounced back into the water. Something had fallen into the water above its position. Was it just debris from the tree or was it something edible? The fish edged forward slightly in order to see more of the surface immediately above its station.

The man let the lure sit where it was for thirty seconds that felt like an eternity, then, with a quick but short move of the rod tip, he jerked the lure forward just a few centimetres. Bloop! Then he let it sit again.

The noise told the fish that whatever had fallen into the water was alive. It was struggling somewhere immediately above and to the left, and, in the area of water the fish could see, ripples were radiating away from the cover. The tree trunk was blocking the view in that direction and so the bass drifted quietly out from the trunk and moved up to station itself under and a little back from the big branch.

Another quick stab of the rod tip. Bloop! The man's nerves were stretched as he focused intently on that one tiny spot in his universe: the popper sitting on the surface, radiating rings into the branches around it.

A slow glide forward and out from under the log and the fish could see something sitting dead still on the surface. By the silhouette, the fish knew it was something it could easily deal with if it really was something it could eat. One more movement would confirm that the form above was alive and in trouble, and therefore food.

Knowing that he had only two or three movements left before the lure would be completely out of the strike zone, the man stabbed once more. This time the little bloop turned into a boil of water behind the lure, then an eruption of the surface as the bass took the lure at the apex of a turn that had it heading back into cover in one continuous movement.

The fisherman saw it coming with the first bulge of the surface immediately behind the lure. He brought the rod up hard as the lure disappeared and took the weight of the fish. He couldn't give the fish an inch in that jungle of snags and the bass was using every ounce of strength it had to make it back to the cover. The man wasn't thinking. He was flushed with adrenaline and reacting to the unfolding situation with lightning-fast reflexes. He held the rod high to keep the fish away from deep cover he couldn't see and kept himself stationed where all the pressure he could bring to bear was directed to reverse the fish into the one opening and back into clear water.

The fish turned its head slightly and the pressure brought it around. The man recovered the slack line this gave him, shortening the length of line between him and the fish and increasing the distance between the fish and the cover. The contest had been decided.

The man worked the fish to the bank and was delighted to see the size of it. A 35-centimetre wild bass was a real trophy, and he admired the metallic bronze flanks and noted how dark the fish had become after living for some time in a pool that saw only occasional dapples of light filtered through the dense leaf canopy above. He eased the exhausted fish within range, then reached down, locked onto the shank of the treble hooks with a pair of long-nose pliers, gave one twist and felt the hook come away. He slipped one hand under the fish and gave it a push forward. It righted itself to a vertical swimming position, then glided out towards the deep water and became lost to sight.

The fisherman noticed that his hands were shaking. He smiled. Fishing doesn't get any better than this, he thought. No matter what else happened along this stream as the light started to fade, the popper strike had made the day. He'd had his fix, but he knew that as soon as the immediate memory started to fade, he'd be back for more. He was just another angler addicted to the business of taking fish on lures.

Introduction

Whether it is the visual impact of a dramatic explosion of water as a bass or barramundi hammers a surface lure, or the sudden dead stop of the line as a big kingfish inhales a jig in 30 fathoms of blue water, there is no experience in fishing to match the adrenaline rush produced by that strike.

Anglers who fish for sport have always been outnumbered by those who fish primarily to harvest food. But since the mid 1970s, the balance has gradually been swinging towards the sportfishing approach. In the last ten years there has been a flood of new anglers coming into the sport, and an accelerating number of existing anglers switching from a catch-and-kill approach to a catch-and-release or selective-harvest ethic.

The popularity of sportfishing is understandable. The extra dimension of challenge adds a spice that transforms fishing into a pursuit with a whole new flavour. This is especially true when fishing with lures. To seduce a fish into attacking an artificial creation is a more active, thoughtful, dynamic and usually much more exciting way to fish than the traditional approach of 'soaking a bait'. Lure fishing can also be a more productive way to fish.

This about-face has been accelerated in recent years by the development of a brand new and highly productive fishery in the form of stocked impoundments. These programs have been a huge success, attracting large numbers of anglers. Because almost all of the introduced fish will willingly take lures as well as baits, these new fisheries have tended to create more dedicated lure fishermen.

To cap it off, one of the most commonly available fish in all of Australia, the humble bream, has recently been found to have a distinct taste for particular lures. This has started off a new wave of specialised fishing and catching bream on lures has taken off to such a degree that Australia now has a tournament fishing circuit dedicated solely to it.

Fishing with live or dead bait is sometimes more productive than fishing with lures, although there are often situations where lures will outfish bait. But that's not really the point. These days we fish with lures because they deliver the highest possible level of angler satisfaction per outing.

A good lure fisherman is a true artist. Making a long cast with a lure armed with six razor-sharp hook points, putting that lure right alongside a snag covered in branches and leaves, without hanging it up on those same branches and leaves, requires real skill.

The selection of a lure to exploit a particular fishing environment, or one particular species of fish, is also an art. How big should the lure be? Should it dive deep or stay close to the surface? How fast should you retrieve the lure? Are there other things you could be doing to make it more attractive to a fish?

To complicate matters a little further, lures that look alike may not be alike. You can take two similar lures and one will be a real fish magnet while the other will hardly raise a fish, no matter how many hours you fish with it. These days you can buy cheap Asian copies of just about every famous lure ever created, but it is rare for any of these copies to work as well as the originals. There are real reasons for this and we'll go into the details of what makes a lure work a little later on.

The way you rig a lure, and the line you choose, may have a dramatic effect on the way even the best lures work on fish. For instance, a floating lure advertised as diving to 3 metres in depth may only dive to 1.5 metres if a heavy line is used and the line is tied directly and firmly to the lure instead of rigging it on a loop or snap.

There is a lot to learn before you can master the art of fishing with lures, but the learning is fun and you will catch many fish along the way. The rewards associated with success make the learning curve well worthwhile.

This is not a catalogue of lures, as new brands and models come on the market so fast the book would be out of date before it went on sale. Rather, it is a guide to lure types and families, because all lures are derived from a small collection of fundamental

TIM SIMPSON

themes with, literally, thousands of variations. Understanding the fundamentals – what lures do, where to use them and how to use them – is the key to understanding the fascinating world of lure fishing.

This book will help you put the pieces together so you can select the right lure for the situation, the best colours, the optimum way to rig the lure, and the delivery and retrieve styles that will fast-track your success when fishing with lures.

If you already have some experience with lures, you might want to go straight to Chapter 5, which groups lures suited to particular fishing situations and examines why they fit within each scenario.

At the end of it all, if you still have questions, we're currently setting up a facility where you can ask questions or get recommendations via email. Log on at www.lureinsight.com for more information.

CHAPTER ONE

Selecting a lure – from the fish's viewpoint

Y ou need to take a number of things into consideration when you set out to choose a lure, whether you are making choices about what to buy in the tackle shop, filling your tackle box prior to a fishing trip, or choosing the lure you will start fishing with. And a key element in making that selection is trying to see it from the fish's point of view: What is going to make the most attractive, and therefore successful, lure?

Factors you have to take into account include colour, shape and size, sound, smell, speed, presentation, depth, ease of casting and, in some situations, strength. And that's just scratching the surface.

Almost any lure will catch a fish eventually – but how long do you want to wait? A little forethought will reward you with much greater success.

Fish don't have hands!

You may ask why fish try to eat lures that look like nothing on earth? Spinnerbaits, for example, with wildly coloured plastic skirts and spinning metal blades, all held together on a piece of wire that looks like a mini coat hanger! The answer to this question is a good example of why you need to think laterally when dealing with lures. Fish strike at some lures because they have been deceived into thinking the lure is something to eat. At other times, a fish may bite something to drive the intruder out of its territory. Then there's the curiosity factor: fish don't have hands with which to prod and feel something new and interesting, so they may 'test' it with their mouths or perhaps just give it a nudge to see what it's all about.

Often, a fish will bite or suck a lure into its mouth when it has absolutely no intention of swallowing it. It is simply curious enough to want to investigate. This may explain why anglers sometimes encounter situations where they get hits on lures with a very low incidence of hook-ups. At these times you often hear it said that the fish are 'biting short'. Even in such situations, there are ways that the fish can be caught on lures. You can start by ensuring that your hooks are seriously sharp. This goes a long way to increase your chances of hooking a curious fish that is only 'feeling' your lure.

You also need to keep in mind that fish often feed successfully in conditions where the target may be sensed rather than seen. More on this below.

Colour

The role of colour in the selection of lures is subject to endless debate in fishing circles. One look in a well-stocked tackle shop will show you that there are no definitive answers, and just about any colour or pattern you can imagine has already been tried. A strong view held in one part of Australia will be dismissed in another, and in other countries the popular colours are often different again. The colours used in Australia are commonly much brighter and more vivid than those used overseas. Japanese anglers are sometimes shocked by the intensity of colour in our lures.

Some lures are presented to catch the angler rather than the fish. It is also sometimes the case that stunningly effective lures are passed over because they don't have 'angler appeal'. Black and dark purple lures are a good example. One reason you don't hear a

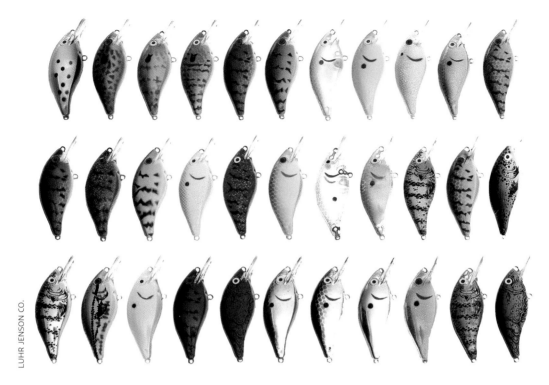

LUHR JENSON CO.

There is no one best colour scheme for all conditions. This is why a single
manufacturer will offer one model in a colour range like this

lot about the success of black lures is that they look boring so very few anglers buy them in the first place; they don't compare at all well with the brightly coloured sparkly offerings when viewed in a tackle shop. But in overcast conditions or any time the light is low, those dark lures are perfectly silhouetted against the surface light when a fish looks up towards the surface and are therefore more visible than coloured lures or lures that rely on reflected light to be seen. The same thing applies to clear lures: there are times when a clear lure, that is almost invisible to the fish, will work best. When pressured, fish are timid and, especially at close range in clear water, they may respond better to a subtle approach. With a clear lure, they can tell that a food item is there, but can't see it clearly enough to know that it is not the real thing. A likely conclusion is an attack, or at least a test bite. Remember the important concept that fish don't have hands; they have to test things with their mouths. Although incredibly successful in particular situations, clear lures are only occasionally purchased by fishermen and so don't have a big fish-catching reputation.

3

Traditional colour schemes tended to be conservative, while modern colour schemes can be quite outrageous. They all have their place in the tackle box

Another valuable lesson is that the fish don't always see what you see when viewing a lure. A shiny silver lure that reflects bright light when you look at it may become almost invisible underwater, where, instead of reflecting sunlight, it becomes a mirror for its surroundings and simply dissolves into the background.

Lures that have high visibility in the world of the fish will be seen more easily, allow faster coverage of a body of water and will probably catch more fish when they are active and aggressively feeding. There are times, however, when the fish will be sedate, wary and selective. They may also learn to associate high-visibility lures with trouble. At times like these, success may require switching to a natural and indistinct pattern with a careful presentation delivered right to the fish's front door.

Naturally, there are fishermen who swear by certain colours. The fact that they put in big hours with just those colours tends to produce a self-fulfilling prophecy: they catch more fish with those colours because they fish with them a lot more than other colours.

The majority of hard-bodied lures have a red throat area (and sometimes a tail highlight), no matter what the other colours on the lure might be. This is probably because the lure-maker is trying to represent the red gill area of a real fish, but we suspect it means more to the lure-maker, or to the marketing of the lure, than it does to a fish.

In our experience, any colour will catch fish some of the time and a broad range of common colour schemes will catch fish most of the time. But there is a big difference between catching *some* fish and catching *lots* of fish. There certainly are colour schemes which, on a particular day, will not just catch some fish, they will catch the *most* fish! These are the lures most anglers are searching for.

As mentioned previously, some fish will bite on a lure as a warning or out of sheer aggression, and the colour of the lure may stimulate this response, but there are two other important factors to consider in the make-up of a lure.

1. Realism. In our experience, this varies from unimportant most of the time to very important some of the time. Many fish are opportunistic feeders, which means they will eat whatever type of prey happens to come along. Sometimes, though, and especially with some species, they will lock on to one particular type of prey, which is one situation when realism of colour may be important.

As manufacturing techniques advance, producers are making lures that, to us, look amazingly like the real prey species they are attempting to imitate. From the fish's perspective though, the lure does not have the living counter-shading that helps the real item blend into its surroundings and camouflage. The lure will still be just a little visible to the predators – perhaps an ideal situation.

For a lure to be eaten, it must qualify by having an acceptable size, shape and movement, but even then a predator will usually want to see it before the final commitment. In most cases, the greater the distance the lure is visible, the greater the number of predators that will see it and the more fish it will catch.

2. Getting the lure noticed. For this task, a naturalised, perfectly real-looking lure is definitely not the answer. It is helpful to remember that the coloration of fish and other prey has evolved over millions of years, with the primary purpose of making them invisible so they *don't* get eaten!

A fish or creature with a colour abnormality or camouflage defect is rarely seen in nature, unless it has additional protection like poisonous spikes. This is not because such fish don't occur; it's because the predators soon remove them from the system.

In an effort to create perfect representations of real marine creatures, lure manufacturers are producing subtle finishes that are part transparent and part light reflective. If the fish can't see the lure clearly, it can't be sure it's a fake

Injury or birth defects can render a hole in their cloak of invisibility and the predators are never very far away, looking for an opportunity or an easy target. The strong are programmed to eat the weak.

Although it is important for a lure to be realistic enough to convince a fish that it is worth eating, if it is so successfully realistic that it also blends in with its background, then it will be seen and eaten far less often, which means you will catch fewer fish. The most important things to entice a strike are simulating the outline and action of the prey and then simply providing enough contrast to the surroundings so it can be seen.

Colour is probably the most complex and difficult to evaluate aspect of lure fishing. Yes, some fish do see colour as we see it, while other fish see all colours as shades of grey. Most species see a combination of some colours and greys, but even then – like colour-blind humans – fish are very good at differentiating between the shades. However, regardless of the way in which fish see colour, you may find that one day they will only eat green lures with yellow stripes and the next they'll eat anything you throw in the water.

In some situations strong colour schemes will help to get a lure noticed

Many factors determine the effectiveness of colour, including the colour and clarity of the water at the time, sky colour or the colour of a dominant prey in the area. The level or intensity of light is also a factor and will vary with the time of day and the density of cloud cover. Some of these things we can take into consideration; others will always remain the secrets of the fish. Colour selection is just one of the interesting challenges associated with lure fishing, and the prime reason why we end up with large selections of lures bulging from our tackle boxes.

Anglers often like to imagine the world of the fish and hold forth with wonderful stories of what works and why. But many of the theories put forward are wild speculation and have been formed with little knowledge of the facts. For a better understanding, let's look at some of the latest science on the subject so we can make some real decisions about how to increase the visibility and contrast of our lures and therefore our success. The sections following will be a little like going back to school, but, hey, if the teacher had told us this stuff applied to fishing lures, we would all have learned it back then!

Light in a dark world

Much of the light that hits the water's surface is reflected off it. Even in full sunlight, perhaps only half the light gets through. When the sun is at an angle, even more light is bounced away, although, due to surface waves and refraction, it doesn't drop as much as you might imagine. It's during the twilight period that the change is dramatic. In the half-hour before sunset, the light level begins to fall. Then, in the thirty minutes after sunset, the light level crash-dives: in clear surface waters it can plummet from moderate daylight levels of 10 000 lux to 0.0003 lux! At sunrise the process is reversed. In the thirty minutes before the sun clears the horizon, the light level again goes through a major transformation.

This twilight half-hour is a major feeding period for many predators, as their eyes are adapted to adjust quickly to the new light conditions. This enables them to discern the contrast of their prey while the prey species is still adjusting. For this brief period the predators have a major advantage: the prey simply don't see them coming.

The total amount of light in the water also decreases rapidly with depth. Even in the clearest ocean water, there is little light at all below 900 metres. In coastal or inland waters, where descending light hits suspended particles, the amount of light getting through is severely reduced.

It works in the same way as the sunlight we get on the ground. When the sky is blue, we get full sun and make a strong shadow. With a little fine cloud, the brightness is slightly reduced and our shadow less distinct. As the particles of water vapour (cloud) become denser and block more of the sun, the shadow fades even more, until, by the time the particles pack down into a huge black storm cloud, our shadow is gone and the amount of light getting through is only a fraction of what it is on the other side of the cloud.

In coastal waters, some light may penetrate as deep as 200 metres, but in rivers or lakes with typical levels of silt and plankton, there may be little light past 10 metres. In really coloured water, it may be dark 0.5 of a metre down!

A keen angler can roughly gauge the penetration of light from the comfort of a boat in much the same way that a scientist might. Lower a white object or disc (termed a Secchi disc by scientists) until it is on the verge of disappearing from sight. The disc is only visible at that point because light has reached through the water, reflected off the disc and then travelled back to the surface and your eyes. By doubling the depth of the white object, you get a pretty good idea of how far the light can travel through that particular water before it is absorbed or scattered.

There will still be some light down to perhaps three times the depth of the disc, but there will be no shadows as it is dim scattered light which is bounced in all directions as it reflects off the suspended particles. Below this level, it is very dark: perhaps less

TIM SIMSPON

We used to stop fishing with lures as the light faded. Now we know that some lures can be highly effective from evening into the hours of darkness

than 1 per cent of the light at the surface remains. But even then, don't think that fish can't see under these conditions. Those with super-sensitive low-light cells (rods) in their eyes are capable of seeing fairly well at close range even on a moonless night.

Despite the darkness, fish obviously feed and seem to manage quite well, although the reality of what they see, even in the middle of the day, is quite different to how most anglers imagine it.

One laboratory test on American largemouth bass (McMahon & Holanov) showed that the bass were able to feed with 95–100 per cent accuracy in light levels ranging from daylight (around 50 000 lux) to full moonlight (0.03 lux). Their accuracy fell to only half that, however, when the light dropped to the equivalent of starlight (0.0003 lux). Interestingly, the bass were still able to catch a small percentage of the prey in total blackness, which shows they have some ability to feed without the use of sight at all. The tests also suggested that the maximum depth a bass would be able to feed visually at night, even during a full moon, would be around 30 per cent of its daytime range.

Colour down below

Sunlight is referred to as white light. White is a mixture of all colours; in fact, if you paint a disc with the colours of the rainbow and spin it on a drill, it will turn white. The various colours travel as vibrations or waves and each has a different wavelength. Sunlight is on a completely different frequency scale, but it travels in a very similar way to sound, except that instead of hearing a (short-wave) high-pitched squeal we see a short-wavelength colour like violet. At the other end of the scale, instead of a long-wave sound like a deep rumble we see a long-wavelength colour like red. It's the same principle but with a different sense organ picking up a different medium. The colour spectrum goes from ultra-violet at the short-wave end through violet, blue, green, yellow, orange, red and far-red to infra-red at the long-wave end.

As sunlight travels through water, the colours are gradually filtered out. It is important to remember that the colours are filtered out by the *total distance* that the light travels, whether that is vertical, as in depth, or simply from a horizontal distance at the surface. A red lure at the surface of clear blue water will appear as red because there is plenty of red light available there. But if we approach that lure from the surface 30 metres away, it will appear as black, then grey, then orange, then red as we get closer.

Which colours are filtered out and how quickly they are removed depends on the type and density of particles suspended in the water. The colour the water appears to us is the colour that is *not* being filtered out; it is being reflected upwards. A similarly coloured lure will therefore appear brighter than other colours, as its colour is not being filtered out either.

To get an idea of how the loss of colour progresses, let's start by looking at the near idyllic situation in clear natural water. In clear water, the reds are removed from the spectrum first. At a depth of 20 metres there will be no more than 1 per cent of red light left, so anything that started at the surface as pure red will have faded through various shades of reddish-grey to be now almost totally black. Even so, although at this depth pure red has been filtered out, all the other colours, including shades of red-orange, remain; however, any colour made from a blend with red will be darker, as the pure red portion will have turned dark grey or black.

Going deeper still, the oranges and then the yellows are removed next. Few shades of yellow exist below 40 metres. Further still, following the yellow-greens, the pure green is next to go, turning to black by 100 metres. The last to disappear are the blues, the dominant colour, until light is almost completely removed by around 900 metres.

On the open ocean, where the water is nearly crystal clear, light can penetrate way down, so the dominant colour being reflected back to our eyes is blue.

The process of filtering out any colour, or blend of colour, is gradual and continuous, just as the colours of a rainbow gradually blend from one colour to the next without any defined edges. In actual fact, the colours do not completely disappear. They get filtered out at a consistent rate that varies with the clarity of the water, but they sometimes reduce so quickly that before long only a tiny fraction remains.

The scientist Curt Mobley studied these effects in his book *Light and Water*. Here is a summary of how he describes the reduction in red, for example: in clear ocean water, red reduces in strength by 20 per cent for every metre of depth. At 1 metre it is at 80 per cent strength; at 5 metres it is down to 33 per cent; by 10 metres it is 11 per cent; and by 20 metres there is only 1 per cent of the colour remaining.

In dirty coastal water the process is the same, except that the increased impurities filter the red out much faster. Here the colour reduces by around 50 per cent for every metre of depth. This means that at 1 metre there is only half of the red left; at 2 metres there is 25 per cent; and at 5 metres there is 3 per cent. By 10 metres there is only one-thousandth of the amount of red that there was at the surface.

When the water itself is coloured, the order and rate of removal of colour in the light changes. With the addition of impurities like silt, algae, minerals, stains, plankton

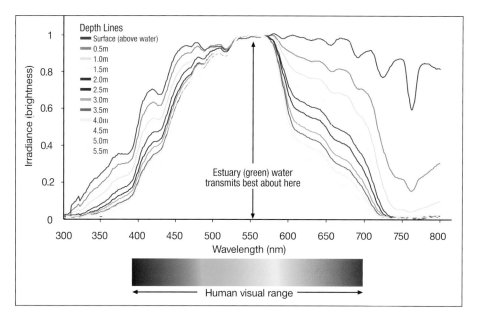

Different water colours filter light at different rates. This chart of green estuary
water sampled at Stradbroke Island in Queensland by scientists Nathan Hart and Justin
Marshall shows how much of a colour remains at various depths after the filtering
effect. To read the chart, select a coloured depth line and then see from the left scale
how much of a particular wavelength (lower scale) is reflected

and so on, the story gets especially interesting. These suspended substances are what
give the water its colour. The particles will absorb (and eliminate) some colours while
reflecting others – which make up the colour we see. By looking at the colour and
clarity of the water, we can estimate what colours may exist below and how far down
they may reach. Let's look at a couple of examples.

Water loaded with plankton reflects green light while absorbing much of the red
and blue light. Some red and blue may reach down to 7 or 10 metres but may also be
lost in the first few metres. When considered more closely, the water is actually a
yellow-green in most cases, therefore yellow and green will reach a greater depth than
any other colour (as the other colours have been filtered out). The particles are also
blocking a lot of the light in general, so even the yellow and green won't penetrate far.
If the water is fairly clear they may reach 30 metres or so, but if it's pea soup the light
will turn black way before this depth.

In another example, a river or lake stained brown with silt and minerals may have a surface visibility of only a few metres. The water will filter out almost all the blue in the first metre or so, then the green, then all the yellow by 3–4 metres. This leaves orange and red as the dominant colours. Red never (or hardly ever) penetrates more than 10 metres and in water like this, because of the silt, it probably won't get past 5 metres, but red will still be the brightest and most dominant colour. Below 5 metres, virtually all colour turns black and the water is near to total darkness. It is interesting to note that in water like this, brown is a popular lure colour, and dark brown is the colour you get when you add a little black to red–orange. The same colour will also result when using a deep diving red lure.

How fish see colour

The range of colour sensitive cells (cones) in the eyes of fish is usually not the same as in our eyes. Fish may be sensitive to different portions of the colour spectrum and some are even capable of seeing colours that we can't see, like ultra-violet. The combination of colours we see may appear completely different to them. They also may not have the resolution that we do.

As an example of how things may be different in the fish world, look at tropical coral-reef fish. They live in crystal clear, bright water where you'd imagine a fish with intense yellow and blue bands would stand out like a sore thumb. As recent research by scientist Justin Marshall shows, at close range the colours are highly distinguishable and the fish use them to communicate with one another. But at a longer range, because the colours are from opposite ends of the spectrum and because of the poor resolution of the fishes' eyes, the yellow and blue actually blend together and become an inconspicuous grey. What started out as intense vivid colours actually turns into camouflage!

The cones in fishes' eyes are usually adapted to see the colours that exist in the waters where they live. For example, fish in murky rivers, which absorb most of the blue and green light, will probably have eyes adapted to sense only the red–orange–yellow portion of the spectrum. Other colours will appear grey to black.

From an angler's point of view, a colour can still be successful on a lure even after that colour has been filtered out by the water, because that colour doesn't actually disappear; instead, it turns black. In a world of green or blue, or even when simply viewed as a silhouette against the brighter light from above, a black lure still gives contrast and stands out.

Contrast

The need for a 'correct' colour is probably overstated. Fish use their limited colour vision to assist them to distinguish the contrast of their prey against the background. Our selection of colour, therefore, can help most by offering the lure greater contrast. If the lure gets seen, it often gets eaten.

For a lure to stand out well in the depth where it will be fished, you need to select a colour that contrasts well against the background light colour yet still exists in sufficient strength so the lure is bright. The colours with the most intensity, that still contrast with the surrounding water, are those that lie either side of the water colour on the colour spectrum.

In blue water, those colours are indigo blue and green, with the addition of yellow if it's green–blue water. Green water is often slightly yellowish, so the strongest contrasting colours there would be blue–green and yellow–orange. Moderately coloured brown water would show greens and reds, and in really muddy shallow water, if any colour was visible at all, it would be red that appeared the brightest.

A pitch-black lure shows up well as a dark silhouette against any background and especially well when viewed from underneath or against a light-coloured bottom. A white lure, especially pure-white, will also contrast particularly well in most conditions, and even more so against a dark background colour.

To summarise: contrast is what will enable a fish to see your lure. You can achieve contrast with a carefully selected colour or the universally successful black or white. Paying attention to the selection will pay off even more in difficult low-light conditions such as deep water, heavily coloured water, and at dawn and dusk.

Shading and counter-shading

Baitfish species, as well as predators, are counter-shaded so they won't be seen. When looked at from above, their back blends into the background beneath them, whether that's the tan of a shallow sandy bottom or the darkness of the depths. Their sides are reflective, perhaps with a subtle pattern that breaks up the outline and blends even better with the side-on background it's mimicking. The belly is also silver, or certainly light in colour, because, when seen from below, the background will be the silvery shimmering surface of the water or at least the lighter glow coming from above.

If a fish can find your lure and see it against the surroundings, it may be temped to bite it. By selecting the right colour that contrasts with the background water and lighting conditions, you can substantially increase the chance of your lure being seen

As long as the fish remain upright and aligned, their reflective sides will make them nearly invisible. If they change their angle even a little, their cloaking is reversed, advertising their position like a beacon.

The shading and counter-shading added to a lure's basic colour pattern can help to get it noticed (or keep it hidden) in the same way. Bars or vertical bands on a lure will also tend to contrast and make the lure more visible in still or deep water with uniform

Fish are intricately coloured with dark backs that match the bottom or depths beneath them and silvery white on the underneath that blends with the surface light or reflects the water colour. This 'counter shading' is to make sure they don't get noticed. Two of these lures are reverse counter shaded — so they do get noticed!

Against a uniform background, striping may help to add contrast to a lure, but remember, striping is used by fish close to a ruffled surface to blend in. In the same situation that a fish would use it, a lure might also be harder to see

lighting, but it may be a mistake to add them to a lure used in the shallows. If you've ever noticed the dancing lines and diamond patterns on the bottom of a shallow swimming pool, you have seen the effect of flickering light caused by wavelets on the surface. These shafts of light give a dappled appearance to the underwater background. This is why fish are often blotched with rippled lines on their backs or vertical bars down their flanks. These help to camouflage them when they move about in the surface layers where there are bright light, shadows and flickering light. For the same reason fish use them, bars or lines will help to hide a lure when the light is flickering from surface waves above.

There's another pattern feature which, although it may seem small and insignificant, can make a serious difference to the detection of your lure. Some specialised movement-detecting nerves have been found in the eyes of fish, which are specifically designed to detect small dots that contrast with the background. The addition of suitably prominent eyes, with distinct contrasting pupils, can add significantly to the chance of a lure being noticed.

Flash

When upright in the water, the sides of a baitfish mirror its immediate environment, making it hard to see. If the fish breaks from that stance its counter-shading is out of alignment and its sides may well catch the sun and flash. When it does, there goes the camouflage … and there goes the dinner bell. Remember that any sign of panic or distress underwater singles a fish out and signals an easy meal to any predator within range.

Incorporating flash into the design and use of a lure not only makes it visible from a much greater distance than colour alone could achieve, it also triggers an attack response in the predators that are conditioned to eat vulnerable prey.

Although many lures have a respectable swimming action built in, top anglers often fish them with a lot of erratic rod-tip action that jerks and throws the lure off balance. This causes the lure to roll a little, creating a sudden flash of light – typical of an injured or alarmed fish.

Some lures lend themselves to flash more than others. A rounded surface will create a steady and thin line of shine, as only a small and consistent amount of the surface is facing and reflecting the sun at any one time. It's like the difference between a street sign and a police car: a steady light does not get noticed anywhere near as much as a flashing one.

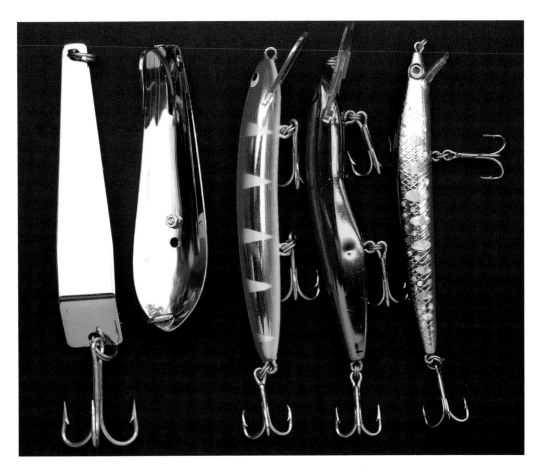

A rounded body will only reflect light on a small area of the lure as can be seen
in the lures second from left and centre. Flat areas on the lure at the left and
the two lures to the right create a far greater flash effect

When sunlight hits the surface of water it is reflected off or bent downwards. Some
light then gets reflected in all directions off suspended particles, but most travels
vertically, regardless of the sun's position.

An angular or multifaceted surface may have many small panels and some of them
will probably be facing the sun at any particular time and reflecting an intermittent
flash. The amount of flash is determined by the reflectivity of the surface as well as the
size and quantity of panels catching the sun. Most plastic holographic and prism tapes
(and inserts) work the same way. These give a great silvery or colourful sheen to the
lure and sparkle brightly, but, as far as flash goes, they can't compete with the range or

intensity given off by a broad, flat mirror-like surface. The greater the flat surface areas and the more reflective those flat sections are, the larger the flash will be.

Lures made from stainless steel or chromed or nickel-plated metal have been available for many years and some are polished to such a fine finish that they shine like a mirror. A lure like this, with wide flat sides, will certainly broadcast a large flash if the panels are at the right angle to the sun.

Interestingly, some manufacturers supplying the recreational salmon fishing industry in North America offer a premium range of metal lures plated with a thin coat of real silver or gold, as the precious metals give a brighter and stronger reflection (and flash) than other finishes. It may seem extravagant, but anglers in situations where the amount of flash decides how many fish they are likely to catch may consider doing a deal with their local jeweller to 'hot up' their lure collection! For the rest of us, it's worth keeping an eye on how reflective our shiny lures are and simply giving them a polish on our shirt or with metal cleaner if they become tarnished.

Manufacturers these days are able to add a metallised 'chrome' finish to timber, plastic and even moulded polyurethane lures. The result is far more reflective than prism tape and gives excellent gleam potential. If incorporated into a thoughtful design, it not only looks realistic but will give off a very intense flash if there are flat panels and a rolling action designed for the purpose.

The colour of the flash is worth considering. It is widely thought that a flash of gold is the most successful in dirty or coloured water and that a silver-based flash will perform better in clearer waters.

One final crucial point to remember: a flash will only occur when the surface is at the right angle to the sun. At all other times, a highly reflective surface will be doing just that: mirroring its surroundings and so becoming nearly invisible. A lure that uses a reflective finish should roll or move so that the flash panels are intermittently facing the sun. Otherwise, a colour may be more successful.

Glowing lures

There are two kinds of glowing lures: fluorescent and luminescent/phosphorescent. Many people confuse these terms, but it is important to get it right as they are completely different. Fluorescent colours require existing light to function, while luminescence creates its own light.

Fluorescence

Fluorescent colours can make a lure brighter and more visible. They can also enable a colour to exist at a depth where it should have been filtered out.

As discussed previously, light is split into different wavelengths, starting at one end of the spectrum with ultra-violet, which has a very short wavelength, progressing through violet, indigo, blue, green, yellow, orange, red and far-red to infra-red, which has a long wavelength.

Fluorescent colours are brighter because, as well as reflecting their own colour, they are able to convert a portion of any other shorter wavelength that hits them and reflect that as their colour too. As long as some other shorter wavelength colours exist at that depth, the fluorescent lure will be brighter and more colourful.

To understand which colours will fluoresce in the water you are fishing, refer back to pages 10–13 to check which colours remain at the depth where your lure will be seen. A fluorescent colour on your lure will only be intensified if light in a colour with a shorter wavelength exists at that depth.

Some fluorescent materials require ultra-violet light to work, but others are modified to fluoresce in daylight. The latter are better for lures as ultra-violet has very limited penetration into any but the clearest of waters.

Even in heavily coloured water, where there is little light and visibility is poor, the slightly brighter colour of a fluorescent may give you an edge and be just enough to help your lure stand out and be eaten.

Luminescence/Phosphorescence

This is the luminous glow-in-the-dark material found on watch dials or anything that requires night-time visibility. These days, luminescence comes as paint, stick-on tape, beads, tubing and lure eyes, or even long-lasting chemical light sticks. It is usually a pale green colour in daylight and glows an eerie green-yellow in the dark, but is available in other colours too. Pale green seems to give the brightest glow, but blue and even pink are also available, and we've even seen plastic lure skirts with luminous additives that appear green in daylight but glow pink in the dark, and others that look pink in daylight but glow green in the dark! The idea of making a lure glow so that it stands out and attracts fish is not new. Many lures, especially Sabiki rigs and night-

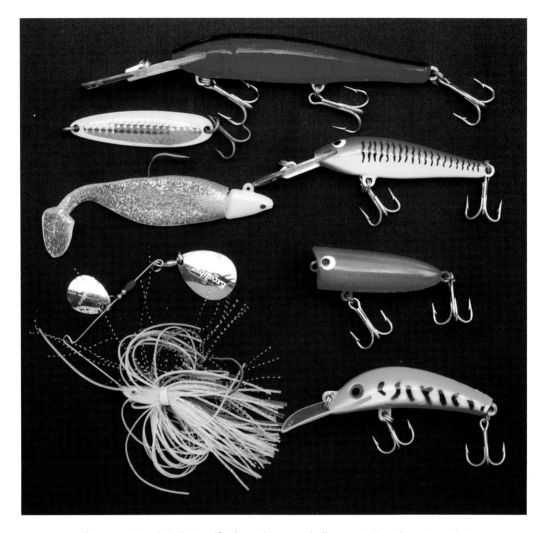

Fluorescent paints intensify the colours and allow certain colours to exist
at depths where they would normally have been filtered out

time or dark-water lures like deep-water jigs and squid lures, have incorporated some luminescence as a standard feature for some time.

Surprisingly, the many anglers who have tried adding chemical light sticks to their lures or painting large portions with lumo paint for night-time fishing have had limited success. Research by former US fisheries biologist Dick Sternberg reveals that the secret may lie in the intensity of the glow. Luminescence certainly seems to help, but too much brightness can scare the fish rather than luring them. Even when using chemical

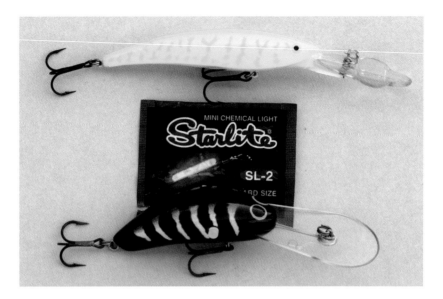

Luminescent lures are designed to glow and be seen in the dark.
The top lure has a luminous finish, while the non-luminous Custom
Crafted lure below accepts a tiny chemical light stick

light sticks, Sternberg found the trick was to activate the sticks in the morning, then use them in the evening when they had settled to a dim glow.

Sternberg's tests with lumo paint, fished alongside regularly painted lures, showed equal results in daytime; substantially worse results when the lure was entirely covered in glow; but often six times as many fish when only a small or faint stripe of glow was applied. The clearer the water, the lower the glow intensity required.

Luminescence certainly seems to be something worth experimenting with, and not only at night. In any low-light or dark situation, like twilight or deep jigging, or in heavily coloured water, a little glow may go a long way towards putting more fish on your lure. Even in bright daylight and clear water, there is growing evidence that luminosity in a lure can make a noticeable difference. The lure may look exactly the same to our eyes, but perhaps the fish pick up on something we don't see. Sabiki jig rigs are nowhere near as effective without the standard luminous bead or paint on the head of each lure, and some of the most consistently successful colour patterns in skirted trolling lures feature luminosity in the skirts.

One last point: if using lures or other tackle with a luminous finish, be wary of leaving them in the sun. Some will 'burn' and turn grey if exposed to too much strong sunlight.

Shape

Many fish are opportunistic feeders, eating anything that happens to come by and looks appetising. While it is sometimes true that a very limited range of colours or colour patterns may be the only things taking fish in a given situation, it is more often the case that fish will be taking lures in a wide range of colours and colour patterns. When fish can't be made to bite on the old favourites in the tackle box, most fishermen start working their way through the box, trying a variety of different colours. However, it might be that the answer lies not in the colour of the lure, but in the size and shape of the body and the depth and speed at which the lure is presented.

In his documentary series 'The Blue Planet', David Attenborough showed some remarkable underwater scenes of fish feeding. A huge concentration of sardines had attracted small tuna to what amounted to a sardine massacre. As time went by, very large tuna arrived to join the feast, then billfish and finally enormous numbers of dangerously switched-on sharks turned up for the banquet. The interesting thing is that the predators further up the feeding chain, which commonly prey on one another, were happy to leave each other alone and feast together on the sardines. Why did all the predators focus solely on the sardines? Surely it would be a better proposition for a shark to take a big and very satisfying tuna rather than chase around after tiny individual sardines?

We're not going to attempt to answer those difficult questions; the fact is, this obsessive focus on an abundant bait is not uncommon predator behaviour. In some

TIM SIMPSON

When fish feed on a particular bait species in any given area, it can be critically important to match the size and profile of that bait, even if it may not be possible to match its colour. Any of the three lures shown here get very close to the bony bream at bottom left

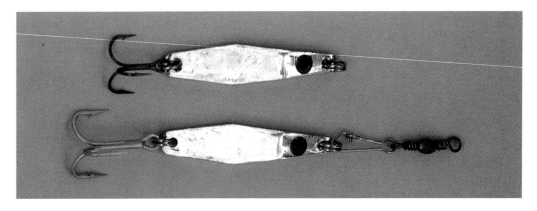

You probably think one of these lures is bigger than the other. In fact they are both
exactly the same size, but the addition of a big hook and snap swivel makes the bottom
lure look twice the size of the top lure. That could cost you fish

cases, it is nature's way of restoring the balance. For various reasons, there may be a
population explosion in a particular species so Mother Nature seems to throw a switch
in the brains of the predators that feed on that species, causing them to ignore
everything else. In effect, nature says: there's a problem over there – go fix it. When the
numbers are back to normal and the balance is restored, the predators go back to their
'regular' setting. This sort of behaviour is often seen during mass migrations and
spawning aggregations.

The tricky part for an angler is that when you come across fish feeding with such
single-minded focus on a prevalent bait species, you're only likely to get them to take
an offering which is exactly the same size and shape as the species under siege.

Interestingly, if you have the size and silhouette right, it often doesn't matter what
colour the lure is. A bright red and black striped lure may be readily taken in the middle
of a school of silver baitfish, but a silver lure that is too big will be ignored every time.

Fly fishermen have long talked about 'matching the hatch': tying flies on the bank
of a stream when a particular insect is hatching and the trout are feeding obsessively
on that single insect. Sometimes the fishing flies bear little resemblance to the real
insect when viewed from our perspective, but when viewed against the light from
below that imitation may look very much like the real thing.

Situations change from day to day, hour to hour, in the underwater world. Today's
obsessively single-minded feeders may be eating anything they can find tomorrow, or
they might be just as obsessive about a different food source. Today they could be

chasing down food as if their lives depended on that single morsel; tomorrow they could watch the same thing swim within a centimetre of their nose without wiggling a fin. The lesson to take from this is that while anglers like to believe a change of colour will always do the trick, it may be more important to make changes on the basis of size and profile, or speed and action.

Size

Even when matching the specific size of a food source is not essential, there are certain advantages to be gained by selecting a small lure or a large one.

A small lure has the advantage of appealing to a wider range of fish species and sizes, and even with relatively tiny lures there is always the chance of a very large fish. For example, we've seen large flathead and mulloway of over 25 kilograms taken on tiny soft plastics while targeting bream. Marlin 3 metres long have taken lures less than 10 centimetres in length, and huge Murray cod have been caught on small trout spinners. Although you never know what might jump on, the main outcome from going small will simply be greater numbers of small fish.

Don't be afraid to use big lures, especially when seeking big fish or when trying to separate the bigger ones from a school. The body of this timber lure is 27 centimetres long and weighs nearly half a kilo, but when you consider the lure in comparison to the reality of the situation, it's not a giant. It's simply proportional to the type of prey a fish like this 14-kilogram jobfish would want to eat

TIM SIMPSON

On the other hand, there can be good reasons for increasing your lure size, especially if quality rather than quantity is your main motivation. A larger lure represents a bigger meal, which gives a fish more incentive to catch and eat it. It can carry larger hooks and a stronger, heavier leader, which makes a hook-up more secure. A larger lure is attractive to larger fish and is often capable of diving or sinking to the deeper level required to reach those fish. It may be easier to cast and, most importantly, it can be detected more easily. A large lure is visible from a greater distance and the pulse its swimming action puts through the water will be stronger and carry further than a smaller lure.

The use of big and very big lures is a great way to attract really large fish. A very big lure will also separate a big fish from a bunch of average fish, as it may be too big for the smaller fish to handle or cause them to hesitate just long enough to let the big one shoulder its way through the pack and nail it. This is a successful tactic for many species, from trout to dog-tooth tuna. Of course, the scale of what makes a very big lure will be in proportion to the species being chased. For the trout, this may be a fingerling-sized minnow of 14 centimetres, while for the dog-tooth it may be a monster lure of 35 centimetres plus and weighing nearly a kilo itself!

Sound – with feeling!

So far we have looked at the colour, shape and size of lures, all of which target just one of a fish's senses: sight. While sight is important to most fish, and particularly important to some fish, good vision is not always available and therefore is not necessarily the dominant sense in all species.

As colour and distance vision is of limited use underwater, for many fish sound is of even greater importance. This is especially true when the water is dirty or dark.

The water's surface reflects almost all sound, so little of what we hear on the ground actually gets through, unless via a structure that passes the sound-wave vibrations from above water through the surface. This interface could be the hull of a boat, a semi-submerged log or rock, or the riverbank itself. Of course, there are lots of sounds that are created underwater too.

It's actually very noisy underwater, especially along the saltwater coastline. Water is almost 1000 times denser than air, which makes it a much better carrier for sound. Sound travels a great deal further and almost five times faster in water than it does in

All of these lures produce noise of some kind. Two have multiple metal
blades designed to bang together, two have loud internal rattles and one pushes
a bubble of air to make a popping sound

air. Interestingly, in his co-authored book *Through the Fish's Eye*, US ichthyologist (fish
scientist) John Clark says that a sound is 150 000 times harder to produce underwater
than it is in the air. Despite that minor technical difficulty, many fish, animals,
crustaceans, natural events like waves, as well as people, boats and lures, are able to
create noise underwater. With a little careful management these noises can be very
useful: while some sound can scare fish away, the right sounds can also be used to
attract them.

Sound is a series of vibrations that, in both air and water, radiate out from the
source as a throb of waves. If you've ever put your hand over a bass speaker when the
music's turned up loud, you'll remember how much of a thump in the air the sound
waves can generate. If you've stood close to the speakers at a rock concert, you were

probably almost blown over by the force of the sound! In contrast, if you put your hand over the tweeter speaker, even when turned up loud, you'll find that high-pitched, or short-wavelength, sounds do not move as much air. These invisible waves, or pulses, behave the same underwater. Deep-pitched sounds and other low-frequency pulses will 'push' more water than the more subtle higher-pitched vibrations.

Sound waves move through the water in two ways:

1. In a series of waves that radiate out from the source as a series of pressure changes. These sounds can travel great distances and are often referred to as the 'far field'. Fish hear these sounds through the vibrating of the otoliths (stone-like calcium bones) in their ears.

2. By causing water particles to move back and forth (particle displacement). Fish pick up these sound waves via their lateral line within a limited maximum range of 5–15 metres, depending on the wave's volume or strength. This zone is termed the 'near field'.

Although their ears are internal and therefore invisible, fish have particularly specialised hearing and can detect sound over a great distance. You might say fish actually have two types of hearing. They hear as we do, through a pair of ears, and they also have a secondary 'hearing' system based in the lateral line on their sides, which interprets low-frequency vibrations in the water, much as we would use sonar.

Just as the sound waves we hear vary in frequency, so these sound waves vary underwater. And, like us, what the fish hears is related to pitch (frequency) and loudness (decibels). Humans can hear sound waves in a range of frequencies from around 20–20 000 cycles per second (termed a Hertz) and, at its most effective, between 3 000–4 000 Hertz; whereas the sensitivity of a fish – that is, the range of sounds it can detect – will vary between species.

The range of sounds that are useful to a fish may depend on the level of background noise of its environment. Fish species that live in quiet murky surroundings, like some calm freshwater environments, are likely to have more sensitive hearing and rely more heavily on sound than fish that live in very noisy habitats, like the clearer waters of the saltwater surf zone.

The perception of sound waves through the ears of a fish is, in most cases, limited to an upper level of 600–3 000 Hertz, but in some species, like minnows and carp, it may reach 10 000 Hertz or more. The range that fish are most sensitive to is usually between 200–800 Hertz. (As a guide, Middle C on a piano vibrates at 261 Hertz and

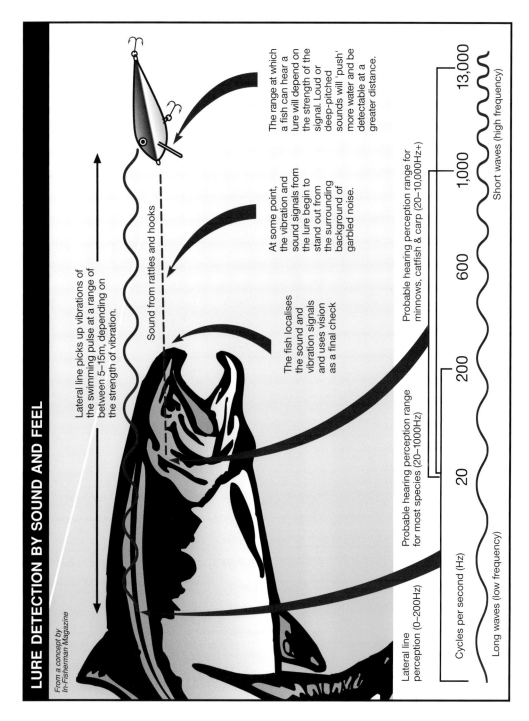

LURE DETECTION BY SOUND AND FEEL

From a concept by
In-Fisherman Magazine

Lateral line picks up vibrations of the swimming pulse at a range of between 5–15m, depending on the strength of vibration.

Sound from rattles and hooks

The range at which a fish can hear a lure will depend on the strength of the signal. Loud or deep-pitched sounds will 'push' more water and be detectable at a greater distance.

At some point, the vibration and sound signals from the lure begin to stand out from the surrounding background of garbled noise.

The fish localises the sound and vibration signals and uses vision as a final check

Probable hearing perception range for minnows, catfish & carp (20–10,000Hz+)

Probable hearing perception range for most species (20–1000Hz)

Lateral line perception (0–200Hz)

13,000

1,000

600

200

20

Cycles per second (Hz)

Short waves (high frequency)

Long waves (low frequency)

When sound becomes feeling

The lateral line which allows a fish to 'feel' movement nearby can be seen
clearly on this impoundment barra held by Ron Calcutt. It was taken on a bibbed
stickbait in shallow water on a near moonless night

the highest note a soprano singer might hit is around 1500 Hertz). The lowest
frequency that fish ears are likely to hear is comparable to the lowest sounds we
humans would hear: around 20 cycles per second.

The lateral line picks up sound in a different way. It picks up particle displacement,
or movement, in the water and is therefore only sensitive to the short distance covered
by the near-field sound vibrations. The lower limit for some fish species may reach way
beyond the ability of human hearing, as low as vibrations of only 1 Hertz, although
most will have a limit of around 20 Hertz. The upper limit of detection by the lateral
line is vibrations of around 200 Hertz. As you may have noticed, there is a crossover
area where some sounds are sensed by both the lateral line and the ears. To get an idea
of how these lower frequencies compare to the sounds we might recognise: the deepest
note a bass singer might reach is around 60 Hertz, as is the deepest note from a cello.
The lowest note on a piano is around 30 Hertz.

The word 'hearing' does not adequately describe what takes place when the fish is
sensing sound with its lateral line. The lateral line picks up pulses via the vibration or
movement of rows of micro hairs in tiny nerve-filled sensors along its length. The

message it conveys to the brain is similar to how we might feel out our surroundings with our hands. The fish receive such an accurate picture from these signals that scientists often refer to this sense as 'distant touch'.

The near-field displacement waves penetrate only a short distance through the water before they fade and become impossible for the fish to detect; just as the range of sound humans hear depends on volume (decibels), the range of the near-field pulse depends on its strength or force.

There is also evidence that low-frequency sound may be weakened or even cancelled out close to the water's surface. Researcher Tom Dunne found that, due to a phenomenon called the Lloyd mirror effect, the water's surface releases pressure from long (low-frequency) sound waves at shallow depths. Recordings of a cruiser made at depths of 1.5 and 7.5 metres showed that at 1.5 metres sound waves with frequencies below 2000 Hertz were up to half the strength of those at 7.5 metres. This may explain why some whales and dugongs are hit by slow-moving boats: they simply don't hear the boat coming until too late, due to all the other noise around them. Interestingly, a fast-moving boat makes higher-pitched sounds and is much easier for them to hear and avoid. This has interesting implications for anglers too, while trolling or positioning!

A strong force, like that from a big fish (or lure), will travel further and be detected more easily than a small fish (or lure). A whole school of fish is also much easier to sense than the more subtle beat of a single fish which may be missed in all the background noise around it. This may explain the success of strong wide-actioned lures that 'push' a lot of water in muddy freshwater, where predators rely more on their lateral line than sight when hunting.

It is commonly thought that the near-field, low-frequency vibrations are detectable by most fish only within a range of 5–15 metres, but scientists Myrberg and Nelson found that sharks are capable of sensing the pulsed vibrations of an injured fish from 250 metres (Helfman, Collette and Facey 1997)!

Even blind fish can find and catch prey using their lateral line, picking up the prey's water movement within the near-field range. This water movement will be strong when near to the prey but will decline rapidly with distance. However, within 1–2 metres the sense is so accurate it can pinpoint a fish and tell its size, shape, direction, distance and, by the way it is moving, whether it is injured or vulnerable.

The lateral line can even be used for navigation. Like sonar or radar, fish can feel the rebound of their own movement off structure or other fish. This is how they are able to swim in a synchronised school or dart through snags without crashing on a pitch-black night or in filthy water. A great lure designer will take into consideration this incredible sensitivity and the range of information fish receive from these vibrations.

According to acoustical engineer Joe Lindell of Boca Raton, who studied the vibrations made by fish, each species makes a unique wave pattern. A predator can sense these patterns and determine the species of prey item before it is even visible. This might explain why a great lure (or live bait) may work well in one area and not in another – the predators may not recognise, or be 'feeling' for, its particular vibrations.

Some lure manufacturers are working with scientists to define the vibrations made by several key bait species so they can duplicate them in the lures. If they get it right, they are sure to have a deadly piece of equipment!

Rattles and other jangling noises from the hooks on their split rings are much higher-pitched than the pulse coming from the swimming action of the lure. They may be heard from a considerable distance, but the fish will have difficulty determining their direction until the lure comes within its near-field range. Unless the sound triggers a hunting response from the predator, causing it to actively seek out the lure, it is likely to be ignored along with other distracting background noises.

The pulse, or vibration, a lure sends through the water can have a huge influence on how often it gets eaten. All lures can be detected, and some noisy ones will be detected from a great distance, but the trick is having the right beat that appeals to the fish.

Think of it the way we hear sound waves in our medium of air. Most sound is simply noise and we just ignore it. Other things we listen to intently. And some sounds are music. Even then, what may be delightful music to one person can be aggravating to another. Take heavy-metal rock, for example. It's the same with fish: find the beat that turns them on and they will come rushing in.

It is entirely possible that the ability to transmit a particular message through the

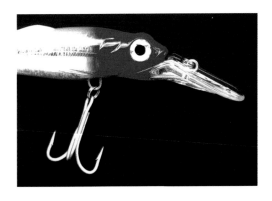

You need to rethink your ideas about sound when you fish with lures. Even the rattle of rings and hooks could be important

vibrations caused by its swimming action may be the single most important ingredient in determining how successful a lure will be. Lures that look identical to our eyes may transmit quite different messages to the lateral line of a predator. This is especially true of the swimming-type lures. A subtle change in body profile, bib shape, buoyancy, tow-point or hook balance will certainly change the swim pattern and consequently the vibrations emitted. An angler may not be able to determine the difference, but fish live or die according to their ability to interpret the messages broadcast throughout the underwater world they inhabit.

The vibrations created by a lure as it moves through the water not only alert predators to the presence of the lure, but also convey critical messages about its behaviour. It could be saying this creature is nervous, terrified, distracted (feeding), wounded, crippled or fleeing from danger, all of which are switch-on messages for a predator.

Predators act very aggressively towards crippled fish as they represent a capture that can be taken with little expenditure of energy. Fish move through the water with smooth fluid motions, but an injured fish will move quite differently and the hunters are able to detect this difference as the target fish will be creating vibrations at odds with everything around it.

In a memorable example of this in action, an underwater camera crew were filming a reef situation where prey fish and predators were swimming together in harmony. A diver netted one of the small fish, then clipped a side fin before releasing the fish. Within seconds of release, the injured fish – while swimming in the midst of hundreds of similar fish – was eaten by a predator, then everything went back to being harmonious again.

There are several factors you can consider when selecting a lure to suit the conditions at hand. As mentioned earlier, size, shape and contrast all play a part in making the lure visually appealing to a fish. What many anglers don't consider, however, is how the lure feels to the fish, what effect it will have on the lateral line. If a range of similar shapes and sizes don't seem to be working, try using different actions before you switch to something completely different. The profile may be fine; you just need the right beat to go with it.

The vibrations don't just change when you switch size or type of lure; they also change when the speed is varied. This might explain the scenario where two anglers are fishing side by side with similar lures and one hooks heaps of fish while the other can hardly raise a bite. The latter may be using a lure that doesn't have quite the right beat for the situation. Even with the same lure on, the angler retrieving the lure at the

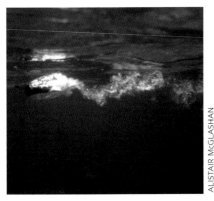

ALISTAIR McGLASHAN

DAVID GREEN

LEFT From underwater, a popper is hard to miss due to the sound as well
as the vibrations and visible splash

RIGHT A hot fish blasting a surface popper is one of angling's most adrenalin-charged moments

speed that creates the best pulse may catch plenty, while the other angler, who is off the pace, may only catch a few. This is more likely to occur when vision is poor, such as in dirty water or darkness, than when vision is the dominant sense. Giving a lure a jerk of extra speed while retrieving, or pumping on the line while trolling, also changes the beat and may transmit a signal of great interest to a predator.

Our little scenario in the Prologue allows us to better understand the role of sound in lure fishing. The Australian bass takes some of its food in the form of insects, and even small animals that fall into the water from the bank or overhanging trees. Any *plop* at the surface is worth investigating. Splashes are noisy and we would imagine that fish are particularly in tune with the vibrations they create. Poppers are particularly effective sonic lures because they can produce a lot of noise without moving very far, pulling fish from quite a depth or some distance away from the initial point of contact.

Some fish are able to hear crustaceans and worms moving about beneath the surface of the sand or mud, so the potency of even low levels of noise should not be underestimated. A small jig lifted then dropped back to bump on the bottom is making a noise that is meaningful to an alert fish.

Here are a few final thoughts to consider on the subject of sound.

Sound, especially close loud unexpected sound, can certainly frighten fish, even when that sound is made by a lure. We saw an example of this some time ago while testing a new loudly rattling model of a large bibless minnow. One of us was diving among a school of dog-tooth tuna on a coral reef about 20 metres down. The fish were patrolling a gutter in the coral and ranged in size from 10–90 kilograms or more. One of the anglers dropped the new lure to the bottom of the gutter and, when signalled that the fish were nearly upon it, jerked the lure up and jigged it to the surface. The lure erupted into a booming burst of loud rattles that completely startled the tuna. They scattered in all directions and were not seen again!

It might be worth recalling this example when casting a rattling lure at a snag in a river. By casting beyond the snag and drawing the lure towards it, not only are you likely to have more depth by the time the lure gets there, you might also gently alert the fish to its approach so it isn't startled and can prepare for the ambush.

On a recent photo shoot we had a 225-horsepower 4-stroke on the back of a boat that had been nosed in to the beach with the motor still running in deeper water at the back. Eight nice bream were observed to come in and investigate where the telltale water stream was hitting the surface immediately behind the huge outboard. Fishermen trolling for small and large game fish with outboard-powered boats have often reported remarkable changes in fish behaviour when they switched from a 2-stroke to a 4-stroke motor, with fish frequently taking lures immediately behind the prop wash just metres from the boat when using the 4-stroke engine.

Sometimes the marine environment itself is full of noises, ranging from breaking waves to pistol prawns, fish scraping teeth on rocks or coral, and so on. In such situations, the sound of a boat's motor, especially a slowly moving motor (below 1000 Hertz), may be ignored.

Motors are not the only negative sounds anglers need to consider. Things being dropped and bumped in the boat are a definite no-no, as are noisy anchoring practices. We often anchor up when we find fish working deep, even in bass waters. Getting that anchor over the side quietly is a critical element in the exercise. If you don't need chain to get the anchor to bite into the bottom, take it off and tie the rope straight to the anchor as it is almost impossible to work quietly with chain. You can also line the anchor-well with carpet or some other noise-deadening material.

Aluminium hulls will always be noisier than fibreglass or timber hulls. Even a slight chop on the surface will make far more noise on an alloy hull than it will against glass. We have been in situations where fish have been so turned on, no amount of noise would deter them. In other, heavily fished areas, attention to noise can make or break the outing.

When working rivers, creeks or impoundments, the best approach is to use the outboard for the distance work, but to operate only with an electric motor once you have sighted a spot you want to fish. Some complex snags may warrant your attention for quite some time and you don't want to have to start an outboard when the wind blows you in too close to the fish-holding cover.

Finally, it's worth knowing that fish can be trained to recognise certain repeated stimuli. In areas where substantial numbers of fish have been taken on noisy lures, especially when the fish have been released, it is highly possible that a learning process may have taken place: the fish may associate the particular sounds (or even the feel) of a lure with danger. This might explain why a very successful and popular lure sometimes stops producing the strikes. In heavily fished waters, or in a fishery where a lot of caught fish are released, it may be a good strategy to try a new lure, especially a 'silent' one, if the strike rate is slow. In this instance, once a particular lure has been given a rest for a period of time, the factors that made it an old favourite should work like new all over again. There are some beauties lying in the bottom of tackle boxes that might warrant being dusted off and tried once more.

Smell

Fish have a highly developed sense of smell (and taste) that is exploited in many forms of fishing. Laying down a trail of berley has long been employed as a method of concentrating fish in one place and getting them in a mood to feed.

American fishermen have used various concentrated scents on their lures for many years now, but Australians have never taken to the idea in a big way. At the time of writing, scents are once again being promoted through the fishing magazines, and it is just possible that the current boom in impoundment bass fishing with specially scented soft plastic lures may get Australian fishermen more interested in scents than they have been in the past.

It is surprising that saltwater anglers do not incorporate the use of berley when fishing with lures. If it makes sense to concentrate fish with berley when bait fishing, why not berley the area when using lures? One angler we know had spectacular success with snapper by retrieving soft plastic double tails through a berley trail. Weighted and punctured cans of sardines or a row of crab pots work with flathead, and when trolling for large fish such as yellowfin tuna consider marking the trolling run on the GPS, then seeding that area with chopped pilchards to bring big fish up to the surface. A lone roaming jewfish can be localised by attracting and concentrating yellowtail, tailor or

TIM SIMPSON

ABOVE The many fish scents available on the market today may be just as important for the smells they cover up as those they add to the lures

LEFT The salmonoids (which include all trout) are known to be incredibly sensitive to smells — particularly the amino acid 'L-serine' from sweat, even at staggering rates of dilution

whatever else it is out there stalking into a small defined area. (Although it is not using scent, it is worth mentioning that this same principle is effective when squid fishing, using surface lights to draw and hold the prey the squid feed on.)

One of the most popular scents used in the US is associated with the sexual activity of fish. When in breeding mode, fish become extremely aggressive and territorial, which works in our favour when we intrude into their space with a lure.

The right scent may also make a difference when an alert fish is in a 'will I or won't I?' frame of mind: that is, wanting to eat a lure, but not entirely convinced that it is genuine food. The application of a scent may be all it takes to tip the balance.

A tackle-store proprietor fitting out one angler for a trout-fishing trip added a bottle of attractant scent to the package. The angler was not convinced of the value of the scent but he took it anyway. Returning to the shop after the trip, he told of a large trout that had followed several consecutive retrieves of a lure, swimming so close that it only had to open its mouth to take it, but each time the fish simply turned back when the lure neared the bank. Frustrated, the angler remembered the little bottle of scent in his bag and, with nothing to lose, decided to give it a try. He rubbed a little on the lure and cast it out into the stream again, where it was taken by the trout the moment the retrieve started.

There is another likely scenario to consider here: the use of scent to mask unpalatable odours associated with the lure. Humans secrete an amino acid substance called L-serine through the pores of their skin; perhaps the same substance that produces a black fingerprint when you hold polished silver or stainless steel? Some people appear to sweat and secrete more L-serine than others and more readily leave an imprint on polished metals. The bad news is that L-serine has been found to be obnoxious to many fish, so those who produce high levels of it may unknowingly be tainting the lures they handle. Some forms of scent additives for lures contain an agent to neutralise L-serine. It is said that human spit can have a similar effect, suggesting that the success of these additives may rely not so much on the scent added as the scent taken away from the lure. It is worth noting that trout and other salmonoids are amazingly sensitive to L-serine. We handle all sorts of things that may or may not have an effect on the way a lure smells to a fish, including things with odours not detectable by us. If the fish seem interested but wary, why not give the lure a quick smear with a masking agent to be on the safe side?

We still have a long way to go in terms of exploiting the olfactory sense of fish when lure fishing. Many of the new soft plastics are impregnated with various scents and flavours, including salt. Aniseed and fish oil are two readily available scents that have proved themselves over many years.

Some of the latest soft plastics have such an effective smell/taste built into the plastic compound that they are really a 'bait with action' as much as they are a lure. We saw one brand being tested in a massive tank of barramundi. Not only did the barra scoff the moving lures, but they also sucked up and ate lures that had broken off and been lying motionless for some time on the bottom.

Speed

Think about what you are trying to achieve when you start to fish any area with lures. First of all, you want to try to fool the fish into believing your offering is edible, in which case you will be trying to match something the fish normally eats

When we think lures, speed is a relative thing. The deep diver in the centre
of the left column is a plodder with real speedsters above and below. On the right
are lures that need very little pace to be highly effective

in terms of visual appeal and the way you work the lure. If you have a school of a thousand little fish swimming around, it will be the one that breaks the pattern that will be taken first by predators. Similarly an injured fish will quickly be singled out. Predators will always attack something that looks like an easy meal, which is why the strange swimming actions of many lures attract fish. A lure presented to represent something that can't get away, or is handicapped in some way, becomes very attractive to a predator. In this case, you might look for unpredictable erratic actions in the lure.

When throwing lures at high-speed hunters such as tuna or mackerel, you might rely purely on speed and flash as these fish are attracted to prey that is desperately

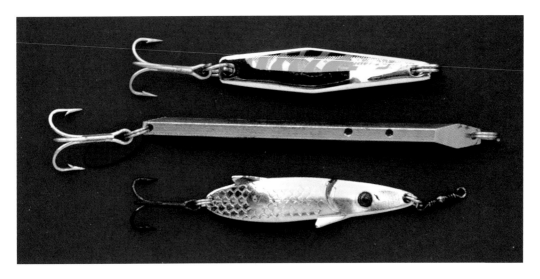

Similar in some ways, these three lures each do their best work at quite different speeds. The light metal spoon (bottom) has a lot of body contour that causes it to flutter at quite low speeds. The slim bar (middle) is ultra streamlined to travel through the water as fast as the angler can wind the reel. Top is a lure where a combination of modest shaping and plenty of weight provides good action at medium speeds

trying to escape. Just as we are more likely to notice a moving object than one that is stationary, so it is with fish. Laboratory experiments show that a rainbow trout can detect a moving object up to 20 per cent further away than it does a similar stationary object. There is also evidence, at least with some species, that a lure moving horizontally across their vision, combined with an undulating dipping motion, has an increased chance of being attacked. This helps to explain the enormous success of lead-head jigs and soft plastics.

In fresh as well as saltwater, shrimp and prawns (and squid) are an important and favoured food source. When these creatures are pursued or frightened they snap their tails and flit away. Their action goes from nearly stationary to very fast but only covers a distance of one tail snap at a time. Depending on the size of the prawn, this flick may be 0.5 metre or less and a prolonged escape attempt will be a series of short flicking movements. A lure that mimics this action is sure to get attention.

Energy is a precious commodity to a fish. A fish eats to top up its tank of fuel, so to speak, and if it uses 1 litre of fuel to catch a meal that only gives it 0.5 litre of fuel in return, it is starting to die. If the fish continues to operate in that fashion it will soon lose condition to the point where it no longer has the energy to chase and catch food, and it will soon become vulnerable to predators. The best lure in the world can have its effectiveness negated by poor presentation or by being worked at a speed above or below its optimum pace.

When trolling bibbed lures, spoons or other lures with a pulsing action, it's an interesting exercise to vary the speed of the boat while watching the lure or the rod tip. If you go too fast, the lure will become unstable and start spinning or come to the surface. As you slow down, you will notice the rod tip resume its trembling or pulsing in response to the swimming action of the lure. You will soon find a particular speed at which the rod tip is most active, which is probably the optimum trolling speed for that particular lure. A sensitive rod like a good graphite will help in this situation.

Similarly, when a lure is cast and retrieved it is possible to feel the action of the lure through the rod, especially when using low-stretch lines like fused or braided gel-spun. Once again, vary speeds to find the point at which you can see or feel the lure doing its job effectively.

While most lures have an optimum speed at which they can be retrieved through the water, not many creatures in the sea swim very far at exactly the same pace, unless they are swimming flat out to avoid being eaten. Stop/start retrieves can attract the interest of a predator, as can varying the speed of the retrieve or using a flick of the rod tip to impart erratic action and direction changes to the lure.

Presentation

There is no one way to fish a lure. You should be prepared to experiment with presentations. Even when you have previously caught fish by working a lure in a certain way, if you are not catching fish on that lure with that technique next time out, try varying the presentation before you change the lure.

Different fish respond to different stimuli. Some need a stealthy approach or they will disappear, but for others you will catch more fish if you 'announce' the lure's entry into their realm. Some barra and Murray cod fishermen insist on a noisy *splat* landing at the end of a cast to ensure the fish take notice and realise the lure has arrived.

You can also be a little creative in the way you rig and present lures. An example is an imaginative rig used for kingfish. These fish often swim deep but are known to be inquisitive and attracted to surface splashing. The lure rig consists of two lures used together to achieve a strike from what can sometimes be a frustratingly difficult customer. At the head of the rig is a chugger popper with its hooks removed. This slow-moving, loud-commotion-producing surface lure is what drags kingies up from their patrolling down deep. To the rear of the popper, a shortish length of leader is attached to a soft plastic curly tail on a hook. The curious kingies rise up for a look at the popper then can't help themselves when they see the wiggly critter following close behind. Without the soft plastic, these playful fish sometimes just follow and tease; and without the popper, they may never have known the soft plastic was there.

We have also seen an adaptation of this technique where a darning needle was used to thread the line through a squash ball with a big saltwater fly tagging behind. The squash ball provided casting weight and acted as a popper when retrieved, and the fly chasing this noise became the focal point for predators. A lead-head jig behind a blunt-topped 'popping' bobby cork makes another good variation.

Floating and sinking lures

Another way to look at lures is to break them down into floating and sinking types. Moulded plastic or timber lures often rely on a bib or angled face set at the front of the head to make them dive, and the size and shape of that bib, plus the placement of the towing eye and the angle of the bib, determine how deep they will dive. The fact that many will rise to the surface if you stop the retrieve is a useful asset in some situations. For example, you can cast the lure over sunken timber then start the retrieve to make the lure dive. When you come to the timber, you back off the retrieve, the lure floats up so you can slowly work it over the obstacle, then you pick up the pace and dive it hard again right next to the timber. You can fish some very difficult fish-holding cover this way without losing lures.

There are situations where a slowly rising or sinking 'suspending' lure produces the best results using a wind-and-stop routine. A cautiously interested fish may repeatedly follow a slow-moving lure. If the retrieve is stopped dead, the fish is suddenly confronted with the lure right in its face. Some species regularly react by striking the lure. This retrieve is particularly successful with golden perch and bream.

A deep-diving floating bibbed lure with slightly more buoyancy in its tail than in

These fizzers and skipping poppers can be worked in different ways. The saltwater fizzer (top) will be effective when used with simple rod tip stabs, or it may be raced back over the surface, much like the skipping popper (middle) which is designed to work right on top in a representation of a fleeing baitfish. Bottom right is another skipping popper that can be tweaked with short jerks or run at speed. The tiny fizzer at bottom left may be worked with extreme subtlety by an expert who will get those small propellers working with very little forward movement

its head can be used to effect around structure with a violent, short-jerk retrieve delivered through the rod with short but sharp snaps of the wrist. Once cranked down to working depth, this retrieve is started with pauses of one to three seconds between jerks. During the pause the lure starts to rise, but since it is sitting at an angle of around 45 degrees and is mostly tail buoyant, it floats up moving backwards away from the angler. This effectively primes it almost back to the start position, ready for the next jerk. The lure has hardly advanced and so can spend a longer time within the strike zone. This is a great technique for barramundi and other structure-orientated ambush feeders.

TIM SIMPSON

Many of the soft plastics that are highly effective on flathead may look like a fish, but they are worked to imitate the action of a prawn. Dropped to the bottom, they are usually given a short rip or two with the rod tip then left to settle to the bottom again. Fish frequently take them while the lure is settling or lying dormant on the bottom

Then there are floating lures, intended to work right on top of the water. Skipping poppers are the most obvious example, along with some fizzers and a number of other styles intended to be cranked across the surface at a great pace. These give a pretty good imitation of fish jumping across the surface to escape pursuit.

Fizzers are a particularly interesting family of surface lures. They are cigar-shaped, tapering to a point at both ends, with a two-bladed propeller fitted to one or both ends of the lure. A skilful angler can cause these small propellers to move, without noticeably moving the body of the lure, simply by manipulating slack line with the rod tip. It is amazing to see one of these little lures inhaled into the bucket-mouth of a rampaging barramundi that has been switched on by the minimal movement of those tiny propellers.

It is also worth noting here that there are times when fish will only show interest in a lure that is barely moving. If a lure is left in the strike zone of a fish like a bass, it will be watched. Giving it just enough of a twitch to confirm that it is alive and not just another piece of debris is all it requires for a strike. The next day the same little lure, with its props really buzzing as it is cranked across the surface at speed, will send fish wild.

Soft plastics

Soft plastics are another family of lures that don't require much action to be highly effective. In fact, most people fishing with them for the first time make the mistake of trying to do too much with them. The plastics, especially the curly-tail grub styles, can even be paused on the bottom quite a lot of the time. Fish will eat these plastics much as they would take a real worm.

You can also fish soft plastics with a rip-and-drop technique, where the rod tip is used to rip the lure along for a metre or so in a series of small jerks, then lowered to allow the lure to flutter back before it's ripped again. This aggressive technique works very well with a stiffish rod and is deadly on flathead as long as the lure is paused on or worked within a few centimetres of the bottom.

A good way to get a feel for just how slow you have to fish these lures is to dangle one in the water then move the rod tip and watch the tail. The merest suggestion of movement is enough to make that tail wiggle, and that is often as much action as you need to get a fish to scoff the offering.

These lures are usually most successful when they have just enough weight to flutter down on the drop. If the soft plastic is intended to represent a worm, keep in mind how slowly even a swimming worm moves in the water.

Another thing to consider when fishing with plastics is that they really are a transition between lures and bait. Impregnated with scents, and in some cases salt, they smell and taste like something to eat, and when a fish bites on them they actually feel like something to eat. Experimenting with presentation will pay real dividends.

Sinking lures vary from ultra-light plastic worms through to 400-gram metal bars used in deep offshore waters. With a sinking lure, you can cast it out and let it drop just as far as you want before you retrieve. This allows you to make presentations at varying depths.

You can also choose to work a sinking lure by bouncing it along the bottom, or perhaps working it in a vertical fashion by dropping the lure to the bottom then bringing it straight back, or yo-yoed to the boat. Lures fished this way are often taken on the drop, especially if they flutter.

Depth – getting it right

When fishing a rock wall, steep bank or even a snag lying lengthwise in the water, if you stand off and cast straight to it there is every chance that your lure will be well out from the fish-holding area by the time it has dived to the fishes' depth. In such cases, it pays to move the boat to a position where a cast can be made parallel to the cover or snag. Cast along or beyond the cover as far as possible, give one hard hit with the rod tip to dive the lure, then start the retrieve. This way the lure will traverse the whole area at its maximum diving depth, which hopefully has been matched to the depth of the predator lying in ambush.

Getting lures to the correct depth is a major factor when fishing. You can set the depth to some degree by choosing lures that sink or are designed to run at particular depths; or, when trolling, you can use devices that will present lures at far greater depths than they were designed to achieve with regular presentations.

With any lure used at great depths, it is important to keep in mind the water pressures the lure will have to work under. As depth increases, the weight of water above crushes down and makes the water much denser. This denser water makes it harder for a lure to move, with the result that many lures with a great action at the surface will be smothered if the lure is taken well below the depth it was designed for. Other lures with a wild uncontrollable action at the surface (like some spoons) are often fantastic when trolled at great depth. If deep trolling a lure whose surface action would be smothered by the depth, you can often restore the action by simply increasing the speed; half again or up to twice the normal speed depending on depth.

One way of getting any lure to any depth is to use a downrigger. A downrigger consists of a wire or GSP line spooled onto either a manual or electric winch with a short boom or arm like a rod. A heavy lead bomb is attached to the end of the wire line, which is lowered to any required depth. The fishing line with lure is attached to the bomb with a quick-release clip so it can be trolled in really deep water, but the line will break free the moment a strike pulls on the release. This means that even very light lines can be trolled with bombs weighing 6 kilograms; also, once a fish is hooked, there is no weight on the line to impede a fight. At some time after the line clip is released by a strike, the downrigger rig is wound back up separately.

Because the bomb on a downrigger is usually easy to pick up on an echo sounder, the operator can register fish at a particular depth and place the bomb at that exact

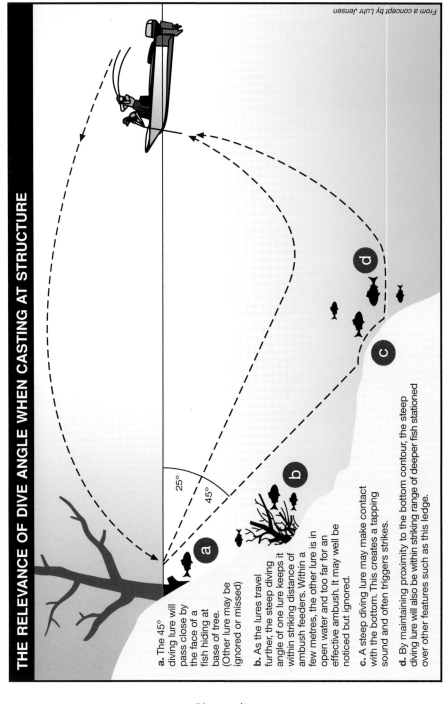

THE RELEVANCE OF DIVE ANGLE WHEN CASTING AT STRUCTURE

From a concept by Luhr Jensen

a. The 45° diving lure will pass close by the face of a fish hiding at base of tree. (Other lure may be ignored or missed)

b. As the lures travel further, the steep diving angle of one lure keeps it within striking distance of ambush feeders. Within a few metres, the other lure is in open water and too far for an effective ambush. It may well be noticed but ignored.

c. A steep diving lure may make contact with the bottom. This creates a tapping sound and often triggers strikes.

d. By maintaining proximity to the bottom contour, the steep diving lure will also be within striking range of deeper fish stationed over other features such as this ledge.

25°

45°

Dive angles

47

RIGHT The heavy line (1) is a 3 kilogram weight (bomb) located on a downrigger and running some 4.5 metres from the sounder transducer. Another bomb (2) located on the other side of the boat and down 6 metres produces a finer signal reflecting its position a little farther from the transducer. All of the 'eyebrow' shapes (3) below the bombs are bass, and the lines angling up from left to right are fish rising to the lures

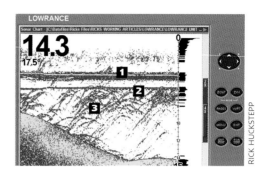

depth. Many downriggers also have a counter which helps to gauge the depth of the lure. With a sounder and downrigger working together, catching fish can often be as simple as connecting the dots!

Downriggers are a little fiddly to use and will cost several hundred dollars to buy, but they are a sensational way of presenting lures (and live or dead baits) at any depth and without the handicap of weight on the line. Many very successful anglers would not be without them.

When trolling a downrigger at speed, the combined water-drag on the cable, the attached line, the lure and the bomb will pull the rig out behind the boat and up towards the surface. At slow speeds of 1–3 knots, the length of cable out is pretty close to the depth your lure will be running, but when the speed is increased to 4 knots the bomb will probably be at a depth of only 70 per cent of the cable length. At 6 knots the rig may be washed out the back to the extent that the bomb is at only half the depth it started at. It will also be that far out behind the boat and so may no longer be within the search area of the echo sounder either. At 8 knots the rig will have 60–70 per cent of the cable length out behind the boat, which means only 30–40 per cent of the cable length is being used for depth. This is termed 'blow-back' and is caused by the water-drag on the rig beneath the surface.

Some anglers have found a way to beat blow-back and troll deep at speed. One trick is to use a very large paravane instead of a lead bomb, as a paravane will dive harder as speed is increased, whereas a lead weight will plane up towards the surface. An American company called Nekton makes the Z Wing 500 paravane which is especially designed to troll large lures at high speeds on a downrigger. The other trick is to replace the usual 7-strand wire cable on the downrigger with a length of GSP line, especially a super-thin-diameter braided gel-spun with a round profile. This is

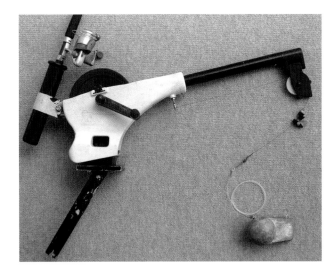

LEFT In some fisheries the ability of the downrigger to locate a lure at a specific depth is crucial to success. The in-boat part of the device is not much more than an elaborate winch with a depth counter to raise and lower the heavy lead weight

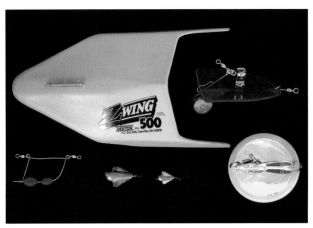

LEFT Not as depth specific as a downrigger, but nonetheless successful in some circumstances, deep running paravanes and trolling weights play an important role in trolling, particularly in freshwater

considerably thinner than the wire and so will have less water-drag.

Something else we have found when using downriggers at speed is that you get a serious hum of vibration off the cable as it drags through the water. This hum travels right down to the bomb and lure and we believe it must put some fish off. The hum is caused by the taut ribbed strands of the cable vibrating against the water flow. A great way to reduce or eliminate the hum is to change the rough stranded cable for the smoother finish of plastic-coated cable or single-strand Monel wire or, best of all, a smooth-finished, round-profile (cross-section) GSP line, which in a comparative strength is much thinner.

Other options include in-line paravanes, leadcore lines and sinker rigs, but none of these offers the same accuracy and versatility of presentation as the downrigger.

Casting

One very exciting form of lure fishing is to cast small metal lures at fish feeding on the surface. Mackerel, tuna, tailor, bonito, queenfish and salmon are just a few of the fish associated with this style of fishing. When the birds start diving and the surface of the water erupts in foam, the bait is under attack and it's time to get a lure into the vicinity.

The angler's first impulse is to throw a lure right into the middle of the bait, but that could be a mistake. When a school of bait is under attack, the safest place for an individual baitfish is right in the middle of the school. Fish on the outside or at the bottom of the ball are the first ones to be hit, so a lure cast beyond the school and worked back under it, or one placed to run along the front or side of the action, could produce a better result.

When surface-feeding fish are on the move as they feed, it may be appropriate to cast ahead of the school. This is often the case when casting to mackerel tuna. The lure should intercept the sides of the school or the lead fish and be travelling in a direction away from the predators. Be cautious about very fast boat speeds or hard manoeuvring in these situations as they can often upset the school. If the school is boat-shy, also be aware of the angle of the sun. The boat's shadow passing over the predators or bait school may be enough to make them cautious, or break up the school entirely and put an end to the action.

It is worth noting at this point that the angler should try to keep himself as far away from the target fish as possible when presenting lures. When trolling a working school of fish, the rule is always to pass on one side of the action with the lures well behind the boat, then, when the boat is well past the fish, make a sharp turn so the lures veer across and intercept, or at least come close by, the school.

Casting at fish schools from a power boat can be extremely exciting and productive, but you should cut the engine short of the action and try to use the wind to drift the boat towards the fish. Many surface fish appear to be wary of the noise/vibration of a 2-stroke motor, but most will demonstrate greater tolerance for the quieter 4-strokes. Any outboard will set up some pretty noisy harmonics within an aluminium hull, especially if loose items are left in contact with the hull. A timber or fibreglass hull may offer more stealth, and carpeting will always help to mute the sounds of people and moved hardware within the boat. In nervous-fish situations, even the noise of waves slapping against the hull can be enough to send them away.

TIM SIMPSON

A swirling mass of birds indicates surface feeding fish. These fish often move very swiftly, and there is an art in getting a lure into the right place without spooking the school

When flighty boat-shy fish like small tuna invade estuaries and bays to decimate a migration or influx of bait species, there are often small patches of fish blasting the surface in all directions. Because they move so quickly and stay at the surface so briefly, a successful strategy is to drift silently in a likely spot and wait for the fish to come to you. Chasing these high-speed predators with the boat and trying to get a cast off is usually frustrating and often fruitless. By waiting quietly, poised and ready when they come past your position, you have a great opportunity to cast to close-range, unspooked feeding fish. There is also the possibility that if the boat is kept very quiet, the baitfish may shelter under the hull, thus bringing the predators right to the boat!

When fishing with fast-sinking lures, such as the metal-bodied lures frequently used from rocks, a common technique is to make a long cast then allow the lure to sink to the bottom, counting the seconds to touchdown. Subsequent retrieves can be made at different depths by using the countdown method to establish how far off the bottom the retrieve is to be started.

Slow-sinking lures can be used to fish deep under snags and other forms of cover. A lure cast well back into cover, then allowed to sink to a desired depth before starting the retrieve, is a very effective fish-finder.

An alternative approach is to draw the fish up to the surface with noisy splashing

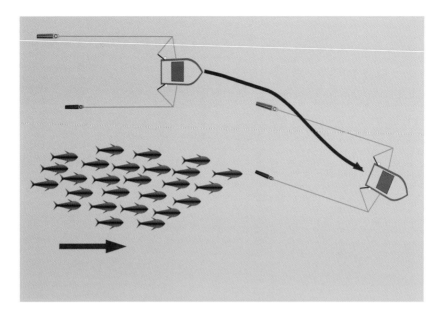

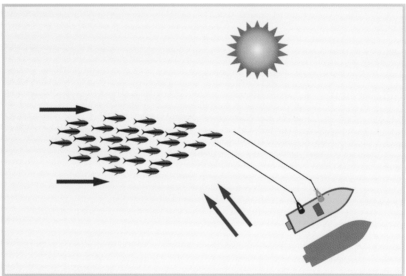

To present a trolled lure to a surface school of fish, the boat should be driven
around the school at a distance that doesn't spook them. Once in front of the school,
cut across and drive in line with the fish. With enough line out, the lures will track across
and pull through the school without alarming them. When casting, position the
boat upwind and in front of the fish. Cast across the leading edge of the school.
Watch the angle of the boat's shadow if the fish are easily spooked

lures such as poppers and fizzers. Once up at the surface and inspecting a lure, if not caught straightaway the fish can at least be seen, sized up and presented with something that will do the trick.

In a session around an exposed and waveswept rock, normally a hot spot for deep-prowling big cobia, a small metal lure was used to hook a tailor in the wash, then bring it out just to the edge of the foam. Within seconds big cobia were charging out after the tailor, and big lures cast in behind the hooked tailor were readily taken by the cobia. This is a fun and successful technique that requires good timing and teamwork. *See Blue-water Teasers, page 193*, for more information about the procedure in relation to the exciting form of fishing known as 'bait (or tease) and switch'.

Finally, berley is a viable option for getting the fish to come to you, if you can't get a lure to where the fish are. Lure fishermen rarely consider using berley but, as we mentioned before, there's a lot to be said for casting lures down a berley trail.

Strength

A common difference between the smaller lures is in the strength of the hardware: the freshwater models carry light hooks and rings, while saltwater lures are often fitted with heavy-duty hooks and rings. Fish like barramundi and trevally can sometimes do an amazing amount of damage to even heavy-duty hooks. So why not just put heavy-duty hooks on everything in the first place? Live-bait fishermen can give you an answer to that when they say there's a big difference between fishing with a 'live' bait and a 'lively' bait. The 'lively' bait will be taken first every time.

We saw a graphic demonstration of this one day up on the Great Barrier Reef. There

TIM SIMPSON

Fish with extremely powerful mouths such as giant trevally, kingfish and barramundi will find and exploit any weakness in a lure, especially rings and hooks

The internal strength of these lures helped land the fish even after
powerful jaws had destroyed their bodies

was a Queensland groper of more than 200 kilograms swimming around the boat
while we were fishing the bottom. Whenever someone brought up a reef fish, the
groper instantly sprang to life and vigorously chased the smaller fish until it was eaten
or lifted into the boat. On several occasions an angler teased the groper by repeatedly
lifting the fish away just as it was about to be inhaled. When the fish was lowered back
into the water, the groper resumed its attack, as eager as ever to climb all over the
luckless bottom fish – until it became tired and slowed in its exertions to escape. Once
the prey's struggling decreased, the groper lost interest and settled back to wait for the
next 'fresh' victim from below. Even when we took the tired fish off the hook and let it
swim free, right past the face of the groper, it was ignored.

We watched this procedure several times as new fish were brought up from the
bottom, and each time it was the same. When the angler eventually let the small fish
go, it was the identical desired food item as before, but once its struggles got weak and
the vibrations of panic subsided, the predator was simply not turned on and motivated.

The groper in this example was probably well fed and lethargic, but it shows what can occur if you happen to be fishing when your quarry is not actively feeding. If a lure does not do things that press the 'attack button' for a predator, even if it represents a preferred food item, it may swim past the predator's nose all day, unassaulted and ignored.

Many lures are delicately balanced to swim or wobble in a certain way. If you add more weight to the underside in the form of heavier hooks it may slow the action of the lure and make it less effective. Some fish species have such powerful and destructive jaws they will demand that you upgrade the hardware, but you must know the capacity of the lure to take those changes or you may destroy the very action needed to get the strike in the first place. The best result is achieved when a lure is actually designed to incorporate such special requirements. Another point to remember is that stronger hooks are usually thicker and thick hooks take considerably more pressure to set into a tough mouth. A large barb is even more of an impediment. For these reasons the thin guage 'chemically sharpened' hooks with their usually very fine barbs are an excellent choice unless the species or tackle demands the heavy artillery.

We'll look into some of the technical factors of lure performance and design in Chapter 3, The Basic Lure Families. With in-depth knowledge of how lures work, it is much easier to select the best lure available and be rewarded with many more fish.

LEFT Fish like this huge dog-tooth tuna have savage teeth and extremely powerful jaws that demand quality hardware. They swim deep along the coral reef edges and are often easier to tempt with a sub-surface lure. In this case, Tim fast-trolled a large deep-diving bibbed lure to present a typical baitfish replica down in the strike zone.

TIM SIMPSON

Most fish relate to structure. A rock like this in the middle of the ocean is sure to attract a healthy population of baitfish and predators, especially in the surrounding white water washes

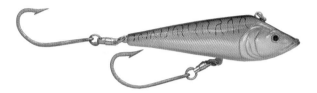

CHAPTER TWO

Finding and targeting fish

You've probably heard the old saying, 'The only thing wrong with fishing is that there is too much water mixed in with the fish', and that's very true. The areas of water that are populated with fish are far fewer than the areas devoid of fish. So no matter how good our lure collection and fishing technique, if we are not putting those lures in front of fish we are wasting our time.

This isn't the daunting problem it initially seems to be. There are quite a few ways we can pinpoint exactly where fish are – or are likely to be. With the help of modern electronics there are also ways to then check if anyone is home when we get there – and even how active they are and whether they are chasing prey. Then, by knowing how and where our lures work, we are able to select and deliver a tantalising offering right into the strike zone of the fish we are seeking.

We associate many lures with particular types of terrain and fish species, so let's first turn our attention to sorting out which places are likely to hold fish, and how to recognise areas worthy of investigation with your lure.

Visual clues

Sea birds

The open sea is a unique environment where the angler needs to be very alert, constantly looking for signs that will indicate the likely presence of fish. A mass of feeding birds and erupting bait at the surface is about as obvious as it gets, but sometimes the signs are quite subtle. For example, a single bird hovering at a fixed height above one area is a positive sign. It is probably observing bait down deep, and waiting for predators to encounter that bait and push it up to the surface where the bird can get at it. The lower the hovering height, the closer the bait is to the surface.

One or a group of hovering birds may also be watching a large fish that it is not feeding at the moment. They know that, sooner or later, that fish will be forcing bait up to the surface.

Sea birds are an excellent guide to the presence of fish, and some birds are much better guides than others. You can generally ignore seagulls, but any of the tern family are excellent signposts to fish, as are gannets, shearwaters and frigate birds. Get to know your local sea birds and watch them closely when they're around.

Currents

Currents are another signpost to fish. There are many occasions when, motoring along at sea, you come across a massive slick that looks like a river of different water cutting through the ocean – which is exactly what a current is. A decent current will have a distinct edge, often speckled with flotsam and jetsam of one kind or another. When there is a temperature difference between the current and the main body of water, it forms a distinctive 'fence line' or barrier to the passage of fish. Most fish are extremely temperature sensitive and will not venture across a sudden shift of as little as 1 or 2 degrees. Small baitfish, with their tiny bodies, are less able to cope with temperature change than larger fish. Predators may pin bait up against this temperature wall to prevent their escape. If the baitfish do go into the cold area they are likely to be slowed enough to allow an easy capture. This situation occurs throughout the fishing

TIM SIMPSON

LEFT For ocean wandering pelagic fish, a current edge where waters of different temperatures meet forms a barrier or fence line. Baitfish and predators bunch up and accumulate along these barriers. The edges are often marked on the surface with a smooth current line
RIGHT Fish love to congregate under floating debris. In this case kingfish are in residence beneath a barnacle covered timber panel — 20 kilometres offshore!

seascape, even in mountain lakes where feeder creeks may be a different temperature from the lake they are flowing into.

Those who spin for surface fish from the rocks are highly dependent on currents, and most land-based gamefish hot spots are headlands or rock shelves located in areas where ocean currents frequently move inshore. In the southern areas of Australia, currents coming from the south can be so cold they completely shut down the fishing for all the normal target species and introduce new coldwater species such as barracouta.

Debris

On the open sea, anything that floats will attract fish. Logs, boxes, palm trees, buoys, big planks and so on. If the object has been in the water for any length of time it may have attracted big fish, like dolphin fish (mahi mahi) or yellowtail kingfish. Debris often creates shade and shelter for tiny baitfish and crustaceans in an otherwise featureless ocean; these in turn attract fish that prey upon them and so on, right up the food chain, until a whole ecosystem has developed. Top-of-the-food-chain predators like marlin and tuna will migrate across oceans following drifting flotsam.

We talked with international tuna professionals who found a tree drifting in the middle of the Pacific Ocean. They attached a marker beacon to the tree then tracked it for months, harvesting hundreds of tons of tuna that had aggregated around it and adopted it as a 'home base'. In a similar scenario, a fairly small drifting tree produced a hot barra bite for us in an open bay in northern Australia.

Shade

Shade can be extremely important in the hunt for a fish. To appreciate the value of shade as a fish attractor, consider this: in the deadly game played by predator and prey, early detection of victim or opponent can have a huge bearing on the outcome. Even a fraction of a second may be the difference between death and survival.

Many predators use shade to gain an advantage, as a fish in shade can spot a fish in sunlight up to 2.5 times further away than it can be seen itself. This is partly because the sensitivity of a fish's eyes to light is determined by the brightness of its environment. Sunlight entering the water is reflected off the suspended particles of silt and organic matter that give the water its colour. These reflections bounce the light in all directions, up, down and sideways, which makes the water relatively bright around the eyes of a fish in the sun. In bright light, the fish's eyes will adjust to the conditions by reducing sensitivity. The eyes of a fish in the shade, on the other hand, will have adapted to the lower light levels and so will be more sensitive to movement in the dimmer distance.

TIM SIMPSON

A barramundi peeks out from under the lily pads where he's been hiding. The camera has overexposed the lily pads that are blasting back sunlight while the fish over the dark bottom is underexposed and difficult to see. Exactly the same thing is happening to the sight of a baitfish as it swims by the pads. Any fish looking out from shade has a huge advantage over those in the sun

To understand this phenomenon, imagine you are entering a dark tunnel from bright sunlight. When you stand in the sun and look into the dark tunnel, you can see very little in the dim light inside. Once you enter the darkness, however, and give your eyes time to adjust, not only can you see your surroundings but you can also see objects out in the sunlight. Your eyes will be around 20 per cent more sensitive than when you were in the sun. Couple this increased sensitivity in vision with the fact that a fish in the light is twice as visible as a fish in the shade and you realise the enormous advantages that shade has to offer predator or prey – whichever uses it first.

This is one reason structure is so important to successful fishing. A bream under a dock, a bass behind a stump, a flathead beside a channel marker, a dolphin fish or baitfish in the shadow of a piece of ocean flotsam, are all using the benefit of the shade. Perhaps even a barramundi, poised on the edge of a dirty creek runoff as it pushes into cleaner and brighter estuary waters on a run-out tide, is gaining the advantage of shade.

There are other points to consider here also. A predator ambushing from a position in shade will be temporarily dazzled when it makes its dash into the sunlight to engulf its prey. This can help an angler, as the fish isn't able to be as critical of the lure and leader in the final closing centimetres of its attack. The converse, though, is that because of the dazzling effect (like walking out of the tunnel), the fish will only travel a very short distance from its shade. Its vision won't be clear enough to attempt a sustained chase, so if it can't line up the fatal blow from where it sits, it will simply wait for another opportunity to come along. This illustrates the necessity of accurate casting or lure placement in many forms of fishing.

Structure

Rocky islands and bomboras are fish magnets, especially when wave action is producing active white water. This white water is similar to shade, affording shelter to baitfish, so predators come looking for them there. Inexperienced boat operators need to take great care in these areas, however, as it is very easy to be distracted by hectic fishing action while the boat drifts or is sucked into the highly dangerous wave-breaking zone.

An island or rock in a strong tidal or ocean current will have a small pressure eddy immediately in front of it. The baitfish may gather here, and the predators will use it as a calm-water launch pad to attack food that washes down in the current. This applies as much to mackerel and marlin in the ocean as it does to trout in a mountain stream.

TIM SIMPSON

LEFT A bird's eye view of a nice location for some inshore trolling. Deep drop-offs
and patches of foam are happy hunting grounds for predatory fish

RIGHT This overview of waterside Sydney suburbia reveals productive hunting
grounds for the alert angler. You would find plenty of bream and baitfish under
the marina and craft anchored in deeper water. The sand flat, channel from
the mangroves and drop-off would all work well for flathead on various stages
of the tide, and small pelagics such as tailor, bonito and salmon would also
find plenty to interest them here

Inshore, the big white washes off the rocks are productive areas, as are headlands, especially when a long headland intersects an inshore current. An eddy will often be created on the up-current side of the headland; this will hold bait schools and the predators will follow.

The area inside training walls can be a happy hunting ground for all sorts of predatory fish taking advantage of the movement of fish in and out of the river system.

The lower reaches of any river are normally a mix of sand bars and channels. In the tropical areas, a fast transition occurs from open shallow waters into rivers and creeks where bank-side snags focus fish. The first snag in the system can be a red-hot spot for big fish.

The drop-offs from sand and mud banks are prime ambush territory for flathead on a run-off tide, with the same fish scattering over the top of the banks on high water. Flathead are also particularly partial to weed beds as a wide range of small creatures will be hiding there.

Once into the stream proper – and this remains true all the way up into the conversion areas from salt to freshwater species – fish will be associated with structure. Bream will hang around jetties, marinas, moorings, pontoons, pylons and wharves in the lower reaches, then start taking cover around snags in the upper reaches. Those same snags will also be home to mangrove jack and, in the upper reaches, wild bass.

Any feature out of the ordinary will attract fish. Lily pads, stands of reeds, steep drop-offs, rock faces, bank-side undercuts, deep shade under overhanging trees – anything that affords cover for them to lie in wait and ambush. The same general rules apply in tropical waters, where the same features will attract barramundi, mangrove jack and other northern species, including real bruisers like the great trevally.

Fish activity is often closely associated with the tide in the tropics, and in many creeks the fish move in and out of the system with the tides. The mouth of a creek can be dynamite on the first hour of the run-in tide.

In areas where there are slim populations of fish, they will only be found in the best cover, and are often difficult to get at unless you are a very good caster. In waters that are over-populated with fish (yes, there are such places) the best cover will be taken up by the biggest, most aggressive fish; as you work your way down the pecking order, you'll find the youngsters virtually out in the open, or trying to ambush from areas where they are largely exposed.

Stocked impoundments follow much the same rules, with fish being associated with structure of any kind. Submerged weed beds at any depth are also great food- and fish-holding grounds, as are dead trees and the usual snags. A unique factor in impoundment fishing is that the fish will treat the old river bed as if it's still a river so this is always worth locating and checking out.

Floodwaters

Floodwaters create some unusual opportunities for the lure specialist. After flood rains, the run-off from a river will eventually form a demarcation line beyond training walls when the tide begins to push in. This is similar to an ocean current where waters of different temperatures form a wall where they meet in the sea. In this instance, it's fresh and saltwater creating a distinct line of demarcation and this area can be red hot for big jewfish in the south and barra in the tropics.

In tropical regions the period after 'the wet' produces sensational barramundi fishing wherever water off the flood plains is feeding back into the rivers. In fact, the junctions where feeder streams join bigger bodies of water remain a hot spot as long as water continues to come out of the feeder.

A feeder creek of heavily stained water spills into the main waterway. This will often flush food items into waiting mouths at the entrance. The coloured edge may also harbour ambush predators hiding in the murky water

Sight fishing is one of the lure angler's great pleasures. Even in relatively clear water experienced eyes will see more than those of the casual observer, and good polarised glasses will make a world of difference to what you can see. Here a tropical feeder creek runs into the river beside a small sand bar. At the entrance is a deep hole beside a sunken tree – a certain predator hot spot!

Looking beyond the surface

When you are searching for fish with your eyes, it doesn't take long to start getting a feel for good fish-holding terrain, but you will see a lot more fish if you learn how to use your eyes on the water.

When inexperienced anglers look at water, all they see is the surface. That sounds trite, but in fact you need to look at the water in other ways if you want to see fish. It's a little like looking at those 'magic eye' pictures where a 3D image is hidden in what looks like an abstract and random arrangement of colours. You have to learn to focus your eyes just beyond the printed image and then the 3D image jumps out at you. It takes a bit of practice to get it right.

Similarly, a fisherman needs to shift his focus from the surface to the water below. If you can get hold of a good pair of polarised sunglasses you'll see how this works. With the naked eye, all you see is light and colour reflected on the surface of the water. Pop on the polarised glasses and suddenly you find you're looking through the surface into the water beyond. The ability to see into the water is not just to look for fish. Seeing what lies on the bottom – like weed edges, timber, holes or rocks – will not only save you from snagging lures but will also give you important clues in the hunt for where fish are likely to be. You will also spot fish following your lures and if you know they are there, you can, of course, do something about it. Anglers can spend a lot of money on top-quality polarised glasses that make it easy for them to spot fish, but it is possible to train your naked eye to look beyond the water's surface, although the result is not as effective.

Some people have very good peripheral vision (the area of vision just outside the point on which the eyes are focused). You can't move your focus to that area, as that defeats the purpose, but you can make yourself more aware of that 'grey area' and get used to monitoring it so that you quickly pick up things at odds with the general pattern. This is a good method when looking out for flocks of birds at long distances, water disturbances or even a subtle but moving shade of colour as a camouflaged fish glides across your field of view. It's a difficult concept to explain, but it works. The key is to be aware of that single thing that is at odds with the general seascape. A colour, a shadow, a slight surface ruffle that is not part of the surface wind pattern – these are all clues worth following up. Anglers refer to 'nervous water', a term that covers everything from the surface 'rippler' giving away the presence of baitfish through to a similar surface pattern indicating an up-welling of water from below, caused by a current striking deep structure.

Targeting fish with electronics

When dealing with structure such as shallow reefs, rocky islands, snags and so on, you will find most of your fish by exploiting features you can see at the surface. But in deeper water – at sea, on big rivers, lakes or impoundments – fish will be associated with bottom features you can't see.

For example, all impoundments have been formed over what once was a river or creek. If you can locate the original river bed, even though it is only the memory of a river now, you'll find fish gathered there.

A common hot spot is the shoulder, where what was once the land running alongside the river plunges down to the river bed. Sometimes you will even find fish suspended high above the old river bed. This is when you need some electronic help to search them out.

Echo sounders

Echo sounders – also known as fish finders or sonar – are your eyes underwater. Operating on the same principles as the sonar used by surface ships to hunt submarines, an echo sounder fires an electronic pulse at the bottom, which bounces back to the receiver enriched with information it has collected on its trip down and back. How it does this is of no concern to us here; we are only interested in the way we can use this information. However, it is worth exploring some of the features that separate highly effective echo sounders from the more basic models.

The computer in the head unit (display cabinet) interprets the returning signal and extracts highly detailed information which is then displayed on a black-and-white or colour screen. The difference between a bottom- and a top-of-the-range sounder is in the intelligence of the software used to interpret the returning signal and the quality of the display screen.

Screen quality is important and is determined by the number of vertical pixels in the display. (Don't worry about the number of horizontal pixels, as this determines how much history the screen can show rather than the actual quality of the image.) Pixels are the building blocks used to create an image onscreen and the more you have, the finer the display detail. These days, many anglers are rushing out to buy expensive

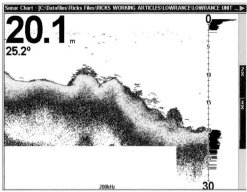

RICK HUCKSTEPP

Two examples of sounder screens showing that fish are working at different depths.
With the fish suspended at between 2 and 8 metres on the black and white screen you
wouldn't catch much fishing the bottom. The black clutter at the bottom of the picture
is weed. In the colour picture the fish are on the bottom along with bait balls.
Notice in both pictures the way the sounder draws a grey or colour line with the actual
bottom shown as a thin dark line — this allows you to separate the bottom from
things that are on or close to the bottom

colour sounders, but the same amount of money would buy a far superior fish-finding
tool with a black-and-white screen.

Consider a situation where a large tree has plunged into a lake from a steep bank or
been carried into deep water in a past flood. Bait schools have taken cover in the mass
of branches and twigs, while larger predators are gathered just outside of the mess, with
a few actually taking up station inside the branches of the tree. A bottom-of-the-range
sounder will be completely stumped by the complexity of a situation like this and all
you'll see on screen is a big blob of something on the bottom. A real blockhead sounder
may decide that the tree is part of the bottom and mislead you completely.

A quality unit, on the other hand, should have the capacity to separate the tree from
the bottom, define the outer branches, show the bait as bait and separate each of the
larger fish from the structure. Experienced sounder-users judge fish-finders on their
ability to separate the bottom from things on or close to the bottom, and to show big fish
as separate individuals when mixed in with a school of bait. A good sounder can also
show the nature of the bottom, be it sand, hard rock, a weed bed, a tree or even an old
car body dumped in a lake. It can also show a thermocline: the band where two layers of
water of different temperatures meet. Naturally, the sounder you use will be the sounder

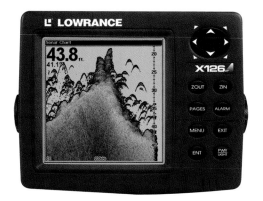

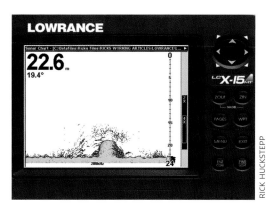

RICK HUCKSTEPP

A good fish-finder with a high-resolution screen is an essential item in a fishing boat

Fish love structure of any kind. In this case a hump has attracted bait (the fine black dots) and larger fish (the arches)

you can afford, but serious anglers should buy the very best unit they can manage.

Sounders are often used to confirm the presence or absence of fish in areas where visual observation indicates fish should be. For example, we were fishing an impoundment in an area where several small bays of shallow warm water ran off the main body of water. It was a pretty good bet that bass would be patrolling right where that warm water joined the colder, deeper drop-off, probably raiding fish sheltering in the shallows after dark. The sounder confirmed that two of the bays were devoid of fish but the third had an abundance of big bass. We had a great fishing session there, but without the sounder we might have wasted the day working the bays that held no fish.

Sounders can also turn up fishing spots you had no idea were there. Working some terrific cover along the bank of a river, the echo sounder showed we had drifted over a big snag that must have been left over from a past flood. Even though this was a complex mass of branches the sounder showed us a number of barramundi gathered there. It told us exactly how deep the fish were, so we tied on appropriate deep-diving lures and trolled back and forth over the snag several times, taking strikes every time until the fish woke up to us and stopped hitting the lures. We would never have known those fish were there if the sounder hadn't been left on.

Sounders are a great help in determining how you should fish an area. Fish may be found anywhere between the bottom and the surface at various times, so knowing where they are holding in the water column allows you to make presentations at the productive depth. Game fishermen often use sounders to locate bait schools down deep, then troll the surface over the schools knowing full well that any major predators in the area will be drawn to the bait sooner or later. An echo sounder used in conjunction with a downrigger can be a lethal weapon. A good sounder will show the ball weight used to get the lure down deep, and the depth can be adjusted to match the level the fish are swimming at. When trolling a downrigger, remember that many fish feed by looking upwards. Don't present your lures at a level below the fish on the sounder. If trolling quickly, the downrigger bomb will be shallower than indicated by the downrigger's counter due to 'blow-back', and the weight won't show on the screen if it's outside the sounder's cone of vision.

Sounders can also be used in conjunction with visual clues to further explore an area. For example, a ridge of rock coming out of a hillside and extending into the water as a rocky point probably continues out from the shoreline for some distance. This is worth checking out as it may well be holding fish.

Don't be lazy about using an echo sounder. Echo sounders are sold to many fishermen on the basis that they are exceptionally easy to use – buyers are told that all they have to do is switch on the power and the sounder will do the rest. That's baloney! You are a lot smarter than any echo sounder and, no matter how good the instrument is, you will get more out of it if you take control. Auto mode on the majority of sounders uses filters and low-sensitivity settings to ensure a lovely clean picture on the screen at all times. For really startling results, you need to get in there yourself: switch off filters, push sensitivity up until the screen starts getting dirty, then pull back until you have an acceptable amount of clutter on the screen. At this point, you'll have some noise on the display, but you should also be seeing fish and bait that weren't there on the auto settings. Whatever you do, get out of that silly 'Fish ID' display and choose the raw sonar display. It takes a little getting used to, but it is the only way to get value out of a fish-finder.

Having given sounders such a good wrap, we must also mention that many good fishermen believe fish are aware of the electronic pulse from the sounder and that some fish will switch off when they detect that pulse (especially when the boat is stationary above them). This is most likely to occur with resident schooling species, where fish repeatedly experience the sonar thump while watching others in the school being caught. In our opinion, the occasional situations where this might occur are far outweighed by the positive results turned up by using echo sounders. Whether the pulse is enough to influence the bite is open to debate, but if you are not actually using the sounder to find fish it's probably better to keep on the safe side and switch it off.

Global Positioning System (GPS)

Another useful electronic instrument for the angler is the Global Positioning System (GPS). Again, we don't want to get bogged down in the detail of how this system works, so let's just say that a GPS uses satellites scattered about the sky to determine its exact position on the face of the earth. These days, a GPS can achieve a position of within about 15 metres (often much better) of dead centre.

The more expensive models show an electronic chart on the screen, and the current position of the boat is shown on the chart as a blinking icon. Basic plotters simply show the position on a plain background. The great thing about GPS is that it allows you to save your current position to memory; when you want to return to that position at a later date you simply select that point from a library of saved positions. The GPS will indicate the direction you have to travel, how far away it is and how long it will take to get there at your present speed. It updates this information as you move along, gently correcting you if you stray off track.

There are two ways to save positions in a GPS set: as a 'waypoint' or as an 'event mark'.

A waypoint is so named because a number of waypoints can be strung together to form a route. You would use this method if the trip you intend to take involves a number of changes of direction. As you reach each waypoint, an alarm sounds and you are given a new course to the next waypoint. You can even reverse the order of the waypoints to take you back to where you started. So a waypoint can be a destination or a point along the way.

A modern GPS will allow you to save locations using event marks. An event mark is not saved into a library as is the case with waypoints; instead, the point where you hit the event mark button shows up as a little icon onscreen. You can navigate to this point by placing a cursor over the event mark and selecting a 'go to' function. What makes event marks even more useful is that you can choose from a number of icons to mark the spot. For example, if you find fish there you might mark it with a little fish icon; if it is an interesting feature on the bottom you might use another icon. If you start fishing a new area, every time you encounter fish or some interesting bottom feature likely to attract fish, you can save that position to memory, then the next time you return you can quickly check out all the positions where you found fish before. And because these event marks are displayed on the screen of a plotter or a chart plotter, you can go to a wide view on the display and see where you are in relation to everything you have marked in that area.

LOWRANCE

A GPS will save all of your special locations in a library. Choose one of these saved spots and the GPS will show you how to get there and let you know when you arrive. Mapping units like this one show both your position and track to get there. They are highly effective and very valuable tools in a boat. Once again good screen resolution is essential

At the time of writing this book, the east coast of Australia was in the grip of a severe drought. Some of the impoundments were down as low as 5–10 per cent of capacity, and the best of them were down to 50 per cent. This meant that a lot of areas normally covered by a considerable depth of water were as dry as a bone. However, with a handheld GPS, it was possible to walk around and save the position of rock bars, snags and all sorts of other things that would be fishing hot spots when a particular dam eventually filled again.

It gets even better when you realise that GPS still functions on a moonless night, in fog or when heavy rain affects visibility. This makes night fishing or getting onto hot spots before first light an easy task.

GPS units are available in a range of models, starting with handheld units the size of a mobile phone and ranging through to desktop-computer size with sophisticated software that enables the navigator to undertake all sorts of complicated manipulation of data. You can also buy models that combine echo sounder and GPS functions.

Other location markers

Without GPS it can be quite difficult to relocate fish once they've been spotted on a sounder. You don't want to be continuously running your boat back and forth over the fish-holding ground to find the same group of fish. One effective method is to make markers from something like plastic juice bottles or corks, with a weight attached to a length of light sash cord. It's a little like setting a crab trap with a white marker to indicate the whereabouts of the trap when you return to pull it. You can set up an area to fish in the dark in the same way by attaching light sticks to the float.

Lures come in a bewildering mass of shapes, sizes and colours.
They each have a distinct purpose and method of catching fish and they can
all trace their origins back to just a few lure families

CHAPTER THREE

The basic lure families

M an-made items have been fashioned from cloth, metal, wood or bone and fished in a way that deceives a fish into biting them for centuries now. The first known reference to the use of an 'artificial minnow' (made from silk) is in the landmark book *The Compleat Angler* by Isaac Walton of England in 1653.

Artificial lures of several types were available from British haberdashers throughout the eighteenth century and perhaps even earlier. In 1754 George Smith in his English *Anglers Magazine* lists a range of lures including wobblers, fly-spoons, plug-baits, true spinners, Devon minnows and so on.

The Americans credit their first lure to a spoon invented by Julio T. Buel, who was thought to be using them as early as 1821 and had started commercial production by 1848. The first 'plug', as we know it, is credited to James Heddon, who started fishing for largemouth bass with his invention in the late 1800s and had begun substantial manufacturing by 1902. The first of the plastic plugs were made of Dupont Pyralin and appeared around 1922.

There are now literally thousands of models of lures on the market, and many more thousands of size and colour variations within the basic models. But if you take the trouble to work your way back through the family tree to the roots, you will find they have all evolved from a handful of basic styles.

In this chapter we deal with the heads of those families so you will better understand the basic lure types and how they fit into the overall scheme of things. At the end of each section you'll find more technical information about the anatomy of a particular lure type. This Anatomy section is where you will learn about the important features of lure design and why two lures that seem nearly identical may perform completely differently in the water. It will also explain why there are many lures that look fabulous but don't catch fish at even close to the same rate as the best of their type; or why excellent lures may accidentally be rendered less effective because of simple mistakes or lack of knowledge about how to make them really perform.

Basically, the Anatomy sections give you the inside story on how lures are designed and work. They may get a little technical at times, but stick with them and you'll find they're filled with logical, easy-to-understand information that will 'switch the light on' and give you an in-depth understanding of lures. With this knowledge, you will be able to walk into any tackle shop in the world and easily work out what each lure will do and which ones you need for a particular scenario. And it's invaluable information for anyone interested in making their own lures.

Bibbed lures

These lures are commonly referred to as plugs. In the US, where they originated, they are also known as crankbaits. This is an old American term for a vast family of lures which are fairly realistically shaped to represent a fish or other creature and are given a swimming action by a projecting lip. In America and England anglers still, confusingly, refer to lures generally as 'baits'. Perhaps this originates from an abbreviation of 'artificial baits'.

As the name implies, crankbaits were originally a lure designed to be cast and retrieved; until you crank the handle on the reel it does nothing. Once it is given forward motion its design moves it with a natural or provocative action. The name is a little misleading, however, because this forward motion can be achieved by dragging it

Bibbed lures are a huge family that very successfully represent the many shapes,
sizes and actions of baitfish species that other fish like to eat

at the appropriate speed behind a boat just as much as by casting and retrieving. Many of these lures are used by trolling behind a boat, and some that are large or awkward to cast are used only when trolling.

Although bibbed lures are designed with a diverse array of body shapes, the slim fish shape is by far the most dominant style and so this lure family is also commonly referred to as 'minnows'. The word is used very loosely, as minnows are actually a family of fish species that are usually quite small. The range of lures that come under this heading are intended to imitate a much wider variety of slender bait species which, in real life, might weigh anywhere between a couple of grams and a kilogram or more.

Body shape can vary from an excellent imitation of a specific baitfish or crustacean through to funny little fat things that don't look like anything we see in this country, although they are still effective on Australian fish. They may also be jointed or manufactured with bodies that will float to the surface when forward movement stops, sink very slowly or sink rapidly.

The thing that defines a bibbed lure, of course, is the presence of a metal or plastic bib at the front of the lure. It is this bib that causes the lure to dive and, at the same time, to come to life with a swimming action. Some have a tight fast shimmy while others have a wide, slow wobbling action, depending on the shape, size and angle of the bib and body design.

Some lures have a small bib mounted at a steep or vertical angle to the head, in which case they will run very close to the surface. A lure with its bib set at a 45-degree angle to the head will dive a little beneath the surface when it is moved forward. Finally, a lure with a larger bib set at a very shallow angle to the head will dive very deeply. Small differences in the design of various parts can determine a whole range of outcomes, such as how deep, how fast, the various swimming actions and even if the lure will work at all! (These are described in detail in *Anatomy of a bibbed lure*, *pages 82–98*.)

Bibbed lures are essentially a slow to medium speed lure, although there are notable exceptions; for example, some blue-water minnows have carefully designed and balanced features that allow them to work as a high-speed spinning lure or at brisk trolling speeds as fast as 10 knots.

A variation in the bibbed lure family is a jerk minnow, otherwise known as a stickbait or jerkbait. This is essentially a minnow with a small shallow diving bib close to the nose of the lure, and, although it has a swimming action, it is fished in a similar way to a popper or surface slider. The stickbait is usually a floating lure or suspending lure and, once cast into a likely spot, is given a series of short but violent twitches with the rod. Because its bib is fitted close to the nose of the lure, when it's given the right kind of a jerk, the lure will pivot around. This causes the lure to dip and wriggle but, more importantly, it will also flick around sideways and roll. By sweeping the rod on alternating sides, the angler can cause it to zigzag. Good rod work will achieve this with a very short pull, and as there is sometimes a pause of several seconds between twitches, the lure can remain in the strike zone for a considerable time. If its body is reflective, the rolling action achieved with aggressive rod work will also create additional flash. Managed correctly, the lure will give a very convincing representation of a critically injured baitfish struggling at the surface – something no predator can resist!

A particular lure requires a particular retrieve speed and rod action and it pays to experiment to get the best result. Some lures work well at a steady speed, although in most fishing situations the odd stop/start or irregular dash in a retrieve will make a following fish strike. The rod tip is generally held close to the water and short flicks with the rod tip, mixed with cranks on the reel, will cause most lures to behave in a highly erratic and provocative manner.

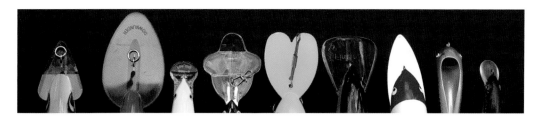

Bibs come in a wide variety of shapes and sizes to make lure bodies do different things.
Wide or narrow wobble, shimmy, dive, don't dive, go fast, go slow — how they all work is a
complex and fascinating business

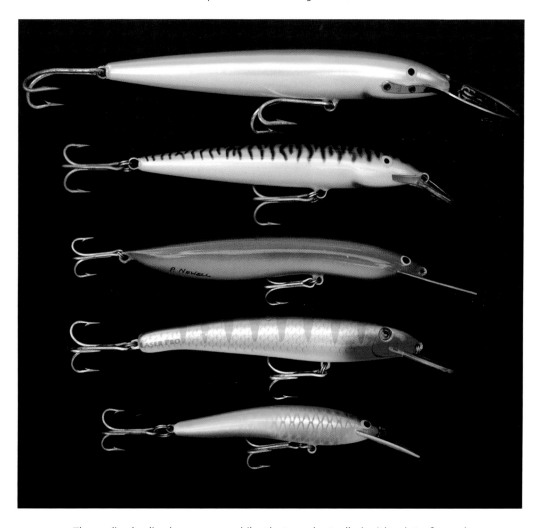

These slim bodies have narrow bibs that can be trolled with a lot of speed

ABOVE These examples of stickbaits (or jerkbaits) have bibs that are designed to destabilise the lure. With small stabs of the rod tip the lures will dart off in different directions, fall on their sides and generally behave just like an injured fish. This means that they can create a lot of flash and stay in the strike zone for long periods of time

RIGHT Factory lure testing at Lively Lures to ensure that the lure is swimming the way it is supposed to. It pays for anglers to test-swim new lures to get a feel for how they should be worked

TIM SIMPSON

When casting with deep divers, it is common for an angler to get the lure down to the required depth with a sharp sweep of the rod tip and a rapid retrieve for a couple of metres, then settle back into a slower retrieve that still maintains the lure's depth.

If casting to fish that are holding close to cover beneath a deep bank, the angle at which the lure dives may be critical to success. If the fish are ambush feeders they will not venture far from cover. The lure will have to get down to their level, but it will also have to get there at a very steep dive angle or it will be too far away from the structure to draw the fish out. Careful lure selection and, more particularly, bib design can achieve this.

With any new lure, it pays to spend some time casting it in clear water to see exactly what it does at various speeds and when paused. This is a good way to get the best out of your lures and to learn which one to select for the job at hand.

Don't forget, you are trying to make the lure look like real prey. Your success will increase if that prey looks especially vulnerable because of injury or distraction. Even a normal healthy fish does not swim in a straight line and at a constant speed for very long.

The lure's body shape and bib will cause it to wobble and 'swim' when pulled through the water, but there are many aspects of design that cause different swimming patterns. Lures that appear physically similar may have a very different movement in the water. The body will swing from side to side in a swimming motion but may also include a nodding of the head or tail, a sideways or vertical shift and a roll – all at the same time.

Even the side-to-side swimming motion will vary. Some lures have a very fast and narrow beat, called a 'tight' action, while others have a slow and very wide sway. The beat is not only visual; its pulse can be felt by the fish's lateral line. A quick tight pulse will usually appeal to fast-moving pelagic species (that primarily hunt by sight), while a slower but more powerful vibration will work best for slow-moving predators as the lure can be detected from quite a distance even in the gloom of heavily coloured water.

The range of subtle variations is enormous, but finding the right match for a particular species will result in consistent large catches instead of the odd lucky one. Some are extremely good for one type of fish or one situation, while for another species in a separate scene a totally different action may be required. Then again, some lures have a motion that doesn't attract and inspire a predator to attack at all. This is why anglers often have a tackle box bursting with different shapes and sizes and brands.

The swimming action of a bibbed lure is reliant on a critical balance of forces around its body. The precision and results achieved by premium lures will usually justify their premium price. (High-priced lures that don't produce, quickly die in the competitive marketplace). Most lures will catch fish straight out of the packet, although some benefit from a little fine-tuning. Unfortunately, due to poor design, manufacturing and quality control, some of the cheaper lures will never swim well. This is not to say that only expensive lures will catch lots of fish; there are some excellent and inexpensive lures made in all parts of the world. However, amongst the bewildering array of lures on the market, only a select few can match the consistent performance of the best.

TUNING BIBBED AND BIBLESS LURES

PROBLEM	SOLUTION

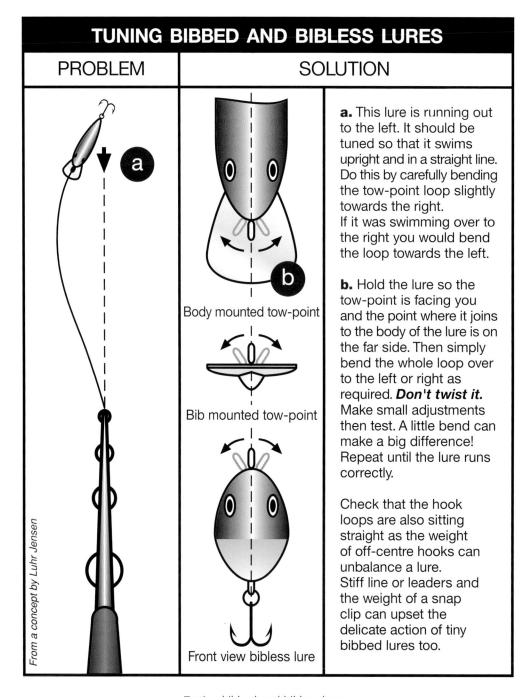

a. This lure is running out to the left. It should be tuned so that it swims upright and in a straight line. Do this by carefully bending the tow-point loop slightly towards the right.
If it was swimming over to the right you would bend the loop towards the left.

b. Hold the lure so the tow-point is facing you and the point where it joins to the body of the lure is on the far side. Then simply bend the whole loop over to the left or right as required. ***Don't twist it.*** Make small adjustments then test. A little bend can make a big difference! Repeat until the lure runs correctly.

Check that the hook loops are also sitting straight as the weight of off-centre hooks can unbalance a lure. Stiff line or leaders and the weight of a snap clip can upset the delicate action of tiny bibbed lures too.

Body mounted tow-point

Bib mounted tow-point

Front view bibless lure

From a concept by Luhr Jensen

Tuning bibbed and bibless lures

Sometimes a lure will swim with a weave to one side and lie slightly over on one flank. In theory this gives the lure an attractive 'injured' appearance. In practice, however – probably due to its altered vibrations – it will not catch fish nearly as well as a lure tuned to swim perfectly in a balanced upright position. With a quality lure this is easy to rectify: as long as the basic design is correct, a slight movement of the tow-point is all that is generally required.

With such a huge range of body sizes, shapes, colours, buoyancy and depth capabilities available, it is not surprising that many anglers are happy to do all their fishing with bibbed lures.

Considerations for bibbed lures

- The length of a typical cast is 20–25 metres. Thin lines cast noticeably better. For each 3 metres less or more than this distance, the lure's diving depth will be reduced or increased by roughly 10 per cent.
- Retrieve or trolling speed will affect a lure's action but not greatly affect its diving depth.
- Achieving a lure's maximum diving depth will require more line out than is usually cast. Lures that are trolled (say, 30–40 metres back) will often run at twice the depth of the same lure when cast.
- Line and trace diameter will affect a lure's diving depth. Each 1-kilogram increase in a nylon line's strength results in a roughly 300-millimetre decrease in diving depth on a typical trolled lure.
- A cast lure will generally take 20–35 per cent of the retrieve to reach maximum depth. That maximum depth is greatly increased with a longer cast.
- Pumping or lifting the rod while trolling – in a full sweep from horizontal to vertical – will cause the lure to accelerate and rise roughly 300 millimetres before settling back to its original depth. Continued sweeping rod lifts will raise the lure up to a new level that may be 25 per cent shallower.
- According to US bass pro Mike McClelland, who performed all these tests, when trolling a diving lure (more than 20 metres back) the height of the rod's tip, whether high overhead or underwater, will make little difference to the lure's running depth.

Anatomy of a bibbed lure

BIB

- This is the lure's 'wobble plate'. The bib's (or lip's) surface area, shape, angle and placement in the head are all significant to the lure's action and diving depth. They also affect the lure's stability, both at speed and when striking the bottom or structure.
- The surface area of the bib, together with the angle it is set at, determines how much water pressure is forced against it. This, along with where it is pulled from, is what drives a lure down and controls the depth it will dive to.
- Generally, a bib set vertically (at 90 degrees to the body) will keep the lure right at the surface, while a bib set horizontally (parallel with the body) will cause the lure to dive steeply. This is not always the case, however, as there are many other factors that affect the performance of the bib and lure.
- The more vertical the bib, the wider and more exaggerated the lure's action and the slower the frequency of its swimming pulse.
- Specially designed bibs (such as an upward-angled lobe at the front) can make a lure dive at an even steeper angle, which is useful for getting to fish that are holding up against deep structure next to the shore.
- While bibs are usually preferred to be clear in colour (to preserve a realistic outline), bibs with a metallic or reflective-coated surface can aid in fish attraction with their flash.
- A metal bib will add weight and affect the balance of the lure.

A bib is not just a bib. Lure designers create a remarkable range
of shapes and sizes to achieve a particular depth and action

- The strength of the bib should be considered if casting the lure at hard objects like rocks or trees, especially if the tow-point is attached to the bib.
- Generally, a narrow bib gives a tight action; a broad bib gives a wide action.
- A bib with a pointed or narrow tip will be more stable at speed.
- A cupped bib may produce a tighter action and will help to stabilise a lure that otherwise might not swim.
- On a lure with its tow-point on the bib, the swimming action will be tighter if the bib is narrow where it joins the body. A bib wider than the body of the lure at the join will make it less stable.
- The closer a bib is set to the horizontal centre line of the lure, the tighter the action.
- Bibs set close to a nose-mounted tow-point create a wider roll than those set further back. A close-set shallow diving bib makes a wide-rolling unstable lure suitable for use as a surface stickbait.

TOW-POINT

- The accuracy of the tow-point's placement at the hydrodynamic balance point will determine whether the lure swims straight or veers left or right. It will also affect the type of action the lure has and how fast it will go before becoming unstable and flipping out. Even a millimetre left, right, up or down can have an enormous effect.
- On a lure with a body-mounted tow-point, the lure's action can be deliberately altered by bending the tow-point down (to make it tighter) or up (to make it wider) with pliers. This can also be achieved by tying a tight, rigid knot to the tow-point in the desired position (although it will reduce the lure's ability to move – see below).
- The lure's action will be inhibited by a rigid connection between the line or leader and the tow-point. This is because the nose of the lure will have to overcome the water-drag as it tows the line back and forth through the water. It becomes more noticeable the thicker or stiffer the line is. A link that allows the lure total freedom to move and pivot around the connection will preserve more of its action. The link should have a rounded arc on which the lure can move: a split-ring or a snap-clip with a wide and rounded loop works well. A loop knot tied small and in stiff enough line that it retains its round shape under pressure is also successful; however, the sides of a longer loop or in a soft line will collapse together and fail to achieve the desired result.
- A lure that is not swimming straight and upright can be retuned by bending the tow-point left or right. (Bend the eye in the direction you want the lure to swim.)

The location of the tow-point has a lot to do with the way a lure behaves in the water

Also check that the hook attachment loops have not been bent.

- A 'floating' tow-point mounted on a bib – i.e. one that is not fixed and can pivot from side to side – will allow the lure to be somewhat self-tuning.

- How well-anchored the tow-point is in the body of the lure may be a concern, depending on the strength of your line. Some tow-point loops are merely a small screw eye which rely on the strength of the body material to anchor them. The strongest connection is a continuous wire or plate that extends from the tow-point to the rear hook – although with modern plastics and manufacturing techniques, a simple figure-eight loop can be moulded in with remarkable strength. Modern plastic lures are commonly made of ABS (acrylonitrile butadiene styrene, a tough co-polymer) but this can be cracked or shattered by strong jaws or impact with rocks. Others are moulded from stronger synthetics like Lexan or Tenite Propionate, but are more difficult and therefore more expensive to produce.

- The tow-point is what connects the lure (and fish) to your line. If you are expecting a fish with an extremely powerful mouth that might destroy your lure, or plan to

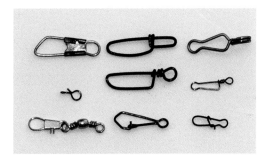 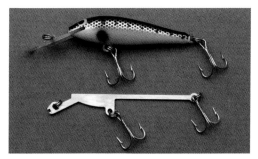

LEFT Lures may sometimes be attached to the line with a snap clip of some kind. You must ensure that the snap allows the head of the lure to move freely and that it is strong enough to handle the fish you seek. An over-large snap may change the body profile of a small lure and the extra weight may dampen its action

RIGHT A one-piece metal frame and strong rings and hooks give this Tilsan lure the overall strength to stay in one piece when monstered by large fish

use a very strong line, it may be prudent to select a lure with a body-mounted tow-point, unless the bib is of adequate strength. Fortunately, many are these days.

✄ A bib-mounted tow-point allows some lures to perform better and dive deeper than a body-mounted tow-point.

✄ The position of a bib-mounted tow-point will vary the lure's action depending on the shape of the body. A curved body will have a wider action if the tow-point is close to the nose. A straight body will have a tighter action the closer the tow-point is to the nose.

✄ In most cases, a tow-point mounted at the front of the bib reduces the diving depth.

HOOK ATTACHMENT POINTS

✄ Whether hooks are attached on or either side of the pivoting point of a lure's action will influence how the lure swims. Belly hooks are a significant weight; if a single belly hook is mounted at the point where a lure pivots in its wiggle, then this weight will not have to be swung through the water by the lure, which frees the lure to have more action. If one or more belly hooks are mounted away from the pivot point, this weight will have to be swung and the lure's action will be decreased. The further it is placed from the pivot – either to the front or rear – the greater the distance the hook must swing from side to side and so the more the lure is affected by this weight.

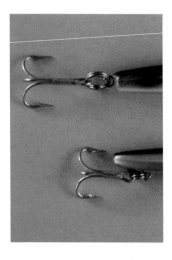 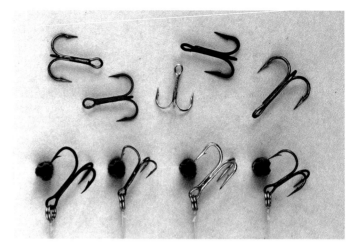

LEFT Attaching the rear hook of a bibbed lure a little back from the tail increases action by reducing the leverage of the hooks weight. It also brings the hook points closer to the body — where the fish is likely to bite

RIGHT Treble hooks are made in a variety of colours. This enables colour matching to lures or low-visibility stealth. The shape of the hook points and particularly the length of their shank will greatly influence how easily they penetrate a tough mouth. Look at the angle of pull on these hook points once they are under load and pivot around. A beak point or the Mustad 'Triple Grip' style (second from left, bottom row) show a much straighter and easier penetration

When the rear hook is mounted at the extremity of the lure, it gives good clearance for the points but positions them away from the body outline. An alternative is to mount the hook slightly forward of the end, so that the hook points sit at the extremity of the lure's body. This may help to keep an accurate profile and keeps the hook points in the region where the fish is likely to bite, not trailing behind. This set-up will also bring the weight of the rear hook back towards the lure's pivoting point and so help to preserve more of the lure's action.

STRENGTH

As with the tow-point, the attachment loops must be securely fixed in the lure or strong fish may tear the hook off.

The attachment points should be spaced far enough apart that the hooks don't overlap; otherwise they may link together during casting.

HOOKS

- Long-shanked hooks add weight and, when at the tail, take the points further away from the body where the strike will be. However, a longer shank will aid hook penetration as it helps to keep the point aligned on the surface it is penetrating.

- Short-shanked hooks are less visible and closer to the body, but harder to 'set' in a hard mouth. Once pressure is on the point of a short-shanked straight hook point, it will rotate until it is almost sideways, requiring considerably more force to pull it in.

- A point that is angled towards the eye of the hook, or a curved-in 'beak' point, makes it much easier to slip the hook in once pressure is applied.

- Although not commonly imported into Australia, hooks are available in various colours. Some colours help to make the tail look realistic; others add brightness or shine that may attract. A dull colour that blends in with the water or background will help to disguise a hook that you don't want seen.

- The size and length, as well as the gauge (thickness) of the hook, will influence the weight and therefore the action of the lure. The hook must be strong enough to handle the line strength and the intended catch, however the gauge will also affect how easy the hook is to 'set' on light tackle. Thick hooks and large barbs are much harder to pull in.

- Some fish will take the lure from behind. If the fish's forward motion is faster than the retrieve speed, the line will momentarily go slack. During this second or two it is possible for the fish to evaluate the lure and spit it out, so you will catch many more fish if your hooks are as fine as possible and extremely 'sticky' (sharp). A fine, sticky hook may catch on the fish's mouth under its own force and hold long enough for the pressure to come back on the line and set the hooks properly.

- There is a left and a right side to a treble hook. If you hold a treble with its eye towards you and look at the points, two will be off to the left or right and the third will face to the other side. Turn the eye 180 degrees and of course the sides are reversed. On a lure with two or more hooks, if the trebles are attached to the rings in opposite ways, the points will be set at six different angles instead of just three, which increases the chances of hooking a fish and also helps to balance a lure if high-speed trolling.

- Hooks decorated with feathers, tinsel or other material will have greater water resistance and so will reduce the movement (action) of the lure.

- Hooks made from high-carbon 'chemically sharpened' steel are much more brittle than regular steel hooks.

WEIGHT OF ATTACHED HARDWARE

✥ The combined weight of hooks, rings, snaps etc must be swung through the water by the power of the lure's action. If too much weight is added, the lure's action will be reduced or killed off entirely. As the lure wiggles back and forth, its nose and tail move a greater distance through the water than its middle, so the effect of the added weight is magnified the closer it is to the ends of the lure.

✥ If the holding power of a large hook is required, but the weight of a treble will upset the lure's action, try using a larger double hook instead, or a large treble with one or two of its hooks cut off. This may achieve the necessary size without adding excess weight. The lure is more able to cope with a larger hook close to its centre (pivot) point than at its tail.

✥ The weight of a belly hook also acts as a keel to stabilise the lure and keep it upright.

LENGTH OF ATTACHMENTS

✥ In all but very poor visibility, a fish approaching a lure will see every part of it. The attachments like hooks, rings and snaps on the lure's body make a visible difference to its outline. When fish are feeding exclusively on a prolific prey item, it is often critical that the lure matches the prey's body size and profile. At other times it simply helps to make the lure look more realistic.

✥ On small lures particularly, the use of a prominent snap or, worse, a longer snap-swivel, may enlarge and change the lure's outline enough to stop it being eaten. Similarly, the hook at the tail end needs to be set to the same proportion as the real prey's tail to its body.

SPLIT RINGS

✥ The rings are an important but often overlooked connection, providing a knuckle-joint between lure and hook to help prevent the hook tearing out.

✥ Rings must be strong enough to withstand the strain of a powerful fish jaw, twisting and the strength of the line they will be used on.

✥ Split rings that have an extra loop of wire – so there are never less than two strands going through the eye of the hook – are usually twice as strong as a similar-sized typical ring that at some point has only one strand to hold the hook.

✥ Tiny rings restrict the movement of the hooks and so may reduce the action slightly. Heavy rings, on the other hand, add to hardware weight and this may affect smaller lures. An overly large split ring may obstruct a small hook and deflect a fish's mouth away from the points.

* Two interlocked split rings will add unwelcome length and weight, but the freedom of movement given by the extra 'knuckle' will reduce the chances of violent head-shaking and jumping successfully levering the hook free.

* A hook can be attached easily without the use of a ring at all. The eye of a treble can be snipped on one side with wire cutters and then twisted open to fit around the attachment loop. Once closed, it is very strong but lacks the movement given by a ring.

CLEARANCE OF HOOKS

* A tail or body section which is broader or deeper than the gape of the hooks can deflect a fish's mouth past the points, preventing the lure hooking up as effectively. A benefit is a more snag-resistant lure which can brush past timber and rocks without the hooks catching.

BUOYANCY

* This is a major aid to action as it helps to counteract the weight of attachments.

* The positioning and surrounding wall thickness (weight) of an internal buoyancy chamber in a plastic-bodied lure will affect balance and action. A moulded-in air chamber may give a lure sufficient overall buoyancy to float, but if the chamber is centralised and does not extend to the extremities of the lure, the ends (which move the most) will be weighed down by the solid plastic and the lure will not swim as freely.

* A similar body shape with buoyancy in its extremities, such as a timber lure, will have a noticeably different action. The tail section of a balsa lure may be ten times lighter than the tail of a similar lure made from plastic.

* A lure made from aerated foam or moulded polyurethane will have almost uniform buoyancy throughout the body (similar to timber) as it does not need a weighty solid casing and reinforcements.

* The more buoyant the lure, the more easily it moves in the water and the greater its action.

* In a timber lure, the type (density) of the timber will greatly affect its buoyancy. Although light, balsa is a favourite for high-action lures, being very buoyant and exceptionally strong for its weight.

* The buoyancy will affect how many hooks a lure can carry, and how big they may be, while still maintaining an effective action.

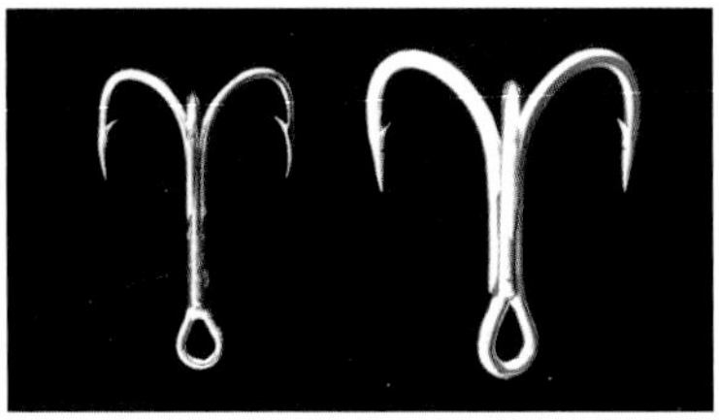

RON CALCUTT

LEFT Stronger hooks are required in some areas, but be aware that stronger hooks are also heavier hooks that may impact on the action of the lure

RIGHT In this see-through picture it is possible to see how the inside of this plastic lure has been created as several sealed chambers, some containing metal balls that act as both ballast and noise creators. This adds strength but any plastic moulding comes with the loss of air space and its buoyancy. You can also see how rings and tow points have been moulded into the body and bib for maximum strength

- Buoyancy determines how quickly a lure will float upwards when the retrieve is stopped, which is important for some paused retrieve styles. The positioning of the lure's buoyancy will also determine whether the lure floats up horizontally, nose up or tail up. A lure that rises slightly tail up (approximately 45 degrees) will actually back up in the water. This is especially handy for some retrieves (rip/pause) as it can keep a lure in the strike zone much longer.
- A buoyant lure, especially one that backs up, is convenient for getting lures off snags.
- A lure with little or neutral buoyancy will have less action but can be very versatile. It can be dived down and then twitched or paused while maintaining its depth. Besides its realistic behaviour, this may provoke an aggression strike from an otherwise dormant fish if the invading lure remains in its territory.
- A sinking lure opens up a whole range of depth options.
- A lure with the bulk of its buoyancy in the rear will travel in a nose-down, tail-up attitude while a lure with most of its buoyancy in the head is more inclined to swim horizontally.
- Saltwater gives more buoyancy to a lure than fresh. A lure in freshwater will have less flotation and perhaps less action.

RATTLES/SOUND

- Some lures incorporate rattle chambers with metal balls. The sound achieved will vary depending on the size and material the balls and their case are made from, as well as the density of the surrounding lure. The weight and placement of the rattle within the lure will also affect the lure's action.

✠ A timber or moulded solid polyurethane lure produces a lower-frequency sound than a hollow plastic lure.

✠ A fish's inner ear can pick up sound frequencies of 20–600+ Hertz from a huge distance, but unless the sound is good enough to go hunting for it will probably be ignored along with the barrage of other background noise.

✠ Lure sound can help by simply alerting the fish to the fact that it exists, but the best sound a lure can make is to mimic prey that is injured, terrified or easy to catch for some other reason.

✠ As a lure swims, the hooks and rings rattle together on their attachment and may produce a noticeable sound.

✠ As the lure wiggles from side to side, the points of any belly hooks will sometimes knock against the side of the lure. The sound this makes depends on the composition and density of the material the lure is made from – the tap of a hollow plastic or the subtle bonk of a timber body. (Just look at the sides of an old high-speed strongly actioned lure to see the wear against the sides from the hook points banging and rubbing against the body!)

✠ At times, particularly in heavily fished waters with re-released fish, the fish may associate the sound of a lure or rattle with trouble. In such situations it may help to

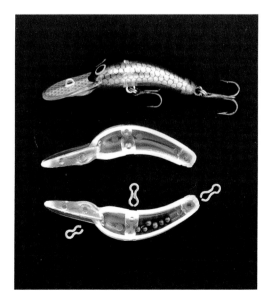

LEFT Another inside view of a moulded lure showing the location of metal balls that will rattle as the lure wobbles along

ABOVE The scraping scars from the hook point on the body of this lure show just how much the hooks can bang against it while swimming. This and the jingling of the split rings add noise to an otherwise 'silent' lure

select a non-rattling lure and rig it for 'silent running'. Bend the hooks on the belly treble so that two are horizontal and the third is vertical (forming a T shape). Also, run a piece of thin spaghetti tubing onto the split ring. This will reduce the jingling of attachments and the body tapping by the hook as the lure sways from side to side.

✢ Sound is particularly useful when visibility is poor in dirty water, in darkness, or when trying to draw fish from a distance.

BODY PROFILE

✢ The cross section and overall profile throughout the length of the lure will affect its action. How water flows around the lure's curves – pushing around the wide contours, then nipping in at the narrow – causes different pressures along the body. This variance in the velocity of parallel layers of water is called 'laminar flow'. When laminar flow moves the lure one way, the pressures along the body change and cause it to move back the other way again. If the lure's body is identical on both sides, these constantly changing, unstable but balancing pressures are what give the lure its wiggle.

✢ The length of a lure's body will restrict and stabilise its movements in the water. A long thin lure will generally have a tight action and a short rounded one will have a wide swaying action.

✢ The difference in body shape above and below the centre line will also influence the flow of water: an aerofoil cross-section creates forces of lift, like a wing, which then act in concert with the diving forces of the bib.

✢ A body with two-thirds of its bulk above the centre line (end to end) is more stable than one with equal size above and below. It will also offer the lure designer more scope for bib and tow-point placement to make the lure either a deep or shallow diver.

✢ A pronounced curve (banana shape) will usually create a strong and wide swaying action.

✢ The outline (and silhouette) of the lure should match that of the prey species you are trying to imitate.

ACTION/VIBRATION

✢ Different fish feed on many different species of prey. Finding the right action and vibration for the species of fish you are seeking is a key element in consistent and substantial success.

✢ The flow of water is different with each different body/bib/tow-point combination,

Three bibbed lures that all have dramatically different swimming actions due
to body profile, buoyancy, weight and bib shape

which gives each model of lure a unique action as well as depth and speed range.

✤ The pulse that the lure gives off should match a preferred prey item if it is intended
to represent food.

✤ The bulk of a big head will push more of a pressure wave through the water than a
slim design.

✤ The action of a bibbed lure is a compilation of different movements – all happening
at the same time. Besides its left–right swimming wiggle, the body will roll (belly to
left/belly to right etc) and the whole lure may shift its position – moving slightly to
the left or right, or up or down, then back again. The tail of the lure may also bob
up and down. An increase in speed will usually tighten up the action.

✤ Water pressure and density increases considerably the deeper you go. At 10 metres
the water is twice as dense, at 20 metres it is three times as dense and so on. As the
water becomes denser, it becomes harder for the lure to move and a lure with a good
action at the surface may have very little action left by the time it reaches its depth.

A lure that dives very deep or a lure to be run deep on a downrigger or weighted line should take this into account.

✦ Some fish species seem to have a preference for a tight action while others prefer a wide slower pulse. For dirty water, and especially for slow-swimming freshwater fish, lures are often much slower and have a strong wide action. With only very short-range visibility, the fish is likely to rely on its lateral line to sense prey so a strongly pulsing lure action is more likely to be found.

FLASH

✦ A shiny or silvery appearance may help to create a more realistic imitation of a prey item. A lure that actually transmits a flash of reflected sunlight is another thing again. A flash will be seen at a much further distance than the lure itself and may give the attractive impression of a fish in distress.

✦ As the lure rolls, a rounded surface will produce a continuous thin line of reflection whereas a multifaceted surface will reflect a series of flashes from a variety of angles. A broad flat surface will only reflect when at the appropriate angle to the sun, but when it does it will give a stronger, broader blast of light.

✦ Highly reflective metallised 'chrome' finishes are available for timber as well as plastic lures.

✦ For many years flash panels have been mounted inside some plastic lures, however their flash abilities are limited by the reflective properties of the material used, overlaid colouring and the clarity of the surrounding plastic.

✦ It is widely thought that a flash of gold is the most successful in dirty or coloured water and a silver-based flash is more successful in clearer waters.

✦ A reflective lure will actually become camouflaged unless there is sufficient light shining off it.

JOINTED BODY

✦ A multi-piece (articulated) body joined by linked attachment loops has a different action to a similarly shaped one-piece body. When the front section wiggles with its swimming action, instead of the tail end being kicked left and right through the water it merely pivots at the joint and is towed in a smooth flowing arc behind the head.

✦ The head section has more freedom, resulting in a wider action.

✦ Overall, the lure's motion is more serpentine and produces a different vibration to that of a one-piece body.

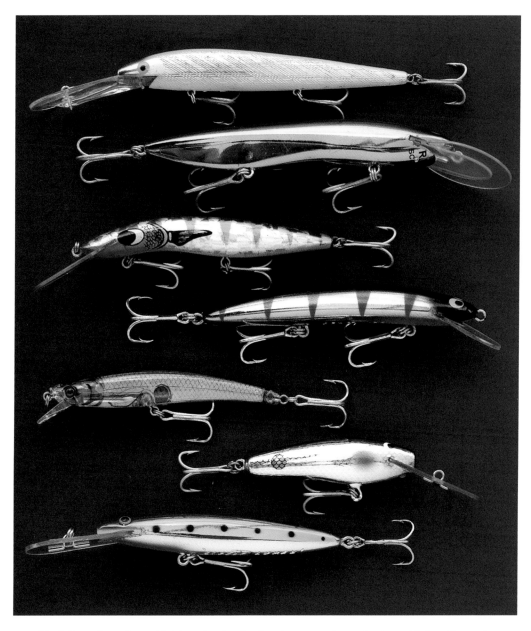

All of these lures have highly reflective bodies, but note how the lure third up from the bottom has no flash due to it being at the wrong angle to the light. Lures with flat reflective planes will throw more flash than a rounded shape

BALANCE WEIGHTS

- These are internal additions (during manufacturing) to aid balance, dive angle and casting weight. They are sometimes incorporated as a rattle.
- Some lures have a small weight attached to a plastic bib. This makes a floating lure sit at rest with its head angled down, which primes it for a steeper dive angle once the retrieve is started.
- Weights set forward in the head of the lure can change the angle at which it runs through the water, repositioning the water flow onto the bib and allowing a lure to dive much deeper than the bib size would seem to indicate. A metal bib is a significant weight at the front of the lure.
- Internal bar or bent-wire hook-hanger arrangements are also a significant weight. If positioned above the lure's centre line they may affect its balance.
- Centring any added weight around the pivot point of the lure's motion will preserve more if its action.

EYE

- In spite of excellent camouflage, fish have great difficulty disguising their eyes. As a result, predators are particularly sensitive to the round shape and centre dot of an eye; in many cases this is the first thing they distinguish.
- Most schooling baitfish have relatively large eyes. A suitably sized, contrasting and prominent eye gives the lure credibility and attracts the attention of a predator.

ATTITUDE

- The angle the lure swims at – horizontally or head down – will affect its appearance as well as its resistance to snagging and hook-point damage.
- A lure that swims head down with a substantial bib projecting out in front will usually strike a snag with its bib first. The hooks will be suspended slightly above it and shielded by the body of the lure in front of them. Depending on the tow-point and bib shape, some lures will then pivot and flip over the obstacle without snagging.
- A diving lure that swims tail up is useful when run along the bottom with its bib digging in to imitate a feeding bottom fish. The bib will stir the bottom while the hook points are lifted up away from damage and positioned well for a predator to easily inhale the tail and hooks.
- If the buoyancy is centred towards the head of the lure it is more likely to swim horizontally, which is more realistic for a surface/midwater baitfish representation.

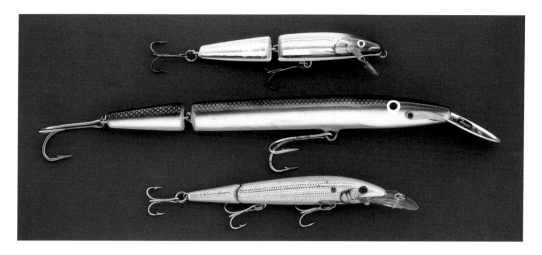

Lures with jointed bodies tend to have sinuous, quite different actions
to those with a one-piece body

Eyes are very difficult for a fish to disguise and so many predators have special sensors in
their eyes to detect the circle and centre dot against the gloomy background. Having a large,
prominent eye on a lure should help to get your lure noticed and give it credibility

CASTABILITY

- A bibbed lure is typically bulky and wind-resistant compared to its weight. This makes it difficult to cast long distances and vulnerable to being slowed or blown off course by wind. A design which tumbles or flutters during a cast will drastically shorten the cast even more.
- Some hollow plastic lures feature a chamber with loose ballast or rattle-ball weights. During a cast these weights run to the tail of the lure and their momentum keeps the lure travelling tail-first, with least resistance, through the air. Once the lure has

settled in the water, the balls run forward and over a small ridge which traps them in the correct balance position for the lure to swim.

✥ A large bib can catch the air like a wing. Besides the drag, which reduces casting distance, it can deviate a cast.

Bibless minnows

A bibless minnow also swims with a fish-like wriggle, but with a different motion to that of a bibbed lure. Instead of pulling from under the nose and using a bib to induce an action, these lures are towed from the top of the head. This drags the lure through the water with its head and back pushing against the water pressure. These forces wrap around the body, causing it to vibrate strongly and giving it a 'swimming' appearance. The forehead of the body becomes a 'bib'.

The swimming action of these lures is more back left/right, belly right/left; whereas a bibbed lure is more head left/right, tail right/left.

The strength of the vibration that can be built into this design allows it to carry a heavy payload of hardware or ballast weight. Some bibless lures contain a large quantity of rattle balls, while others are loaded with lead to handle extreme trolling speeds or sink like a rock for use as a jig. They are commonly made from timber, hollow plastic or moulded polyurethane, but the same vibrating action can be achieved with a nose weight on a thin vertical sheet of metal.

Bibless minnows are a useful fast-trolling lure, especially for big fish when large hooks and a heavy trace are required. Some varieties will stay swimming beneath the surface at extreme speeds of over 15 knots! This makes it a real possibility to keep trolling even while travelling out or between spots.

The slower, pulsating varieties are useful for dropping down beside structure. They can be fished at any depth and either jiggled to antagonise a sleepy cave-dweller or given a volatile retrieve at the whim of the angler. The strong pulse these lures put out also makes them suitable for poor-visibility situations such as stained water or low light.

One variation with an exceptionally strong action is the Flatfish style. These lures have a very strong pulse at very slow speeds and have found enormous success with anglers trolling for trout in all parts of the world. They are particularly good when trolled deep on a downrigger where the water pressure tames their wild action back to

These are examples of bibless lures. Like the bibbed lures, they can be designed
to be used at a variety of speeds. Their movement is a swimming wobble,
but it's slightly different to that of the bibbed lures

a very effective swimming shimmy. Another variation of a bibless minnow is the darter.
This is a surface twitching lure with a sloping face, often with a 'mouth' cut into it
which gives an erratic darting action when jerked with the rod. On floating models,
these lures also benefit from the splash attraction of a popper.

Two dramatically different shapes for highly specialised jobs. The sliders (top and bottom) have no built-in action at all and rely entirely on erratic rod tip action to dance on the surface and interest fish. The flatfish (centre) swims with a strong pulse at very slow speeds and was a freshwater favourite for trout and cod fishermen for many years

A completely different variation is the slider (not the soft plastic version). The slider is a floating cigar-shaped lure with no built-in action. It doesn't splash and relies entirely on the angler's rod work to create its enticing jerky motion as it slides across the surface. These are usually used with a very slow retrieve and a series of short violent twitches, keeping them in the strike zone for long periods and giving an excellent representation of a struggling baitfish.

Anatomy of a bibless minnow

TOW-POINT
- The position of the tow–point on the face of a bibless minnow will affect its balance and so influence its action and maximum speed. It will also determine whether the lure swims horizontally or how far nose down/tail up.
- Some lures have two or more tow-points: one for fast trolling and one or more for

slower speeds. The further forward the tow-point is placed, the faster the lure needs to be towed to produce a swimming action. It will also cause the lure to ride more horizontally.

FACE
🐟 This becomes the 'bib' of the lure. The surface area and the angle of the face will determine the resistance of the lure against the water, which will influence the action, the amount of weight (hooks etc) it can swing through the water and the minimum speed required to make the lure swim. It will also affect how deep the lure will dive and how fast it can be swum before it becomes unstable and flips out.

🐟 A flat face will achieve more resistance against the water and so will have a bigger action and a lower speed than a similar lure with a rounded or ridged-face surface. A ridged face, with less resistance, will not reach its action potential until it is travelling much faster.

BACK
🐟 If the lure travels nose down/tail up, as many do, its back will form part of the resistance to the water and so its profile will affect the action.

RATTLES
🐟 The strong and shaking action of the bibless minnow make it an ideal vehicle to carry the weight of rattles.

🐟 The chamber the rattling balls are enclosed in and the material they are made from will affect the pitch and volume of the sound. The sound will also be influenced by the material of the surrounding body.

🐟 A timber lure will usually give a lower-frequency sound than a plastic lure.

🐟 Fish will only react to certain frequencies, so if the rattle doesn't make the right kind of sound it may all be in vain!

🐟 Sound vibrations travel further than swimming vibrations, so whether the sound actually excites the fish to strike or simply attracts attention, it has greater potential if the lure designer can achieve the right noise.

VIBRATION
🐟 Bibless lures are usually deep-bodied with relatively flat sides so when they swim they move a lot of water. This pulse can be detected by a fish's lateral line and may

excite and alert your quarry to the lure way before it can see it, especially in darkness or dirty water.

🐟 As with sound, it is important that the pulse is of the right beat to trigger particular fish. Fast-moving fish that eat fast-moving baitfish often prefer a tight narrow beat while more docile predators chasing slower food respond well to a wide sway.

🐟 Sinking versions of these lures are often fished with a rip-and-pause jigging action. This is usually more effective if the lure has a fluttering vibrating action on the drop.

FLASH

🐟 The broad flat sides of these lures (in contrast to most narrow rounded-bodied lures) enable them to deliver not just a shine but a full-on blast of flash if the sides are reflective. This will obviously help to get your lure noticed and may be an advantage where fish are feeding boldly or in coloured water.

🐟 A flash is visible at a greater distance than mere colour and outline, and may also give the impression of a fish that is injured or in distress.

See also Bibbed lures, Flash, page 94.

HOOKS

🐟 Most bibless lures will be armed with treble hooks. On really large blue-water lures, or when using tackle stronger than 10 kilograms, these hooks may not have sufficient size and strength to stay connected to the fish. In these instances, a gamefishing-strength single or double hook may be a better option.

🐟 The (usually) strong action of this type of lure gives it more scope to accommodate a large hook, but excessive weight can easily affect a lure's action, so if replacing hooks keep in mind that the new hook should probably be similar in weight.

🐟 With a treble hook, the holding power is largely determined by the size of the gape on each of the three hook points. If the treble hook is enlarged so that each of its hooks is big enough to handle serious pressure, the hook may be too heavy and physically too bulky for the lure. After all, a single hook will have a width nearly half that of a treble hook with similar gapes.

🐟 A double hook has excellent holding power, covers two approach angles, sits balanced and cleanly against the belly of the lure, is less than double the width of a similarly sized single hook and is much less bulky than a treble. When using large sizes, remember that a double hook will have twice the weight of a single, which may affect the lure's action.

These bibless minnows vary from high-speed models with a tight swimming action
to slow-speed models with a strong vibration. The metal blade (second bottom, right)
also vibrates with a strong action. The bottom lure is used as a suspending jerkbait,
where it darts and flashes according to manipulation by the rod

≈ If a single hook is used, it must not be curbed or it will cause the lure to roll or spin.
To keep both the belly and tail hooks riding vertically (and balanced), they will need
to be attached to the lure with two interlocked split rings or brazed solid rings. On
larger lures a twisted micro shackle or two connected singles could be used.

≈ Another strong factory-fitted connection is via a ball-bearing swivel. In this case,
one end of the swivel is attached by its solid brazed ring to the lure while the ring
at the other end is attached to the hook. The brazed rings of a strong swivel do not
allow the hooks to be changed easily, however, and unfortunately add unwelcome
length to the hook arrangement and set the rear points further back from the body
of the lure.

See also Bibbed lures, Hooks, page 87.

As bibless minnows increase in size they move into a category where game fish strength
hooks become more appropriate. Singles or doubles are more practical than huge trebles

BUOYANCY/WEIGHTING

※ The strong action of this vibrating design overcomes some of the need for buoyancy
that is so helpful in a bibbed lure. The more buoyancy a bibless minnow has,
however, the more easily it will carry the weight of large hooks and associated
hardware and still retain an action at the lower speeds.

※ An internal weight orients the lure in an upright, head-down/tail-up position that
primes it for diving and swimming. High-speed trolling models use a substantial
weight in the nose to keep the lure keeled. In the smaller sizes, the added weight also
assists with casting.

※ Most of these lures sink. Some of the smaller ones contain a rattle of metal balls
which adds centre weighting and balance; these are often used as a jig.

*See also Bibbed lures, Hook attachment points, page 85–6; Length of attachments, page
88; Split rings, page 88–9; Eye, page 96.*

Surface lures

While the bibbed lures are designed to seek out fish at a range of depths, the surface lures are designed to encourage fish to come up to the surface or to appeal to fish that are already feeding at the surface.

A prey item on the surface is a very attractive thing to a predator. The attack will naturally come from underneath and, when it does, the prey has only a hemisphere of air where their escape route would normally be. Add the appearance of distress or injury to this vulnerability and it's easy to appreciate the effectiveness of a top-water lure.

Poppers are the most common of the surface lures and there are two distinct and separate types: the chugger and the skipping popper.

The chugger (also known as a blooper) is a stocky barrel-shaped lure with a large, blunt and usually concave face. The idea with a chugger is to slowly work it across the top while tearing great holes in the surface, splashing and making as much noise and commotion as possible.

Depending on the location and the species, the retrieve may involve nerve-racking pauses of many seconds between each 'bloop'. Predators cruising below can hardly miss the fuss and, because the lure is worked so slowly, have ample time to rise up from the depths to climb all over it. This makes for spectacular strikes! In fact, even at times when a chugger is not the most productive style of lure, some anglers will trade the excitement of a popper strike for twice as many sub-surface strikes.

There are times with some species, however, when the fish may not be interested in feeding at all but are so infuriated by the crazy intruder that they smash it out of aggression or as a plaything. At such times, a popper is the only thing that works. Yellowtail kingfish and giant trevally are suckers for this type of lure.

The face of a cupped chugger can make an audible 'pop' if the angles are right. Others will lack the benefit of sound but still create a large surface commotion. If retrieved with any speed, these lures will usually dive just beneath the surface and wobble with a strong shaking motion, often with a bubble of air streaming behind.

A slow twitching retrieve is commonly used to work snags where fish will be hiding amongst a tangle of branches. The long delays between pops encourage a fish to believe that something has fallen in the water close to its hiding place. The delay allows the lure to be kept in the critical strike range for a longer period than any lure that has to be moving to work. You need to be patient as there are times when a number of casts

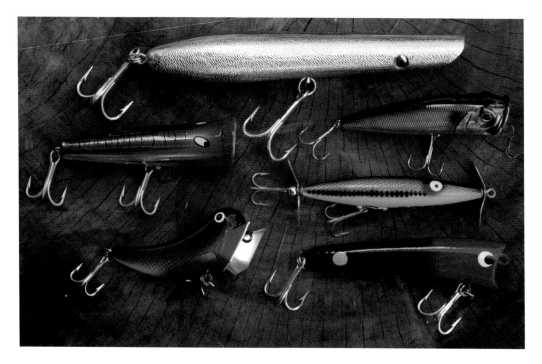

Surface lures are designed to behave in different ways. The skipping popper (top)
does not pop so much as skitter across the top imitating an escaping baitfish. The two
chugger poppers (middle) boil the surface at slower speeds making plenty of noise and bubbles
as they go. The fizzer with propellers fore and aft can be a more subtle lure that spends a
long time in the strike zone with the spinning blades churning the water and attracting fish.
BOTTOM LEFT Waddlers rely on strange attachments to the head to
cause them to waddle and plop across the surface.
BOTTOM RIGHT A cross between a blooper and a skipper — for use at speed

and patient retrieves will produce nothing, but then, suddenly, a fish will explode
through the surface to hammer the lure. It's exciting fishing!

The skipping popper also splashes across the surface but with a completely
different modus operandi. In fact, skipping poppers never actually 'pop'.

When baitfish are being chased at the surface by a predator they often jump out of
the water in a desperate attempt to get away. With the attacker hot on their tail, they
frequently spend as much time in the air as in the water. Garfish, for example, will
greyhound across the waves in a frenzied display that covers many metres, until it ends
with escape or a swirling boil where the final jump landed. Even a prawn in the weed

LEFT Flicking a popper back to a school of rampaging giant trevally on a coral reef edge is not for the faint hearted. Few angling situations deliver the same nerve-jangling excitement as seeing very large fish exploding on a surface lure

RIGHT Chugger poppers are particularly effective on the giant trevally (GT). GTs reach sizes more than five times as big as this one. They demand heavy tackle and very strong lures

beds being chased by a bream will skip across the top. This is what a skipping popper imitates. Some of the most exciting moments in sportfishing can be had when a big trevally, queenfish, kingfish, mackerel or any other fast pelagic comes storming across the surface in pursuit of a high-speed skipping surface popper.

If poppers can draw fish up from the depths by being loud or brash, fizzers can sometimes do the same thing by being quiet and extremely subtle. A fizzer is generally a cigar-shaped body fitted with a little propeller at the front or rear. Some have a propeller at both ends. When the lure is moved the propellers spin and make a 'fizzzzz' noise, hence the name.

Although fizzers can be jerked across the surface fairly briskly, their real value lies in their ability to attract fish sitting in cover with barely any movement at all. It takes no more than a small rod-tip movement twitching the slack in a line for those little props to buzz. The forward movement of the lure is so small that the lure can be kept active in the strike zone for a very long period of time.

Fizzers are great lures to use when ambush feeders are hunting for insects or small animals beneath overhanging banks or trees. In these cases, the fizzer's prop is what makes the distinction between something that is alive and just another stick or piece of debris.

The other common form of surface lure is the waddler. These stubby lures have a blade or wing across their face that catches on the water, dipping first to one side and then the other as they rock back and forth on their belly. This waddling motion can be worked very slowly in short spurts or at a steady pace across an open stretch of water. It is highly provocative to fish feeding on frogs, mice or large insects that have fallen from above. Waddlers make an attractive 'plop plop plop' sound as they walk across the surface. They are usually used in twilight or at night when ambush feeders roam into the open to hunt.

Anatomy of a chugger popper

FACE
- The face of a chugger is usually large and cupped, to tear as big a hole in the surface as possible.
- In many chuggers, the face is dished and angled to trap a bubble of air which 'pops' under the force of water being blasted against it.
- The size and depth of the cup, as well as its angle on the face, will influence how much water the lure moves and how much it pops.
- The face should run at an angle from the tow-point in order to keep it at the surface and not diving or pulling beneath. This is particularly important in lures which are to be used on heavy ocean chop.

ATTITUDE
- The lure should sit at rest either horizontally or angled slightly upwards.
- The cup should be primed with its bottom lip just underwater, ready for its next assault on the surface.
- The popper should grab water and pop the instant it is moved or it will be dragged out of the strike zone too quickly.

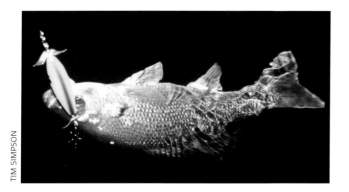

TIM SIMPSON

A skilfully twitched fizzer is a great way to imitate a struggling insect or animal that has fallen onto the surface beneath an overhang. They can be subtly tweaked for extended periods while still remaining within the strike zone. Bass love them!

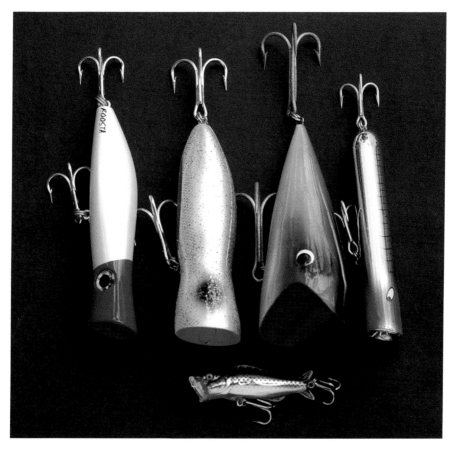

Chugger poppers all have scooped faces of one kind or another, designed to tear a big hole in the water as they are ripped with the rod tip. They make a lot of noise and splash as they go and their slow speed allows deep fish time to rise up before they are pulled out of the strike zone

BUOYANCY

- As these lures are often used at very slow speeds, it's much easier to keep them at the surface if they float.
- A lure will have much more buoyancy in saltwater than in fresh.
- A heavily weighted sinking popper may be required for long-distance casting. It will remain at the surface due to its water resistance as long as a continuous retrieve is maintained.

Anatomy of a skipping popper

FACE

- The face is usually angled forwards to make the lure rise to the surface and then plane (skip) on top.
- A cupped face will help to enhance the splash, although these lures rarely 'pop' the way a chugger does.
- The larger the face area above the tow-point, the greater chance it has of planing above rough conditions and not becoming smothered by the surface chop.

ATTITUDE

- The lure should sit and run face up/tail down, so that it planes up to the surface easily.
- A lure that runs with its tail sub-surface will be easier for a fish to connect with and result in a better hook-up rate.

TOW-POINT/BALANCE

- The lure needs to be balanced around the tow-point so that it maintains its attitude in the water and doesn't spin, plough underwater or flip over and dive.

Anatomy of a fizzer

PROPELLERS

- There are various shapes available. The angles not only need to catch the water and revolve at the desired speed (often very slowly) but must also throw water into the

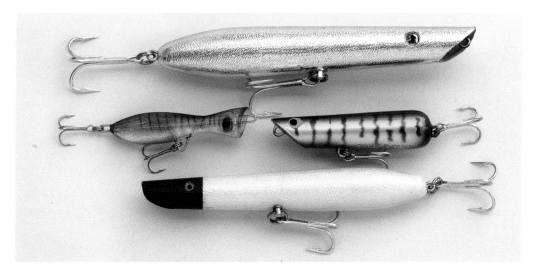

Skipping poppers come in a range of sizes and shapes but they all do much the same thing — skipping across the surface at speed to represent fleeing baitfish

Fizzers range from small, very subtle lures that are gently tweaked to splutter on the surface while hardly moving within the strike zone, to large fast models that can at times be streaked across the surface like a noisy torpedo — in the same manner as a skipping popper

Waddlers are a funny little family of lures most often used when fishing for bass
or Murray cod from evening to dark. A variety of appendages around the head cause
the lures to flop from one side to the other as they are retrieved, doing a pretty
good imitation of a small terrestrial or amphibian moving across the top
of the water. The strikes, in the dark, are heart stopping!

air and beat the surface on their re-entry. As these are a surface commotion lure, the
opposite of 'silent running' is required.

✠ The blades should be long enough to reach the water when the lure is lying flat on
the surface. The fatter the lure's body, the longer the blade needs to be. At the same
time, a propeller at the rear of a lure will greatly obstruct the points of a hook
immediately behind it and so the blade length should be kept to a minimum.

✠ Sharp edges on metal blades should be rounded so they don't cut fishing line.

✠ Clear plastic blades are available which give the fizz of a propeller but are not visible
to the fish.

✠ The hole through the centre of the propeller should allow easy rotation without
restriction but should not allow the blades to flop into the way of the hook.

🐟 Metal spacer beads may assist as a bearing for the blades and at the rear will help to space the tail hook away from the obstruction of the propeller.

Anatomy of a waddler

BODY
🐟 The body should be shaped and sit with an attitude that allows it to roll from side to side.
🐟 If the tail sits below water level, the lure is more likely to be swallowed on a strike instead of merely bumped.

FACE PLATE
🐟 This is a wide blade attached at right angles to give the lure a wing extending on either side.
🐟 The plate should create noise as well as surface disruption. As with a chugger, the plate is usually cupped or angled to spit water forwards and trap a small bubble of air to create a pop. The rapid succession of small pops as the face rocks from side to side, dipping first one wing and then the other, will sound more like a 'plop plop plop' than the 'bloop' of a popper.
🐟 The larger and more wind resistant the face plate, the harder it will be to cast.
See also Bibbed lures, Hooks, page 87; Rattles/sound, pages 90–2; Castability, pages 97–8.

Metal lures

Spoons and cobra-style

The longest-standing form of metal lure is the spoon. Allegedly originating from the bowl section of a real spoon, these lures have been refined into a multitude of sizes and designs. The basic metal spoon shape is a highly adaptable pattern as, besides its length and curves, the thickness of metal used to create the lure will determine how much action it will have, how much speed it will tolerate and how well it will cast.

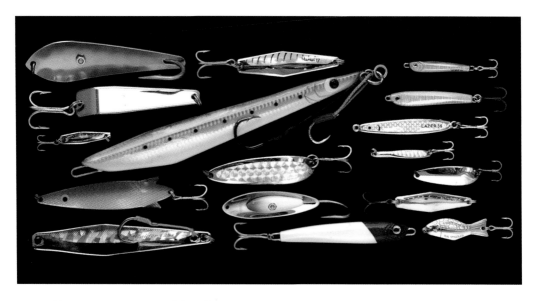

Metal lures are very successful at delivering a compact, castable baitfish representation with an unlimited depth range. They vary from simple, straight tracking metal bars for very fast retrieves to carefully contoured shapes with vibrant actions at very slow speeds

The cupping or dishing of the metal sheet will induce action, as for a spinner's blade. An S-shaped bend will add a different type of wobble, and the degree to which it is bent will determine how strong this action will be.

High-action lightweight spoons with a rounded and cupped shape are popular as a slow trolling lure for freshwater anglers. Even when taken down into the depths on a downrigger – where the denser water and high pressures smother the action of many lures – a lightweight spoon will still attract strikes.

By extending the body outline into a long slim shape – more suggestive of a baitfish – and reducing the curves and cupping, the spoon's action is tightened into a narrower pulse. This is generally more attractive to the pelagic fish that prey on fast-moving bait species. In a thin metal body this will make a very attractive lure for trolling or short-range casting at slow to medium speeds. A thicker body will offer more castability and its reduced action gives the option of increased speed. These versions can be used for trolling, jigging or casting.

There is a uniquely Australian adaptation of the spoon which has found enormous success with trout fishermen around the world. The 'cobra' style was first made by Brian Johnston of Tasmania in 1949: a lead tube moulded inside a plastic spoon-shaped shroud.

Spoons come in many shapes and sizes and are a lure style with a very long history. They catch everything from small trout in streams through to big game on the blue water. The trolling lure (top left) is made of plastic (originally bone) but is based on the spoon design

The various brands of cobras offer several advantages over regular pressed metal. They have considerable weight, which helps to achieve depth at slow speeds, and the weight is centred, which allows the lure to rock around its centre keel with an attractive weaving wobble. In many models the lead centre and flexible exterior allow the lure to be bent so an angler can adjust the curve for various actions. They are also commonly rigged free-running on the line, so that when a fish jumps they will run up the line and deny the thrashing fish the weight that can often tear a hook loose.

Perhaps their main advantage is their clear 'wings'. The lure moves through the water with the large attractive pulse of a spoon but, as only the thin centre tube is visible, it has the appearance of a smaller prey item – much more to the liking of many trout.

There are many reasons why a spoon of some sort is a mandatory inclusion in every lure box. They are castable, durable, have a great action and can be easily fished at any shoreline depth. They can be retrieved across the surface, jigged through the middle or sunk and flicked across the bottom. When retrieved with a 'rip and sink, rip and sink' action, the fluttering as they drop is a great imitation of a dying baitfish.

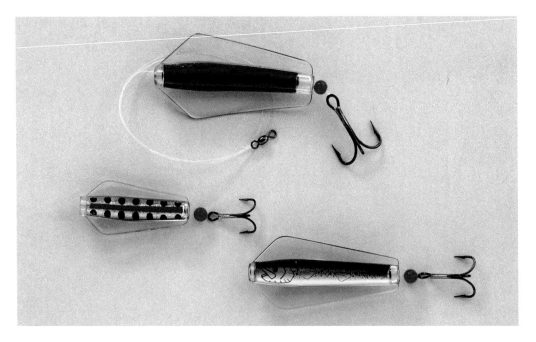

The clear wings of the cobra-style spoons offer the strong pulse and action
of a spoon with the appearance of a slim baitfish

Another major bonus is that, being metal, they offer an excellent opportunity to incorporate the attraction of flash. The greater the surface area that is flat, the stronger it will flash. A multifaceted surface will face the sun more frequently so it will flash more often, but as each facet is smaller the intensity will be reduced. A rounded surface will have a continuous shine, but as the outside of the curve is constantly reflecting a thin band of sunshine it won't achieve the same effect as a broad flash.

Anatomy of a spoon or cobra-style lure

ACTION
⌦ The shape of the lure will determine how water flows around it and so establish the lure's action. The greater the difference in laminar flow, the greater the action. Like an aerofoil or wing, the flow across the outside of a cupped surface will be at a different speed to the flow underneath. This and turbulence cause a wobble. Additional curves or bends will add their own contribution to the movement.

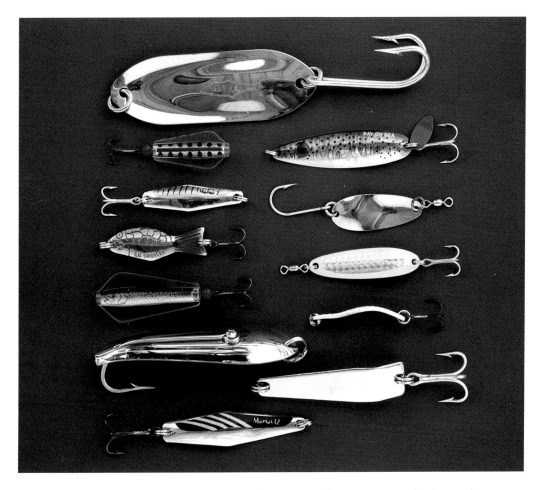

The potential for flash and strong pulsed actions from spoons and cobra-style
lures can be very effective in a wide range of situations. Their usefulness is probably
underestimated by many anglers these days

✼ The wobble of a spoon will move a lot of water and create a strong, usually slow
   pulse.
✼ A spoon should wobble through the water, not spin. A spinning (line-twisting)
   spoon may indicate too much speed for the design to handle.
✼ The length of the lure will stabilise the wobble. A longer spoon will have a more
   subdued and tighter action with a different pulse than a similar but stubbier shape.
   It will probably be capable of more speed – before becoming unstable and spinning
   or flipping right out of the water.

- The action caused by the lure's design will be dampened by the weight of its body and any hardware attached to it (hooks, rings etc). A thin lure, or one made from a lighter material, will have less weight to move around and so will have more action than the same shape with a heavier body.
- Spoons for both spinning and trolling are often fished with a rip/pause jigging action. In both cases, a lure that is thin and light enough to flutter down during the pause will often outfish a lure that simply sinks.
- If the tow-point is on the convex side of the lure, just back from its nose, the leading edge becomes a bib that will paravane the lure to greater depths.
- A lure to be used at depth (e.g. on a downrigger) should have a very strong action at the surface, as its action may be severely reduced once down deep where the pressure is higher and the water denser.

SPEED

- Most spoon lures are used at relatively slow speeds due to their strong action and high water resistance.
- A long narrow spoon will usually handle more speed (due to less action) than a short round one.
- Long-bodied, deeply cupped saltwater trolling spoons often feature large and heavy hooks which help to keel and tame their action. They are capable of reasonable speeds despite their strong pulse.
- A heavy-bodied lure will have less action and so will be able to handle more speed before spinning or flipping out of the water.

HOOK CLEARANCE

- If the lure's body is wider than the hook, especially just in front of the hook, a fish's mouth may be deflected past the points. In this situation a larger hook may help, except that the added weight will decrease the lure's action.
- A wide body will help to deflect the lure through obstacles like timber and weed without snagging.
- A single hook in place of a treble will greatly reduce snags in amongst the timbers.

CASTING WEIGHT/BALANCE

- The cupped and usually lightweight design of some spoons makes them difficult to cast long distances due to wind resistance. They may flutter in the air which makes

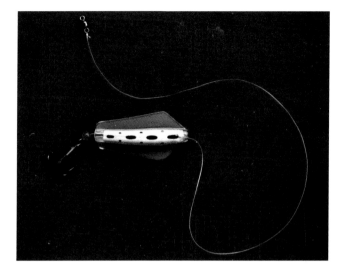

Normally rigged on a centre wire, cobras can also be rigged as a free running
lure like this. It helps to stop jumping fish from throwing the weighty lure

distance, accuracy and use with an overhead (baitcaster) reel very difficult. A
thicker, heavier spoon will overcome this but at the sacrifice of action.

❧ If the lure has more weight in the rear than the front, it will usually cast more easily
and without tumbling.

PROFILE

❧ The outline of a metal spoon will determine the shape of the creature it represents
to a fish.

❧ A cobra style has the advantage of clear wings that enable a small thin baitfish
profile while keeping the action and pulse of a spoon.

RIGGING OPTION

❧ The hollow-tube construction of a cobra-style lure enables the option of removing
the centre wire and rigging the lure to run freely on the line. Allowing the lure to
slide up the line when a hooked fish is jumping stops the weight of the lure from
pulling the hooks free. In this case, a bead or split ring should be used as a buffer
or knuckle between the hook and the rear of the lure.

*See also Bibbed lures, Hooks, page 87; Clearance of hooks, page 89; and Long-range
casting slugs, Flash, pages 128–9.*

Long-range casting slugs

These are metal lures, usually based on lead or brass, which, due to their compact weight and aerodynamic shape, offer exceptional castability. They are successful on a wide variety of fast-moving predatory fish and especially useful in situations where long-distance casts need to be made to access distant water or timid schools of fish.

They are usually long and slender in shape, which gives them an excellent baitfish profile and very little wind or water resistance. An action is created when water pressure is forced against their curves or any angles in their shape, so lures with bigger facets or pressure-catching areas will have a greater action.

The more streamlined their shape, the better they cast. Even those whose streamlined form does not offer much in the way of action are still highly effective at speed.

This type of lure appeals to fast-moving pelagics that use sight as their primary sense. The baitfish they chase are also fast-moving and have fast narrow swimming patterns so a strong throbbing action is not required.

Besides profile, speed itself is a large part of the attraction with this type of lure. Speed not only increases the water pressures, which accentuate action, but also leaves the predator very little time to carefully evaluate a lure: they have a moment to react or the opportunity is gone. The fact that the lure is usually running just under the surface makes it seem more vulnerable. A fish at the surface has lost half its escape route.

Some of these lures have an appealing action at moderate speeds, which suits any predator that chases active baitfish. Even slow-hunting species like trout can be tricked by the flicking darting action of one of these lures when they are feeding on lively food like smelt. In this case, the lure would be worked with a series of flicks causing it to dart short distances with pauses or flickering drops in between the dashes. At the other end of the scale, a species like tuna that swims on a perpetual high-speed rampage may require a retrieve speed at the absolute extreme of reel and human ability!

There is much ground in between. These lures can be used fast with a straight and constant retrieve, they can be given exciting bursts with a sweep of the rod tip during a moderate retrieve, they can be given a rip-and-pause retrieve to imitate a crippled appearance, or anything else the angler thinks appropriate. They can also be dropped to any depth before the retrieve is started, so the entire water column can be explored. They can even be used as a jig.

Another benefit is their compact size. When predators are locked on to a tiny bait species and are refusing to look at any alternatives, the compact weight and castability

Coming under the general heading of 'slugs', lures like these are chosen for their ability to deliver maximum casting range. They accept fast to very fast retrieve speeds and can also be fished vertically as a jig

of a tiny metal sliver will usually do the trick. When the spring run of micro baitfish invades the bays and river mouths of the lower New South Wales coast, the boiling mass of Australian salmon is an excellent scenario for the use of spinning with tiny metal lures. When this and other species are feeding on bait smaller than a matchstick, these tiny lures are the only option – short of a fly rod – that combine compact size with castability to get results.

The great versatility of these lures, together with their broad appeal and extreme castability, makes them a lure variety that most anglers won't leave home without.

Deepwater jigs

There are many exciting fish of all sizes that live close to the bottom at the deep offshore reefs. For many years they have been caught with live or dead baits. Now a growing number of sport anglers are discovering the thrill of catching these fish with lures.

The difficulty is simply getting a lure to them: the water being fished is often between 30 and 100 metres deep, way outside the capabilities of most lures. Deep water and long lengths of line can also lead to problems with current: if the lure is not heavy

These lures are used as deepwater jigs. They sink fast and some have shapes that cause them to flutter on the drop, often taking just as many strikes on the way down as they do on the way up

and compact enough to cut through the current and plummet straight down, it will be washed away – which leads to even more line out and a distinct loss of feel.

This kind of fishing is usually done in conjunction with an echo sounder, which pinpoints the reef and the fish on it. If the lure is carried away by the current, the fish may be under the boat but the lure will be way off in the distance. Deepwater jigs have a similar shape to the long-range casting slugs as they need to have low drag. As with the distance casting lures, they also have little in the way of a wobbling action. Their profile is long and straight with no curves or bends. They are usually thin and of a width comparable to that of a similarly sized garfish, although many have a flared section at the bottom for tail-weighting. In deeper waters it is essential that they sink like an arrow.

Deep water adds a further difficulty, putting the lures under enormous pressure. For every 10 metres of depth, the pressure increases by the equivalent of an atmosphere. At 60 metres, the water will be seven times as dense. This dulls the little action the lures may have had.

Tail weighted metal lures sink vertically and quickly. In smaller sizes they also cast very well

As with the long-distance casters, the deepwater jigs rely on speed for much of their attraction. The retrieve is often very fast from bottom to surface; much like regular spinning except vertical. For fast-moving pelagic species, the most popular and successful option is to rip the jig upwards with a fast sweep of the rod, then lower the rod while retrieving the slack (like pumping), before continuing with another upward sweep. The rod's arc can be a long sweep, which will move the lure several metres at a time, but many will find that a very short, quicker stroke that flicks the lure upwards will produce the most strikes. A productive technique with either style is not allowing the jig to fall backwards; it must continue to travel forwards even though it is moving in spurts.

It may also help to have a slight angle in the line, say 20 degrees, rather than keeping it exactly vertical. If the angle is much more than 20 degrees, though, it reduces results so a heavier or slimmer jig should be used. In deep water it is common to use long thin tail-weighted jigs weighing from 180 grams to as much as 300 grams.

When the wind is blowing, the boat will drift with it regardless of current. To reduce the angle in the lines and allow more accurate targeting of the fish, the boat will often need to be motored into the breeze at a slow pace to maintain position. This requires the full concentration of a skipper, who will not be able to fish at the same time, but by taking turns at this task everyone will catch more fish.

For fish particularly partial to speed, the fast jerky retrieve may provide the best results. For others, the appearance of a flickering injured baitfish down near the reef may be an irresistible attraction, including many that are not even considered regular lure candidates. In some areas anglers have woken up to the possibilities and are regularly bouncing jigs along the bottom and catching fish such as snapper, John Dory and cod.

For slower bottom species this jigging motion can be performed without retrieving at all, which keeps the lure within a few metres of the bottom at all times. The effect on the lure is a rapid spurt followed by a pause or flutter downwards, which, even when the lure doesn't have much action, gives a great impression of a baitfish in serious trouble. With this style of jigging it is an advantage to have a shorter, slightly broader, centre-weighted lure – like a flat-sided pilchard – so that it flickers as it drops through the water.

Anatomy of a long-range casting slug and deepwater jig

ACTION

✥ A swimming wobbling action is produced by different water pressures acting on various parts of a lure's body. The long slim design of these lures creates very little air or water resistance. This helps with a long cast or a quick sink and an easy low-drag retrieve at high speeds, but it doesn't give the lure much in the way of action-producing pressure points. High speed will magnify the pressures it does have, so at a fast pace these lures will have some wobble or weave even if the body is only slightly angled or tapered.

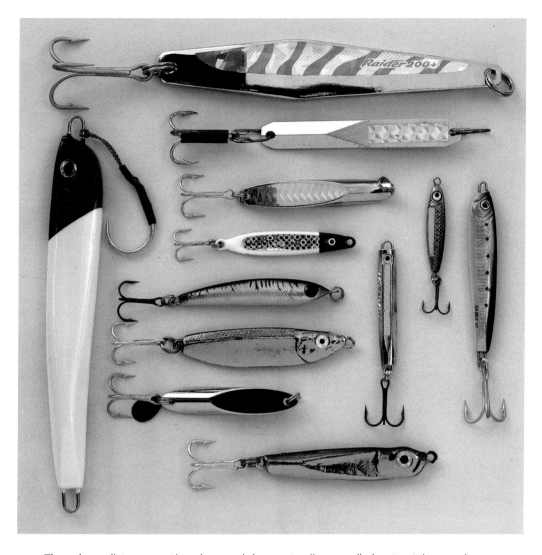

These long-distance casting slugs and deepwater jigs are all about getting maximum casting distance or depth. They are shaped to offer minimum resistance to wind and water and rely on through-water speed to attract strikes

- The larger the angled facets or curves on the lure (relative to weight), the more action it will have. An identical body shape in a lighter-weight material will have more action.
- The larger and heavier the attachments, like hooks and rings, the less action the lure will have.

- Part of the action that attracts predators to these lures is the speed itself. A fleeing baitfish is usually only moving at speed because it is trying to escape. It is trying to escape because it is good to eat and has spotted the hunting predator. A fish that is not good to eat does not flee; it simply moves aside.
- If the lure is to be used for very high-speed surface spinning, a slim profile and very little in the way of broad planing surfaces or action-producing angles and bends is often the most successful choice, as the lure is more likely to stay sub-surface where it can be taken accurately. Features producing action will also create drag; at speed this will lift the lure up and cause it to skip across the surface.
- Breaking the surface and leaving a streaming trail of bubbles adds to the illusion of a terrified baitfish trying to escape. A cupped face on the very front of the lure can achieve this while actually helping to keep the lure in the surface film without skipping out.
- Versions of these lures with little built-in action can be used either with a 'flat out' retrieve or jigged at any depth, from surface to the bottom. This can vary from an occasional sideways sweep of the rod during a fast retrieve to a rapid lift/flutter back/rapid lift yo-yo retrieve.
- A lift/sink jigging retrieve will often work best with a flat-sided lure with most of its weight in the centre. It will flutter a little as it settles in the water, sending out flashes and vibrations which give the appearance of a dying or injured fish. Most of the strikes will be on the sink. (These retrieves appeal more to slower demersal species than high-speed predators.)
- The pressure and denser water of the depths will restrict the movement of a lure. A lure that has a slight action at the surface may have little or none when sunk into the deep. The attraction of the lure may then rest on its speed or on a jigging action imparted by the angler on low-stretch line.

PROFILE
- The outline of these lures is usually long and slim. This matches the shape of most baitfish and maximises castability by reducing air drag.
- A lure that flutters or tumbles during a cast will be slowed down very quickly by wind resistance. For a long cast the lure will need to travel through the air like an arrow. This will be helped by having more weight in the tail end of the lure (or by slightly more wind resistance in the head of the lure).
- A fluttering or tumbling lure will be extremely difficult to cast with an overhead reel, as the momentary pause will quickly lead to a backlash or overrun.

TIM SIMPSON

LEFT Flashy lures retrieved at high speed have special appeal to the super-fast predators like mackerel

RIGHT This is an example of a well-designed high-speed slug. The body is tail-weighted to give tumble-free long casts and its flared face has a small concave scoop which helps grip the surface and maintain contact — without skipping out. It will also create a bubble trail to attract attention. The asymmetrical belly forms a keel which keeps the lure upright and stabilised. Prominent eyes give a finishing touch to this great lure

⚓ When sinking the lure into very deep water or through a strong current, a slender tail-weighted shape with little in the way of curves, action or flutter will get down much more easily and quickly. This gives more direct contact with less line out.

⚓ A lure rising nearly vertically is often more successful than one jigged up at an angle. It will also have less water resistance and so be easier to retrieve at high speed.

⚓ When wary or size-sensitive fish require the use of micro lures it is necessary to minimise hooks and attachments as these add to the overall profile of the lure.

⚓ To achieve a large profile with a castable metal lure – such as when targeting very large fish or those feeding on large prey – a similar lure made from a lightweight alloy rather than the usual heavier metals can be used. This will give you a similar casting weight in a substantially bigger size. A lightweight lure like this will have more action, but more air and water resistance also, and will not sink as quickly.

HOOKS

⚓ The slim profile of these lures gives great exposure to the hook points.

⚓ Most lures will feature treble hooks. These work well and cover attacks from all angles; however, a single hook may be more suitable if snagging on the bottom or fighting large and powerful fish is expected.

⚓ The hooks on these lures are highly visible when near the surface. Even if the lure is moving quickly and so is difficult to see clearly, it can often help with wary fish to use a coloured hook to match the representation (blue/green or yellow), be provocative (red) or camouflage into the background with a neutral colour.

✎ These lures usually feature one hook which is attached to the tail of the lure. This covers attacks from behind but does little to hook fish that attack the head of the lure. A growing trend (from Japan) is to attach a dangling hook to the front ring, either as an addition to the tail hook or, more commonly, as the only hook. This hook (often termed an 'assist hook') is usually positioned in the front third of the lure. Its benefits include a better profile, fewer snags and an increased hook-up rate on head/body strikers. If the assist hook is used without the tail hook, the lure will also have more action because it can pivot around the tow-point without having to swing the weight of the tail hook through the water.

✎ Some assist hooks are available with the barb on the outside of the point. This stops the barb of the swinging hook from catching and locking on the body of the lure while being jigged.

✎ For species with sharp teeth, the assist hook can be attached with a loop of soft flexible wire instead of the usual Kevlar or Dacron. Even when using a mono leader this is usually sufficient to stop a bite-off.

See also Bibless minnows, Hooks, pages 102–3; and Bibbed lures, Hooks, page 87.

VISIBILITY

✎ A lure retrieved in the surface layer will have all colours appearing as we see them because the water won't have filtered out any colours at this depth. Once a lure drops below the first few metres the colours (starting with red) will gradually be filtered out and turn to black. Depending on the clarity and colour of the water it will be completely dark somewhere between 4–300 metres.

✎ If a reflective (chromed) jig is used in deep coloured water where very little light exists, it will have nothing except the surrounding water to reflect and so will be extremely difficult to see. A white or black lure will give more contrast.

✎ In a deep or dark environment some luminosity from paint, tape, beads or a chemical light stick will help to make the lure visible and get it noticed.

FLASH

✎ As these lures are usually made from moulded or cut metal they offer a great opportunity to incorporate flash as an attraction.

✎ A shiny or silvery appearance may help to create a realistic imitation but a lure that actually flashes will be noticed from much further away.

- A flash is a reflection of the sun, hence the lure will only flash when a reflective surface is at an appropriate angle to catch and reflect sunlight.
- A rounded lure will reflect a continuous thin line of shine whereas a multifaceted surface will reflect a series of flashes from a variety of angles. A lure with a broad flat surface will only reflect when at an appropriate angle to the sun, but when it does it will be a large strong blast of flash that is hard to miss.
- It is widely believed that a flash of gold is the most successful in dirty or coloured water and that a silver-based flash is more successful in clearer waters. Lures plated in real silver or gold are more reflective and so give a brighter flash than the chrome equivalents. These are available from some manufacturers in the US.
- To maintain a bright flash, the lures should be given a quick rub with a cloth (or shirt) at the start of fishing.
- When fish are edgy, especially when the water is very clear, a sudden strong flash may alarm them. In such situations a more subtle approach may help.
- Adhesive prism tapes will give a shimmering and colourful appearance with their refracted colours, but will not have the same intensity or reach of reflected flash as a flat polished metal surface.

See also Bibbed lures, Eye, page 96; Length of attachments, page 88; Split rings, pages 88–9.

Lead-head jigs, jig heads, tail spinners

Besides soft plastics and the slim metal deepwater jigs, there is another small group of very successful lures that are basically a lead-headed jig hook – the same as those used with many soft plastics, but with a body of animal hair (usually bucktail fibres) or feathers. These traditional jigs have been around a long time and are a standard in many fisheries in the US. They have never gained much popularity in Australia, perhaps because they rely heavily on a thoughtful presentation by the angler's manipulation of the rod to induce action.

They are basically designed and fished the same way as a soft plastic on a jig head and the design and weight of the jig head will have a big influence on how the lure behaves in the water.

Lead-head jigs are a very old style of lure. They are, and always have been,
a particularly lethal lure in a wide range of situations, yet in Australia they have never
enjoyed the reputation they deserve as fish takers. Now that many anglers are learning
advanced retrieve styles, they may well find new appeal

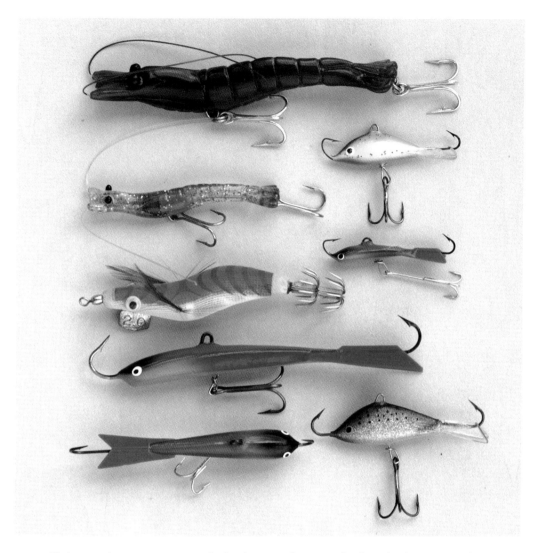

Shrimp and prawns are a staple food source for many fresh and saltwater species.
These jigs are used with a flicking motion and are a deadly weapon in the right hands.
The ice jigs (bottom) have been particularly useful on dams for suspended
schools of bass, and prawn-type squid jigs (third down on left) have revolutionised
squid fishing in recent years

An uncommon little family of lures, the tail spinners are a combination of a flashy
blade spinner and a fast sinking jig. They are very useful in that they cast like a bullet,
have a strong vibration and can be fished effectively at any depth

The supple or buoyant tail undulates and pulses when jigged with a rise-and-fall
action. When pulled straight through the water, the tail slicks down into the profile of
a tapered baitfish. Although these lures aren't usually fished quite as slowly as soft
plastics, they are castable and very versatile. They can be fished with a variety of angler-
induced action retrieves and at any depth from surface to bottom.

Perhaps now that soft plastics are finally being understood and fished successfully,
and Australian anglers are rapidly learning far more sophisticated action retrieves, we
may see a revival of this time-proven lure style.

There's another kind of jig that's starting to find pockets of use in the developing
impoundment fisheries: the ice jigs. These strange-looking lures are lowered into a
school of suspended fish, spotted with an echo sounder, then jiggled or flicked to gain
attention and give the impression of a darting shrimp, before a short pause which is
usually when they are taken. Although the lure is jigged vertically, the special fin on the
rear causes it to dart sideways then glide back to the starting position when the line is
relaxed. As you might imagine, a continually flicking shrimp on the nose of even an
inactive predator will not be ignored for long.

There are several other realistic prawn or shrimp-shaped lures that might be referred to as a jig. These crustaceans are a favourite food of most fresh and saltwater species and a good imitation is useful in many situations. Some are made of plastic, while others are moulded from transparent shades in resin, but they all sink slowly. They can be used at any depth from the surface to across the bottom and give a convincing performance when flicked with a thoughtful presentation by the rod.

Tail spinners have a short moulded body, usually made of lead, with the blade of a spinner attached to the rear. They have the versatility of a jig or soft plastic, but with added flash and the pulse that comes from the frantically spinning blade. The shape and tow-point of the body will influence how the lure behaves when ripped upwards on a jigging stroke and also when falling. Some will flutter and flash while others will sink like a stone.

The weight of these lures gives them great castability and an unlimited depth range. The concentrated weight gives them a fast dipping or nodding action when they are allowed to sink during a drop or pause in the retrieve. They are usually used in freshwater lakes for species like bass and with a similar retrieve to jigs or a faster soft plastic. A typical retrieve may involve a couple of seconds of fast cranking, then either a pause and sink or a flick with the rod tip, or both. Once this is finished, the sequence starts again. Their popularity may well expand as more anglers give them a try in other waters.

Lead-head jigs are available as a ready-made 'dressed' unit or as a component of an easily assembled, readily changeable lure.

Anatomy of a jig head

HEAD
✎ The shape of a jig head is an important aspect of this lure; the head can be much more than just a sinker. Its functions may include:
- action on the up-lift
- action on the drop
- sinking rate
- hook orientation
- snag resistance
- profile
- water resistance
- stance on bottom – at rest

ACTION
✎ As for other lures, action with a jig head is caused by water pressures acting on its

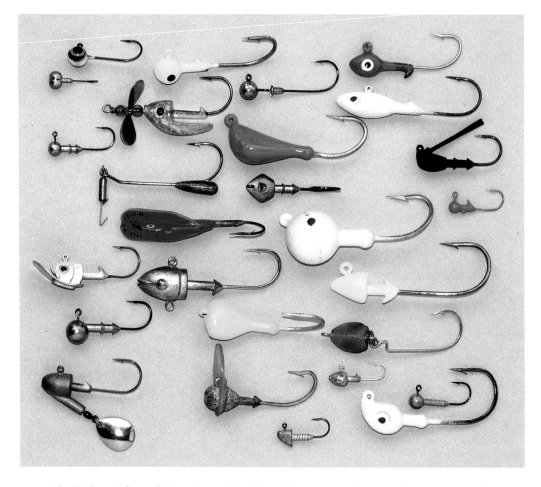

The jig heads for soft plastics and lead-head jigs are much more than just a weight
to get the offering down to the bottom. They can also impact on the lure's action
on the lift or drop, orient the hook in different ways, snag-proof the hook and
make the lure sit on the bottom in a particular way

shape. These pressures must be forceful enough to move the bulk and weight of the
lure through the water or nothing will happen.

🐟 The relatively slow speeds these lures are usually used at, coupled with their
concentrated weight, makes it difficult to achieve an inbuilt action. However, these
lures are extremely effective and versatile, as most of the fish-attracting movements
are imparted by the attached tail or directly from the angler's rod tip.

🐟 A wobbling action on the up-lift can be achieved by a broad head or one that has a lip-like projection in front of the tow-point, providing a large surface (relative to its weight) for the water pressure to act on. The closer this surface sits to a right angle to the direction of pull, the more water pressure will act upon it. Speed will also add more pressure and so more potential for action.

- A broad head is likely to dart on the up-lift and glide or flutter on the drop.
- A deep, very thin head (like a coin standing on end) will rise easily and smoothly on the up-lift and is likely to flicker on the drop.
- Some heads have an action 'lip', either moulded in or attached afterwards.
- An angler can enhance the action of the lure with the nodding of a rapid sinker or the subtle wavering of a fluttering/gliding head.
- Much of the action with this type of lure comes from the attached 'tail'.

TOW-POINT

- How the lure sits in the water and how the water pressures flow around it will depend on where the line is attached to the head. This will affect the lure's action and how much water-drag it has.
- A tow-point over the central balance point of the lure will drag it at right angles to the direction it is facing. Both ends of the lure will rise at the same time. The section of the head in front of the tow-point will, to some extent, act as a wobbling lip and a diving paravane.
- A tow-point at the front of the head will lift the lure up by the nose, giving it more of a nodding action when lifted and dropped.
- A forward tow-point will induce the lure to lift and plane upwards at speed.
- Attaching the line to the head with a loop or snap will allow the head to pivot freely, which gives it more of a nodding action when the angler lifts and drops the lure.
- A firm knot attached to the head will give the lure a slightly more undulating flowing action, as the attached leader provides a little resistance as it sinks through the water.

SINK RATE

- In shallow water, it is sometimes preferable for a jig to settle slowly through the water column. This can be achieved with a bulky skirt or a head that glides or flutters down.
- In deep water, particularly where there is a current, it may be essential that the head plummets down quickly and can be retrieved with the least resistance possible. This is achieved by a slim tail coupled with a head that also has low water-drag. A head

Lead-head jigs are snag-resistant due to the hook riding upright, and most of them have a surprising action on both the lift and drop. In the hands of a thoughtful and imaginative angler they can be used very successfully in a wide range of environments

that is weighted forward of the tow-point will tip the lure downward on the drop so it can sink with the least resistance.

❧ A long, narrow and streamlined head will offer less water resistance and so sink faster.

HOOK ORIENTATION

❧ The hook in nearly all jigs will be set with its point riding upwards. This helps to avoid snags and positions the hook for effective placement in the upper jaw of the fish.

❧ Trailing hooks are sometimes added, either by ganging or on a dropper. These may be set with points up or down.

SNAG RESISTANCE

✤ Most jigs are very snag resistant as they ride with the hook pointing upwards. Some designs are particularly capable of deflecting their way through or over obstacles.

✤ A rounded head is good at bumping its way through rocks and rubble without wedging into cracks. A hook eye towing from the top of the head (90 degrees) will pull out more easily than one pulling forward.

✤ A pointed broad head will separate weed and sticks to allow the hook to pass through unhindered. If the hook's eye runs parallel with the body of the lure (i.e. the line runs through the eye from the side not from the front), the lure will be more weed resistant than one with the hook's eye turned across the head.

✤ A head with an angled bevel at the front, that slopes upward from the belly to the tow-point, will skim up over most low obstructions.

✤ A weed guard is sometimes added, often in the form of bristles that rise at an angle out of the head to stand in front of the hook point. They should be stiff enough to deflect weed but soft enough to allow a fish to bite down and get hooked.

PROFILE

✤ The jig head usually forms a significantly visible portion of the lure so it will be noticed by the fish. At times they will not react to its appearance; however, on other occasions it may be important for the 'head' profile to match the body of the prey it is imitating.

✤ A thin deep head will have excellent visibility from side on, but very little from above or underneath.

✤ A broad thin head will be very visible from above and below but difficult to see from side on.

EYES

✤ The eye of a fish is a highly visible outline that predators often notice before they see the camouflaged body of their prey. A prominent eye on a jig may help to give it credibility and act as a trigger to attract the attention of a predator.

SOUND

✤ Plastic jig heads are available with rattling balls inside to create sound. Other heavy heads are available with attachment points for add-on rattles (usually in small sealed glass tubes). All of these rattles produce a very subtle sound. The jig head striking the bottom will usually produce a much louder noise.

STANCE

- Jigs are sometimes allowed to pause on the bottom during the retrieve. A head with a broad underneath will allow the jig to rest while maintaining the same attitude.
- Some heads feature an angled 'foot' or resting platform at the front of the head, under its 'chin'. When settled, the lure is then positioned with the tail and its hook standing up off the bottom. This allows the tail freedom to move and puts the lure in a prime position for hooking-up if it is sucked off the bottom by a predator.
- A narrow or rounded head will roll or lay over when settled on the bottom. This may look unnatural and will also put the hook point out of optimum hooking position.

TAIL

- The tail of the jig forms the body of the lure. In many cases it imparts action – even to a stationary lure – by the way it moves in the water.
- A tail of feathers will look unnatural when dry, but when wet the feathers slick down into a tapered outline similar to that of a fish. To achieve this profile the feathers should be selected to match the length, width and bulk of the baitfish. The feathers of male fowl are a slimmer shape and more suitable than those of a female.
- A soft fluffy feather with a thin and supple stem will move freely in the water. It will also pulsate as it narrows down when pulled, then fluffs back out when paused. Feathers such as marabou are often selected for small jigs to be used with a slow jerky retrieve.
- Soft fibres and hair are also selected for similar lures. Natural bucktail (from a deer) is a favourite as it is a hollow fibre. The trapped air gives it buoyancy, which in turn gives it more freedom to move and billow in the water.
- Stiffer materials can be used on jigs intended for high-speed use. They may not need to give a pulsing movement, only the desired outline and more durability.
- For feathers and fibres, the jig head should have a flared collar at the rear of the head so that the material can be securely bound or glued into place.
- For the attachment of soft plastics, the rear of the jig's head should have a slim but prominent spike or rib to anchor the tail.

Soft plastics

Soft plastics of one kind or another have been around for a long time. Europeans have used rubbery fish or eel imitations with T-section (paddle) tails since at least the late 1950s. However, the newer soft PVC versions have only gained universal acceptance in Australia in relatively recent times. The first concerted effort to bring this lure style to Australian fishermen was in 1977 with the simultaneous introduction of the American Mr Twister curly tails and the Vibrotail brand with its T tails.

Soft plastics now enjoy extraordinary popularity for a number of reasons. The first attraction is that they are generally quite cheap: a packet of bodies and jig heads can be bought for less than the price of a single hard-bodied lure. This helps give anglers confidence when throwing them into the snag-ridden areas that, as we all know, are where many fish live and feed.

The second reason is that they have great appeal to fish and account for an amazing variety of fish, including species that normally never look at a lure. They show particular appeal to slower-moving ambush feeders or bottom species that don't normally like to rise up or swim fast enough to chase and attack some of the other lure styles.

Finally, they are extremely versatile. They can be rigged with a wide variety of methods on jig heads or bare hooks, which allows them to be presented at any depth and even used in snaggy situations when set up as a weedless rig. They can be fished with great finesse and at such slow speeds that they are down in the strike zone far longer than other types of lure. In fact, it's the incredibly slow speed at which some of these lures can work that is opening up so many possibilities and attracting new species for anglers. That said, many anglers have trouble coming to terms with plastic because they simply can't bring themselves to fish the lures slow enough. Of course, it's important to present your lure where the fish are and, while prospecting or searching, a lure with speed will help you cover more area. But when you know you are in a likely spot, or know the fish are there, with a soft plastic you can keep it right there, in their faces, until they pounce on it!

By creating a realistic outline – which is easy with this mouldable material – and then giving it an action that appears alive even in the gentle waft of a barely perceptible current, these lures can be placed right beside slow-moving timid demersal species until they become convinced or just take an inquisitive bite.

With the addition of scents or flavours moulded in, these lures become more of a man-made live bait than anything that has previously been classed as a lure. Soft plastics have stepped right over the border that separates lures from real bait and many lure purists must be asking themselves where these things stop being a lure and become simply a moulded synthetic food product with action. Soft plastic enthusiasts even hook a lot of fish when the lure is stationary; the fish comes along and eats it just as it would take a natural bait.

The textures of the plastics and the scents and flavours with which they are often impregnated have a lot to do with their success. When the fish clamps down on the lure, it feels and tastes like real food, and for that reason the attack is carried all the way through with no last-moment second thoughts. Often, fish that miss the lure keep coming back until they get hold of it.

Sometimes the lures contain pheromone-like additives – chemical substances that stimulate or affect the behaviour of the fish. Some are sex-related, which at times cause an aggressive response to perceived rivals. The usual way for sex rivals to chase away their opponent is to snap at them, which often results in a hook-up.

Soft plastic lures are a composite of several components: the body, the hook and a weight. Usually a jig head is used, which incorporates an appropriate weight moulded onto the hook. Jig heads come in a variety of shapes and lend their own action characteristics to the assembled lure, depending on their shape and the way they are attached. Some soft plastic lures come with the hook and weight already moulded into the body, but most are sold as individual components. This allows the angler to match the soft body to the most appropriate size, type and weight of head along with the size and gauge of hook to suit the situation. (*See Anatomy of a jig head, pages 133–8.*)

Soft plastics can also be rigged with a small sinker running on the line ahead of the lure, although this will give you less feel. Another way to rig them, especially in shallow water, is to use a hook with no sinker. These virtually unweighted lures will glide or slowly flutter down under the weight of the hook itself. Because the weight is distributed further back and isn't pulling the nose down, the lure will have a different movement in the water. A tail can even be rigged to gently glide in under overhanging structure.

The bodies of soft plastics come in a bewildering array of shapes – everything from prawns, spiders, worms, squid, maggots, lizards, fish eggs and crabs through to various fish representations. Most will have arms, tails or extensions of some kind to give movement and hence the impression of life. For the many that are designed to represent a swimming fish, the most common action devices are a curly tail or a T tail.

Soft plastics have been around for a long time, but recent developments in plastics, designs, actions, scents, flavours and techniques have made them explode in popularity. They are now available in a bewildering array of shapes and sizes, some of which appeal to species that have never been caught on lures before

Curly tails are a long thin extension of the plastic that curls up like a hook at the end of the body. When moved through the water this supple flap bends back and develops a twist that curls and uncurls as it is pulled through the water, giving an obvious appearance of a wriggling eel-like tail. They are sometimes referred to as a 'grub' because the body is often short, fat and corrugated, a bit like the shape of a

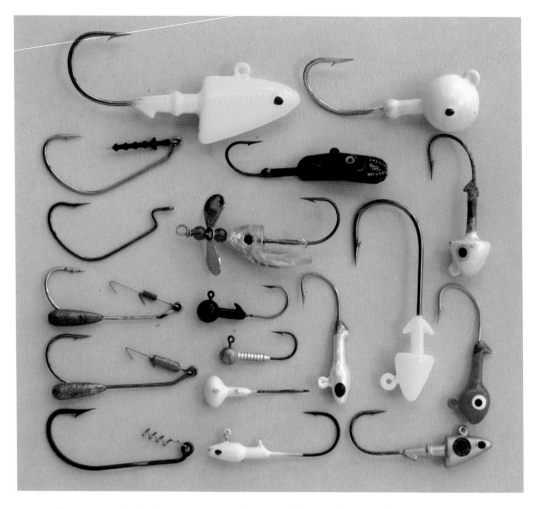

Because most don't come as a ready-to-use lure, soft plastic bodies are married
to a wide range of heads and hooks to do particular jobs

garden grub. We find this term a little confusing though, as it ignores the equally
obvious tail on the back end and, besides, they are hardly meant to represent or look
like a real grub in the water. The extended length of these curly tails takes the end of
the lure quite a distance from the hook point, which means a secure hook-up relies on
a fish engulfing the entire lure.

An alternative swimming tail is the T – a T tail is a short wedge-shaped block or flap
sitting at right angles to the end of the body and connected by a thin, very flexible
membrane of the plastic material. It looks a little like a T lying down, with its top

Most of these plastics are sold as bodies that can be rigged in a number of ways
while the lower two are sold with hooks and weight built-in

extending left and right either side. They are also widely known as a paddle tail, but
this term can cause confusion as several major US manufacturers also use it to refer to
a horizontally flattened tail, like the end of a canoe paddle. The advantage of a T tail is
that they do not extend and so keep the hook closer to the end of the lure. They also
maintain a fish profile.

Each tail puts out a different pulse of vibration. A T tail gives a tight fast beat, more
in line with a baitfish, while a curly tail will probably move more water at a slower
frequency.

Soft plastics have different actions in the water according to the stiffness of the body
and the shape of the tail. The three tails at top right are all paddle tails – named after the
shape of a (canoe) paddle. They undulate when jigged. The most popular swimming
tail styles are the T tails – like the two at top left – and the curly tails – like the remaining
six in the lower half of this picture

With both of these swimming tails, the minimum speed at which they become
effective is determined by the water resistance captured by the tail design and
particularly by the flexibility of the curly tail or the hinge between tail and body in the
T tail. A stiff or thick membrane requires a lot more speed before the tail starts to do
its thing, and if the tail isn't working, the lure, to some extent, goes back to looking like
a dead piece of plastic and is less effective. When fishing at slow speeds this is often a

key element and separates carefully designed lures from the cheapie look-alikes. At the same time, if too much speed is used these tails will blur and lose the enticing realism of a tail swimming. With either of these action tails it is worthwhile spending some time watching them to become familiar with their critical speed range.

Some soft plastics are designed without an inbuilt action. These 'stickbaits' are often no more than a sliver of the flexible plastic in the outline of a slim baitfish. They are still very effective and usually have some sort of action due to their extremely supple composition. The action will be the darting erratic rip-and-fall motion of crippled or terrified prey, imparted at the whim of the angler with flicks of the rod.

Some have a broad horizontally flattened end, sometimes referred to as a beaver tail or paddle tail (canoe-paddle type), which will undulate as the lure is lifted and dropped.

Yet another variety of soft plastics is the development of realistic baitfish – some as big as small tuna – which are used as an artificial bait or teaser when fishing for marlin and other blue-water gamefish.

Before the addition of a hook or jig head, the bodies of soft plastics are usually buoyant or have neutral buoyancy. This gives the tails more freedom to move in the water and opens up the full spectrum of fishable depth. They can be fished like mini live baits on the branches of a paternoster rig or fitted with a bare hook or light jig head to slowly glide across the surface or through the shallows. Alternatively, they can be rigged on a heavier jig head to give a dipping and nodding action. Sometimes it's beneficial to have the lure skim and settle gently while at other times it's best if it plonks down and crashes into the bottom. With a variety of hooks and jig head shapes and weights, the possibilities are vast. New techniques are being discovered all the time.

Soft plastics with really sensitive tails that will react to any movement at all can be fished at any depth with anything, from a dead slow lift of the rod tip with a flutter back to a static jiggle that goes nowhere if the lure is placed amongst a school of non-active fish. A fast rip that causes any fish-like lure to suddenly dart forward is a great way to get attention, but with soft plastics the lure should then be allowed to drift down a little and show its tail working.

When fishing for flathead, the plastic may be cast out, allowed to sink to the bottom and then retrieved with a series of short, sharp 'snap' lifts, before allowing the lure to bang back onto the bottom after each lift. The flathead will usually pounce on the lure as it drops down after a lift, but you have to be alert at all times.

Experiment with the retrieves and remember what the fish you are seeking usually feeds on and how it feeds. Also keep in mind how the type of prey you are trying to imitate would behave. There is no point trying to deceive a fish with a worm that looks as though it's just acquired a rocket pack. Some of the creatures you will be imitating move in spurts of a quarter of a metre or less. Some don't even do spurts! Your new big move may hit the jackpot, but don't forget – soft plastics can be lethal with very little movement at all.

Many anglers using plain non-scented tails add to the attraction of their soft plastic by dunking them into or injecting them with commercial scents sold for exactly that purpose. You can even get scents in fluoro colours to make sure the fish don't miss the offering.

The soft plastic bodies are not designed to last; their soft flexible composition is often torn or nipped to pieces. In fact, many anglers take packs of tails for a day's fishing and expect to go through them the same way they would through packs of natural bait. If you don't regard them as disposable you will soon be disappointed.

The greatest challenge facing soft plastic manufacturers at the moment is the race to find suitable biodegradable materials. The remnants of millions of partly destroyed tails have already prompted authorities to ban their use in several countries. The fact that free fish are willing to swallow attractively flavoured pieces is also a concern, unless the tails are non-toxic and digestible. Fortunately the leading brands seem to be making great progress in this area and some biodegradable soft plastic lures are already starting to appear on the market.

Fishing soft plastics tends to be addictive. You may find your old favourite hard-bodied lures starting to gather dust in the tackle box as the available space is taken over by a wild and wonderful assortment of squishy-squashy things.

Anatomy of a soft plastic lure

BODY ACTION

✄ The flexibility of the material these lures are made from gives them an undulating flowing movement even without the addition of a swimming tail.

✄ Body tapers influence the water's flow around the lure. The varying water pressures flowing around it as it moves can cause the body itself to waggle or roll. The bigger the curves and the longer and more supple the body, the more noticeable this will be. The addition of ribs or protrusions that catch the water flow may cause additional movement when drawn through the water.

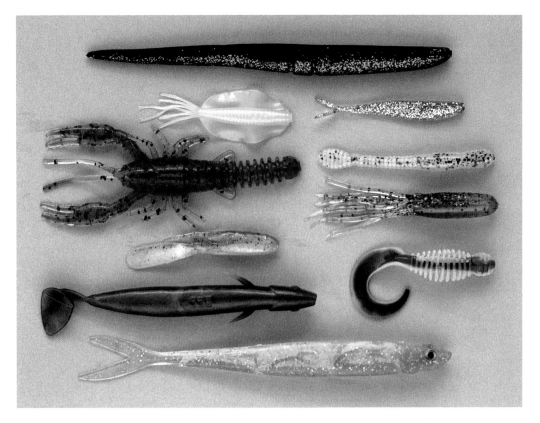

What appear to be very basic body shapes cause plastics to do all sorts of things in the water. While many anglers focus on tail action, they are much more subtle than that

❧ Especially prominent ribs or folds give the lure a more compressible soft texture and provide a greater surface area in contact with the water. This aids with scent transmission, and may also generate some movement at rest as tiny air bubbles trapped in the folds move together and break free.

❧ For lures with a straight tail section most of the appearance of life and motion will be dependent on rod work by the angler. This can range from a subtle jiggle while stationary to a rip/sink darting action.

❧ For 'jerkbaits', designed to be jerked and twitched at speed, a stiffer material may help them to glide and dart with erratic direction changes. The amount and placement of weighting (from hook or lead) will also greatly affect their action.

❧ The thinner and longer its body parts and the more flexible the material it is made from, the more movement the lure will have at very low speeds.

❧ The more bulk and water resistance a shape has, the more water will be moved when it passes through. This movement may be sensed by a fish's lateral line.

❧ A bulky body or a large tail that moves a lot of water will have increased water resistance and so will sink more slowly.

SWIMMING TAILS

❧ These are usually in the shape of a curly tail (flat-sided hook shape) or a T tail – also known as a paddle tail – which is shaped like a horizontal T or wedge at the end of the body.

❧ The flexibility and length of the membrane that joins a T tail to the body will determine how easily and how far the tail can move, as well as the minimum speed the tail will work at.

❧ T tails with broad flat faces and ones that sit perpendicular to the water flow (vertical) will have more resistance to the water and so will move with less speed.

❧ A T tail keeps the body compact and creates a realistic fish shape.

❧ For a curly tail, the thickness and flexibility of the plastic tail will determine how easily it can fold out into its water-screw shape and the minimum speed at which it will start to work.

❧ A curly tail will open out into a wriggling ribbon. A short body with a long curl means that most of the lure will be wriggling when the lure is retrieved. The motion of a large tail will also pull a small body left and right through the water. A long body section with a small curl at the end means the lure will appear as a static body with a short wriggling tail.

❧ A long curl adds length to the lure and takes its end further away from a hook point in the body. These lures usually rely on a fish attacking the head or engulfing the whole lure in order to get a secure hook-up.

❧ A broad curl will push more water as it moves and so may be more detectable by a fish's lateral line.

❧ Curly tails can be mounted on a jig head with the curl up or down. To the fish it makes very little difference, but when casting there is less chance of the tail fouling on the hook when it is mounted facing away from the hook point.

❧ The pulse of vibrations created by these tail styles each have a different feel (and attraction) to the fish.

TIM SIMPSON

LEFT Flathead love soft plastics, with many anglers catching their 'best ever' flathead since switching to this style of lure

RIGHT The angle and shape of the tail and the flexibility of the joint between body and tail can make a huge difference to the action and particularly to the minimum speed at which the tail will start to work

BUOYANCY

❧ Many soft plastic materials are either naturally buoyant or of neutral density. This means that in the water they will waft around naturally or very slowly start to rise. Of course, once a hook is added they become weighed down and don't actually float, but even so, with a light hook they can be worked while very slowly drifting down through the water column.

❧ A buoyant plastic, or one with air injected into it with a small syringe, will cause the tail end of a lead-headed lure to rise up and waft in the current when the lure is paused on the bottom. This technique can be used for a convincing imitation of a yabby's defence stance.

Most modern soft plastics are impregnated with salt or various scents. These scents add to the attractiveness of the lures, but they do wear off after a period out of the packaging. A wide range of commercial scents are available to boost the smell of new lures or to rejuvenate lures that have been in use for a while. Some even include colouring to further enhance the offering

SCENT AND FLAVOUR

❧ Scent and flavour not only add realism but are a powerful attractant to draw fish in. They commonly come as a coating on the lure, as an aftermarket additive in spray, liquid or gel form, or impregnated throughout the plastic itself.

❧ Exterior coatings have a limited life underwater and may need to be reapplied, but they offer a strong constant stream of the attractant while it lasts. A plastic impregnated with scent will last much longer but must allow the additive to disperse into the water or it will remain trapped inside and be of no benefit. If the plastic is porous, a fish may get a burst of the attractant when it squeezes down on it.

❧ Prominent ribs and filaments give substantially more surface area to a lure and allow additives to be applied where they won't wash off too quickly.

❧ Salt is a common and effective additive on many soft plastics.

RATTLES

❧ Rattles for soft plastics are available in the form of small closed cylinders of glass containing several metal balls. Their pointed ends are pushed inside the soft plastic.

STRENGTH

❧ Flexibility is extremely important for action in most soft plastics, but you also need to ensure the plastic material isn't too soft and easily torn.

❧ Many of the cheaper soft plastics will tear very easily. At best, this may mean you only catch one fish per body, but it may also mean that if a fish hits the lure and misses the hook it may not come back because the lure is torn and doesn't sit correctly on the hook or won't swim properly.

❧ Some companies make soft plastics that are both flexible and tough. A new gel polymer called 'Cyberflexxx' is remarkably supple and yet extremely resistant to breakage or tearing.

RIGGING

❧ The soft plastic body can be rigged on any type of hook. It can be used weighted only by the hook, or with a separate weight, or on a jig head that incorporates both the hook and an action-producing weight.

❧ If rigging on a bare hook, the body can be secured by pulling the eye of the hook into the end of the body and then pinning it with a short length of stiff nylon line (20 kilograms or so) through the plastic body and eye of the hook.

❧ A drop of superglue on the hook's shank while rigging will stop the plastic tail pulling down when a fish grabs hold.

❧ The hook should be run carefully straight down the centre of the body when rigging so that the lure maintains its shape without bulges or bends.

❧ Soft bodies can be rigged to be weedless or snagproof by inserting the hook diagonally for a short distance, then exiting the body and running underneath it until only the point of the hook is reinserted at the appropriate distance down the body. Just the very tip of the hook's point will be protruding from the plastic. When a fish grabs hold, the hook will push through. The hook must be big enough so that, once pushed through, the gape is still sufficient to hold the fish, even with the lure body in the way.

❧ If rigging a jerkbait on a jig head, the weight at the nose will give it a nodding action. To achieve a gliding jerking motion, rig the body by pushing the eye of the

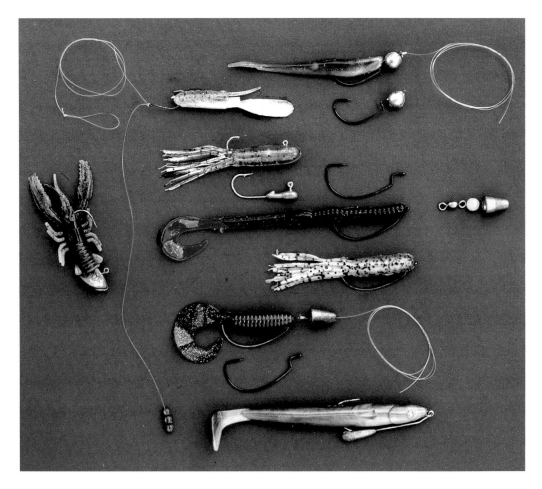

Soft plastics can be rigged and used in many different ways; each will give a different effect. Some of the more common ways to rig them are shown in this picture. A hook and weight are simply added by sliding the body onto a jig head — as with the crayfish (far left) and the weedless jig head (top right). The paddle tail (second from top) is rigged on a dropper hook with split shot down the main line. These will pull off if it becomes snagged. This set-up is called a 'drop shot rig'. The tube lure under that has an internal jig head. The worm is shown rigged weedless on a worm hook, and the sliding sinker, normally separated 20 centimetres or so above the swivel is termed the 'Carolina rig'. Below that is another tube rigged weedless on a worm hook. Under that is a curly tail also rigged weedless and with a sliding sinker for weight instead of a jig head. This is known as the 'Texas Rig'. Bottom: a fish shape rigged centre-weighted on a Mustad Power Lock Plus hook which allows it to sink horizontally and be twitched and darted erratically

TIM SIMPSON

Soft plastics will sometimes produce fish you've never even seen before. This lionfish was jigged-up in a coral lagoon

jig head up through the plastic a little back from the front (5 millimetres). The jig head will now be sitting underneath the body, which distributes the weight further back and gives the lure the effect of a small bib.

STORAGE

- Soft plastics should be stored separated by colour so they don't run and stain each other.
- Chemicals in regular soft plastics can melt or react with cheap plastic storage containers. Store them in plastic zip-top bags or 'worm-proof' tackle boxes. Soft plastics made of the newer 'Cyberflexxx' polymer will even react with other soft plastics – or their residue in previously used tackle boxes. They should be kept separately.
- Soft plastics are often soaked in scented or moistening oils. They may dry out unless stored in sealed bags.

Sabiki (bait) jigs

A Sabiki jig is basically a paternoster rig with lures or 'flies' on the end of the branch lines instead of bait. In the last couple of decades they have revolutionised the catching of bait species like yellowtail, slimy mackerel and herring.

Using a Sabiki allows an angler to catch bait quickly and without the mess and fuss of light lines and bait. The string of multiple lures is simply lowered down to the appropriate depth then jigged with a rise-and-fall action. Because it is a representation

TIM SIMPSON

LEFT Strings of Sabiki jigs represent the fastest way to load up with live bait

RIGHT The Sabiki idea has been extended to offshore fishing where larger lures on stronger rigs account for a surprisingly wide range of bottom dwellers

of a school of tiny shrimp or baitfish, the angler can move it constantly while searching for the correct depth. In fact, most of the fish will jump on while the lure is dropping rather than when it is on the upstroke of a jig. This is much easier than trying to gently float down a lightly weighted bait in a berley trail.

The use of berley will help, as it gets the baitfish into feeding mode, but these jig sets are highly successful even in very deep ocean waters beyond the reach of a berley trail. Schools of fish like slimy mackerel can be found with an echo sounder and effectively jigged with the aid of a suitable sinker in depths of 150 metres or more!

A by-product of fishing for bait species over offshore reefs is the frequent catch of a fascinating variety of reef species which were unheard of on lures until recently. Species like dory, nannygai, morwong, flounder, cod and many other unknown bottom-dwellers are joining the list of regulars like snapper, trevally, flathead, pike and so on. And these are just accidents when the Sabiki is lowered to the bottom. We wouldn't be at all surprised if larger, more appropriate Sabikis are used with increasing regularity in the next few years as anglers realise the potential of a school of tiny prey jigged down on the reef bottom.

Anatomy of a Sabiki jig

MAIN LINE
- This is the vertical line that attaches to the fishing line at the top and a weight at the bottom.
- It needs to be strong enough to take the strain of a complete string of struggling fish as well as the weight.
- The length of the main line should allow the rig to be swung aboard when the connection is wound to the rod's tip.

BRANCH LINES
- These are the short lines that attach to the main line at one end and a lure at the other.
- Since the branch line only has to hold one fish and none of the sinker's weight it can be significantly lighter and thinner in diameter. This is a great benefit because the thinner line is less visible and fewer fish will be wary of biting the lure on the end.
- The branch lines are knotted to the main line in such a way that the branch (and tag end) finishes up parallel to the main line. The rig is then fished with the branches on the rod side of the knot and the tag end facing the sinker. As the lure is jigged it bends the short length of line over in an arc and its stiffness helps to keep

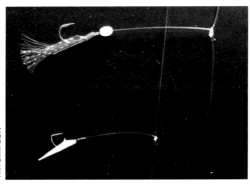

The branch line to the lure can be lighter than the Sabiki main line. This helps considerably when the fish are shy. A luminous bead at the top of each lure will also substantially improve the effectiveness in most cases — even in broad daylight!

TIM SIMPSON

Sabiki jigs can be used on everything from baitfish to reef fish

it away from the main line. For this reason, a thin but stiff line is most suitable for the branch lines. It is also wise to keep them short.

LURE

❧ The lure (or fly) at the end of every branch line should represent a prey item that the fish you are targeting likes to eat. These are commonly shrimp or tiny baitfish.

❧ The Sabiki should be fished in a way that imparts a suitable action to mimic whatever prey item is represented.

❧ One of the most popular baitfish representations has a wing of white, coloured or reflective substance folded over the hook. This can be made from plastic or any other material, but the most successful seem to be those made from a dried sheet of real fish skin (if you look closely you can see the indentations where the scales used to be), perhaps because the skin imparts a scent or flavour to the lure. The effectiveness of the skin seems to decrease after a period of use, probably once the scent or flavour has washed out.

- There is usually a green luminous (glow-in-the-dark) bead sitting at the head of each lure. This seems to make a significant contribution to the effectiveness of the lure, even when used in shallow water in bright sunshine. The quality of the luminous bead will determine how brightly it glows and how long it holds a charge.

WEIGHT

- The sinker at the bottom of the rig may also aid in fish attraction if it is coloured or covered in something that entices the fish, such as luminous paint or silver glitter.
- The weight should be spaced far enough below the rest of the rig that it doesn't inhibit fish from taking the bottom lure.
- It's much easier to handle a string of wriggling fish if the weight at the bottom of the rig is sufficiently heavy to hold the main line straight while you work on the branch lines.

Blade spinners

Blade spinners have been used for centuries but enjoyed a huge surge in popularity when the modern French blade version was invented in 1938 by Andre Muelnart. They are enormously popular with freshwater anglers in all parts of the world and a staple for anglers who fish for trout.

The use of these lures in Australia has been dominated for decades by one or two brands in only one of the common blade designs. The fact that there are at least three other different and productive designs that have largely been ignored is probably due to a lack of understanding of what they do and how they fit into a fishing situation.

These lures feature a blade that spins around a central wire shaft. The differences come in the shape of those blades and how they rotate. Each shape spins at a different speed and different angle, with different water resistance and a distinctive pulse. Most weave their way through the water, while one style tracks straight. Understanding what these lures do and which blade to use will open up a whole new range of fishing options and better presentations.

As the blade whirs around its shaft it creates an indistinct profile which is three-

Blade spinners are highly specialised lures. Each blade shape gives the lure a
particular action and purpose. Their strong pulse at very slow speeds makes
them particularly useful in freshwater fishing

dimensional, symmetrical and somewhat teardrop-shaped. The width of its body is
dependent on the type of blade. Most give the illusion of some form of baitfish.

The indistinct profile and flash, together with the strong pulse, seem irresistible to
many trout; even so, many will simply follow the lure unless the angler adds a variation
like an occasional spurt or pause. It is often the angler's manipulation of the rod tip and
retrieve speed that clinches a strike.

Blade spinners come with many differently shaped blades. Each shape behaves
quite differently in the water and has a specialised application for a knowledgeable angler.
The most common shapes are, from left: Colorado, Indiana or French, willow leaf
and the convex-concave

Aside from the salmonoids (trout/salmon), these lures are often used in other
freshwater environments for slow-hunting coloured-water species like bass and perch.
In a giant size they are even used for gigantic Murray cod. They are successful because
they work at a very slow speed, allowing these fish to find and catch them, and they
put out a strong pulse which the fish detect and home in on with their lateral lines.

The shape of the lure's blade will greatly affect how it travels through the water.
Different blade shapes are selected for different fishing situations. The four most
popular blade styles and their features are:

1. COLORADO

🪝 An elliptical, almost round blade that is quite dished. This design has the highest
blade angle (around 45 degrees) which gives a wide body profile. The angle of
rotation and the curved surfaces also reduce the amount of flash.

🪝 It also has the strongest pulse. This makes it good for coloured water as the lure is
easily detected even when visibility is poor.

🪝 The high water resistance of this blade will lift it towards the surface making it
good for shallow snaggy waters.

🐟 It needs a lot of water pressure to keep the blade from stalling, making it difficult to fish down-current.

🐟 The distinct beat coupled with a slow rotation gives this lure a strong erratic weaving action. Good in open water but it makes it difficult to position near structure without snagging.

2. INDIANA OR FRENCH

🐟 A longer elliptical blade, like a wide water drip.

🐟 Intermediate blade angle (around 30 degrees). This, combined with a broad blade surface, gives excellent flash and a medium-width body profile.

🐟 Has a moderate pulse with a fairly fast blade rotation.

🐟 Some swimming action but can be fished close to structure.

🐟 It has moderate water resistance but still allows some depth.

🐟 The low minimum speed for blade rotation allows easy down-current spinning.

🐟 This is the most popular blade style as it is very versatile. It can be fished fast or slow, deep or shallow.

3. CONVEX-CONCAVE

🐟 An oval-shaped blade with the shaft running through the middle of one end rather than attached via a clevis. The shorter top end is concave (dished) whereas the larger lobe on the other side of the shaft is convex.

🐟 A good pulse and flash even at very slow speeds.

🐟 Popular for spinning down-current due to its low minimum speed.

🐟 Spins helicopter-style when dropping through water. This often attracts strikes even when sinking.

🐟 Moderate water resistance will keep the lure suspended above the bottom and snags even at slow speeds.

4. WILLOW LEAF

🐟 A long, narrow oval-shaped blade.

🐟 This design has a low blade angle (around 20 degrees) which gives a long, narrow (fish-shaped) profile that is highly visible from side on.

🐟 The blade sits at a good angle to catch the sun and the fast blade rotation results in a high-frequency flash. Its narrow curved surface reflects a thin band of flash.

🐟 The low-drag blade gives a more subtle pulse but with a high-frequency beat.

- Rides in a straight line.
- The low water resistance from this blade will not lift it to the surface. This, coupled with an often heavy body, allows deep retrieves, even at speed.
- Prone to snagging in shallow water unless fished fast.
- Requires a moderate rate of retrieve to keep the blade turning. This makes it difficult to fish downstream if there is a strong flow.

Blade spinners are ideal for probing a flowing stream to find where active fish are stationed. Fish in this scenario are facing into the current, waiting for a food item – from a worm or insect to larger prey like minnows – to be washed down to them. The trick in this situation is to have a lure that works well at extremely slow speeds because it will need to appear as a food item being carried by the current. To achieve this the lure is cast upstream and wound back with the water flow.

If the stream is flowing and the lure needs some water speed to work, you'd need to retrieve the lure really quickly to get action from it. This is not ideal when fishing for trout; in that situation, a slower presentation will be more productive, which is where a blade spinner comes in.

A spinner cast up and across the stream can be worked down at just above current speed and used to slowly sweep across and probe around rocks, under banks or amongst fallen timber. By selecting the appropriate blade and body, you can work it deep into the bottom of a pool or keep it suspended at the surface to hover in the current in front of a shallow log. Blade spinners' high water-drag is a very helpful feature, allowing a belly of line to drag in the current and position the lure behind, along, underneath or in front of likely ambush positions.

Spinners can also be jigged for stream trout that are holding up in holes or under timber or undercut banks. The lure is cast slightly upstream then allowed to wash into

Blade spinners are a favourite with trout anglers

BILL CLASSON

position before a short vertical retrieve. Another technique is to use them running fast just under the surface, where they 'bulge' and make a disturbance on the surface.

The flash off the metal blades can be a great attractor, but the amount of flash (surface area/reflectivity) should be matched to the light and water conditions as well as the mood and sensitivity of the fish. Coming into contact with many anglers will make them more wary. Large blades offer the most attraction as their size gives a greater area of flash and a stronger pulse, but the same lure in a smaller size will be more subtle.

Line twist is a constant battle with this type of lure. There are several designs that help to reduce it, but in the end it usually requires an angler to let the line flow back in the current with nothing on the end so that it can untwist itself. Adding a snap-swivel to the front of the lure will do little to help with the twist but will certainly elongate and change the appearance of the lure's profile.

Anatomy of a blade spinner

PULSE
- This is the vibration that the lure puts out. It is detected by the fish's lateral line from up to 15 metres away. In coloured water the pulse may attract a fish's attention long before it can be seen.
- A blade style that runs at a steep angle away from the body will push a lot more water and so have a stronger pulse than a blade with a shallow rotation angle.
- A small blade will have a more subtle pulse than the thump of a large one.
- A blade that rotates slowly around a lure will produce a different beat to another shape that rotates quickly.

FLASH
- The amount of flash will depend on how much of the blade is angled towards the light filtering down from the surface. This varies according to the angle at which the blade spins around the shaft and the shape, size and reflectivity of the blade itself.
- A blade that spins close to the lure's body will travel through the water fairly horizontally and so most of its surface will be exposed to the sun. A blade that spins further out from the body will be at a greater angle to the light and so will have less flash. Its flash will also be reflected forwards.
- Blades with flat sections or panels that catch the sun will have more flash than a

Blade spinners are very useful in freshwater as they are small but castable, sink but work at very slow speed, flash and have a strong, attractive vibration. On many of these lures, when the blade is spinning around it actually forms the indistinct outline of a baitfish

rounded surface. A dimpled or corrugated surface will have a more consistent but more subdued reflection.

How quickly the blade rotates around the lure determines how often a flash is given off. The most suitable amount of flash will depend on the mood and sensitivity of the fish and also on the available light and water clarity.

Small lures usually have a subtler flash because of their smaller surface area.

Flash and colour is reflected off both sides of the blade.

See also Anatomy of a long-range casting slug, Flash, pages 128–9.

Most blade spinners have their blade attached via a horseshoe-shaped clevis.
This must be free to spin around the centre wire supported on bearing beads.
An alternate set-up is the convex-concave spinner, where the centre wire runs
through the middle near the top of the blade

PROFILE
As the blade spins around at high speed it creates the indistinct illusion of a three-dimensional body. The blade's size and especially its rotation angle will determine the shape of the 'body', both from side-on and from behind.

DEPTH
The weight of a lure's body will help it to sink and stay deep; however, even a heavy lure will rise quickly to the surface if there is a lot of water resistance from the blade. To stay deep a lure must have body weight and a blade with low water resistance, such as one that rotates close to the body.

WEAVING ACTION
The pulse produced by the spinning blade may also cause the lure to weave in the

water. A strong, wide and slow blade rotation will throw the lure in an erratic action – up, down, left or right – similar to a propeller with a blade missing.

🐟 The faster and closer to the body the blade rotates, the less it will move the lure.

🐟 A lure with a strong weaving action may be attractive in open water but will be difficult to run close to cover without snagging. Straight-running spinners may be placed to run through tight cover.

BODY

🐟 The body or barrel of the lure adds colour and shape to the lure profile.

🐟 The weight required for casting or running at depth can be achieved through the body design. A heavy compact shape will sink quicker. However, even a heavy body will rise quickly to run near the surface if it has a high-resistance blade design.

🐟 The body may include a rattle or have a certain resonance when struck by the blade. Some bodies have an integral geared noise-making device.

🐟 A ribbed or hollow-ended body makes it easier to apply a fish-attracting scent.

CLEVIS

🐟 This is a U-shaped device that attaches the blade to the central wire shaft (except for convex–concave spinners). It should allow the blade free movement to swing to its rotation angle as well as around the shaft.

🐟 A clevis usually comes as a folded metal U or a solid wire loop with flattened and drilled ends for the centre shaft. This latter version is considered superior as it spins more freely and is less prone to clogging.

BEADS

🐟 Metal beads and shaped spacers add weight to the lure and keep the blade separated at the desired distance from the body and hook. Most importantly, the bead or shape immediately under the clevis acts as a bearing, providing a low-friction surface for the blade to spin on.

🐟 The bearing bead should be perfectly smooth with no burs or anodising lumps to hamper the blade's rotation.

🐟 For extra weight in a home-made lure, the typical brass beads can be replaced with Tungsten beads (available from fly-tying shops) which are the same size but considerably heavier.

SHAFT

✦ The wire shaft must be strong and stiff enough to withstand the strain of fighting without bending. A bent shaft may restrict the rotation of the clevis and may also promote line twist.

HOOK

✦ The way a hook is attached to the lure will determine how much flexibility it has.

✦ A hook fixed inside the hollow end of a lure's body will not have much movement. It will sit in line with the body even at very low speed and help with penetration in tough mouths by holding the points in alignment. It will also maintain the lure's profile and may be more snag resistant than a free-swinging hook.

✦ A hook dangling on a split ring will be easier to replace and allows much more movement, which may help to keep a jumping thrashing fish connected, but may also allow the hook to droop below the body at low speeds.

✦ The points of the hook should sit below the blade so the blade doesn't obstruct the fish's bite.

✦ A single hook will give more snag resistance than a treble.

See also Bibbed lures, Hooks, page 87.

Spinnerbaits

Spinnerbaits are another family of lures that were slow to take off in Australia. Like many lures of American origin they were associated with the small and largemouth bass that populate many of the freshwater lakes of the US, which may have put off Australian anglers because those species don't occur in Australia. In years past, they probably had it right, because we had no fishing environments to equate with the American lakes, even though native Australian bass are very similar in habits to the bass of the US.

All that changed when the stocking of Australia's east coast impoundments created a whole new fishing environment in which fish that acted like the US freshwater sport fish could at last be found in quantity. Where Australians had been used to fishing wild streams and casting lures at snags and structure to catch bass, all of a sudden the fish existed in these big water systems, where they not only enjoyed rapid growth rates but

Spinnerbaits took a long time to catch on in Australia after being a basic lure in
American bass fishing situations for many years. Apart from their ability to attract fish
with flash and vibration, they are a very useful lure because they are also particularly snag
resistant. This allows them to be cast into areas that although known to hold fish,
would otherwise be avoided

also adapted to a new feeding environment – as did a wide range of other native fish
introduced into these waters.

Australian anglers now found themselves working on fish suspended over weed
beds and old river channels, hiding in the branches of drowned trees, weaving through
reeds and lily pads as well as working deep rock bars and so on. This was a new
environment which could be exploited with a whole new boxful of fishing tools.

Initially, spinnerbaits seemed too outrageous to appeal to anything, even a very
hungry fish. A wire coat hanger with a jig body encased in a multi-coloured plastic
skirt, with metal blades twittering away above as the lure is retrieved – which part is
the fish supposed to strike, if it is silly enough to strike at all?

Well, you could look at it another way. Perhaps it could be a lure with its own teaser/attractor built in. Bass can be territorial and downright aggressive little devils, which could explain part of their interest in spinnerbaits. Whatever the fish think of them, spinnerbaits take a lot of fish.

You've probably been sharp enough to notice that we keep talking about 'time in the strike zone' when we refer to the way lures work. The amount of time a lure spends where fish can see it is critical to the degree of fishing success you will enjoy. Lure fishing is often about working the percentages. An angler who makes 100 casts will hook more fish than the angler who makes 50. A lure that spends 50 per cent of its time in the strike zone on each cast will account for more fish than a lure that spends 10 per cent of its time in the strike zone. So the maximum number of casts with a lure that spends most of its time in the strike zone must equal better fishing.

One of the great things about spinnerbaits is that they can be kept in the productive zone for most of a cast. Suppose those bass are over a weed bed and you go after them with a deep diver: the first part of the cast will be wasted diving the lure down to maximum depth, then, soon after you start the retrieve, the lure will be gradually planing back towards the surface as the angle between the lure and the rod tip steepens. A spinnerbait, however, will sink straight to the bottom at the end of the cast, then a lift of the rod gets it off the bottom where a hopping or steady retrieve will keep it running along just above bottom until it gets right under the boat.

In use, the supple-skirted tail billows and flows with the motion imparted by the angler while the blades throb above and impart a vibration that feels good enough to eat. The blades are large and push a lot of water. The vibration they create travels well beyond the range of visibility in most of the coloured waters they are used in and is one reason they get so much attention.

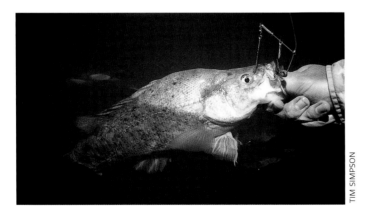

The strong vibrations from the whirling blades of a spinnerbait make it ideal for heavily coloured water where limited visibility forces the fish to rely largely on feel to find their prey

TIM SIMPSON

Although similar in appearance to a spinnerbait, the buzz bait relies on a particularly noisy propeller arrangement to run at the surface and attract fish. They are very snag resistant and work well over weed beds and through lily pads

Spinnerbaits are extremely snag resistant and so can be cast into particularly hostile water where big fish lurk but few anglers dare to cast. By using a sensitive rod and line system you can 'feel' your way through sunken timber and rock edges, dropping down to probe immediately behind where many of the fish will be lying in ambush. That really is working the structure and maximising time in the strike zone.

Spinnerbaits are used in other ways too. A popular retrieve is the 'burn and kill' where the lure is cranked at speed for a couple of seconds before being allowed to free-fall back towards the bottom. The speed gets the attention of the fish, but most of the strikes will come when the lure is paused or on the drop. To notice a bite like this an angler will need to be watching carefully and, again, will find great benefit in a sensitive system like a graphite rod and gel-spun line.

The blades used for spinnerbaits are the same as those for blade spinners; similarly, the correct selection of shape is important to achieve the right pulse, speed and depth for the lure (*see Blade spinners, pages 159–61, for more information*).

A variation of a spinnerbait is the buzz bait, a hybrid between a surface fizzer and a spinnerbait. The buzz bait is essentially the same as a spinnerbait in appearance except the blades are exchanged for a style of propeller. The water resistance on these sinking lures quickly brings them back to the surface where the propeller runs sputtering along and creating quite a fuss, while the skirted lure runs neatly along underneath. The combination gives the attraction of a surface fizzer with the better hook-up of a lure running cleanly sub-surface. Buzz baits are very snag resistant and great for running through lily pads or over shallow weed beds. The strikes are explosive!

Anatomy of a spinnerbait

HEAD
- The head provides the lure's weight. This should be considered not only for casting but also for how quickly you want the lure to sink. To sink quickly the head must overcome the water resistance of the blades.
- The shape of the head can affect the lure's balance and motion during free fall and retrieve. Lead is the most common material for the moulded head, but other metals like tungsten – which gives a heavier head for the same size – are available.
- Some lead heads have a barb moulded in to enable the addition of a soft plastic curly tail for use inside or without the regular skirt.

HOOK
- The hook is usually a single. This gives a more secure hold on a fish than a typically sized treble hook because of the large hook gape, which is a benefit when working hard on large or tough fish with heavy line.
- The upturned hook gives excellent snag resistance, especially as it rides behind the lure arm.
- A second hook, or 'stinger', will help to catch timid fish that nip the ends of the skirt, but makes the lure more prone to snagging. A stinger can be added by ganging the first hook's point through the eye of a second hook (with a suitably sized eye). To prevent the second hook falling off again, a small soft bead of plastic or rubber is then added. Another method is to slip a small piece of silicone tubing around the eye of the trailing hook before forcing the lure's hook point through both.
- The gauge of the hook is worth considering. On light tackle, the large hook may be difficult to set in a tough mouth; a light gauge (wire) will make it much easier to set. A thick heavy-gauge hook is more suited to large fish and strong line. On heavy

line, the flexibility of a light-gauge hook may give the option of partially straightening it when snagged so you can get your lure back. The danger with this, of course, is that you don't want it to happen when fighting a powerful fish. Another danger is that when you bend a straightened hook back into shape, the temper of the steel may be changed, resulting in a substantially weakened (or broken) hook.

SKIRT

- The shredded skirt can be made from all sorts of materials but is usually rubber or latex. A thin or supple material allows the skirt to flutter and pulse as the lure rises and falls during a retrieve. A stiff skirt will restrict this action.
- Some skirt materials, particularly tinsel and those with a tacky feel, may be prone to tangles or matting.
- The skirt should not extend too far past the end of the hook or fish may bite the tail and miss the point. A good length is 20–30 millimetres.
- A thick bulky skirt creates more drag and so is heavier to pull through the water. It will also slow down the rate at which the lure sinks. The addition of a soft plastic curly tail will also slow the lure down, but helps to make it attractive at slow speeds.

WIRE ARMS

- The design, angles, stiffness and material the arms are made from all make a significant difference to the performance of the lure.
- So that the lure's hook remains horizontal during retrieve, the length and angle of the arms must be sized to ensure a balance between the water-drag of the blades and the weight of the head. However, the blades should not extend far behind the end of the skirt or they may obstruct fish from hitting the lure. Also, if the top arm does not reach as far back as the point of the hook, the lure will not be as well protected from snagging.
- The position of the end of the top arm is important when the lure is falling and helicoptering down. At this time the blades will be vertical above the lure and should be positioned over the skirt.
- The thickness and type of metal the wire is made from will influence the pulse that is transmitted, both in the water (felt by the fish) and through the line (felt by the angler). A soft metal produces a bigger vibration but is easily damaged or bent by fish or heavy tackle.
- Titanium and stainless-steel wires are the most commonly used. Titanium has an

advantage in its ability to resist damage or being bent out of shape. Titanium's extreme strength also allows it to be used in a much thinner gauge; this enables more vibration as there is less water resistance. It is considerably more expensive than stainless steel, however, and adds substantially to the price of a lure.

SWIVEL/CLEVIS

- ✺ The blades of a spinnerbait are connected to the wire arm via a clevis or a swivel.
- ✺ A clevis is a horseshoe-shaped loop of metal that attaches the mid-arm blade to the wire and allows it to rotate around it. Cheap lures sometimes use a folded clevis which is wrapped around the arm. These are weaker than a solid drilled clevis and also more prone to clogging with algae or mud.
- ✺ The swivel at the end of the arm gives the blade its freedom to move: it can rotate or spin as easily as the swivel will allow. The quality of the swivel dictates how little water pressure (speed) it takes to make the blade move and ultimately how much action it can perform. You can get some lures where the mid-arm blades are also attached via swivels.
- ✺ There is a substantial difference in performance between a regular swivel and a ball-bearing swivel. There is an equally large difference between a top-quality American-made ball-bearing swivel (from SAMPO or Worth) and lesser brands. These swivels make a big difference to the performance of the lure but are expensive and will noticeably increase the price of the lure.

BLADE SHAPES/SIZES

- ✺ The blades are a key factor in the success of a spinnerbait. They are available in several different shapes, each with different characteristics and purposes, including speed, sink rate, flash and pulse.
- ✺ The surface area and shape of the blades will affect how easy the lure is to cast through the air.
- ✺ The greater the number of blades, the greater the surface area or the wider the blades' action, the more drag through the water the lure will have. Although the vibration is increased, the water pressure will slow the sink rate of the lure and, when the retrieve is started, will quickly draw the lure back up towards the surface, making it hard to maintain depth.
- ✺ Blade action is achieved through water pressure on the different surfaces of the blade. The thinner the blade or the lighter the material, the less weight the water

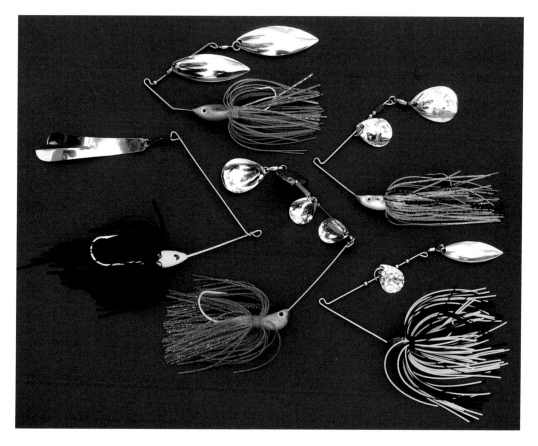

Spinnerbaits are bizarre looking lures, but excellent at holding a particular depth
for the full length of the cast. Their snag resistance makes them ideal for presentation
to fish holding in heavy timber, over weed beds and so on

pressure will have to throw around and so the greater the action. Lighter weight will
also enable the lure to work at a lower speed.

✄ The more rounded and dished (cupped) the blade, the more action it will have, the
more pulse it will create and the slower the speed at which it will start to work.

✄ The high-action slow-speed Colorado blade is great for probing around structure, and
its strong pulse makes it ideal for use in low visibility such as murky water or at night.

✄ The Indiana (or French) blade is a good all-rounder that has a fast action with a
good pulse and flash at even low speeds.

✄ For a deep or fast retrieve, the best blade shape would be the long thin willow leaf
design with its tighter action and much lower drag.

Spinnerbaits with an 'R bend' tie-point in the wire are less likely to foul up with
the line. However, a twisted tie-point will stop the line from riding up one of the arms
while fighting a large fish on heavy line. Trailer hooks can easily be added when fish
are only nipping at the tail of the lure

- The water-drag from the blades needs to be balanced to the weight of the head, otherwise the blades may pull the lure over backwards.
- Blades that occasionally bang into each other create noise which may help to attract the interest of a fish.
- Flash is reflected off the blade area when it is at the right angle to the light filtering down from above. The greater the flat surface area, the more of it will be facing the light at one time and so the larger the flash.

❧ A dimpled or hammered finish will give a consistent but more subtle flash as one of its many tiny surfaces will nearly always be facing the sun. This delicate flash is often more successful when the fish are easily spooked.

❧ Some spinnerbaits are now being made with clear plastic blades for use in very clear water with very nervous fish. They have a pulse but no visible blades to scare the fish.

❧ Blades for buzz baits are designed to operate half in and half out of the water. They must be light and bulky so water-drag quickly lifts them up to run at the surface. Big water-resistant blades coupled to light heads allow a slower retrieve.

❧ Different shapes of buzz bait propeller blades will give differently spluttering surface effects. The sound that each makes will also vary.

TOW-POINT

❧ The bend or loop in the wire arm where you attach the line comes in several different styles. Any of the twisted or coiled (overlapping) tie-points would seem to be the most secure, however there are several advantages with the simple 'R bend' tie-point. A twisted or coiled tie-point will allow the line to jam and become damaged; with a bend this cannot happen. Also with a bend, if the line does wrap around it will easily pull off.

❧ With some wire bends the wire becomes acutely kinked. This will weaken it and may lead to a breakage.

❧ If a snap is to be used to connect a lure with an R bend, it can be locked in place by slipping a tiny loop cut from a small plastic or silicone rubber tube over and to the back of the tie-point to prevent the snap sliding up one of the lure's arms.

❧ A twisted tie-point or an R bend with a locking loop is a good idea when using very heavy tackle as it stops the line from slipping up the arm under pressure.

❧ Although a snap is a convenient way to quickly connect the lure, a more sensitive way is to tie it directly to the line. This allows the vibration to pass into the line which enables you to monitor its performance, ideal speed and bumps from structure or fish.

BEADS

❧ Metallic beads act as spacers between the blades and clevis. They also help to create noise.

See also Anatomy of a Blade spinner, pages 162–5.

Skirted trolling lures

These lures range from small metal bullet-headed 'squid tails' of 5 centimetres to massive shaped resin action heads on shredded tails over 30 centimetres long. They are usually aimed at the faster-moving pelagic species that hunt at the surface and respond well to a high-speed lure.

Although·they have a shredded plastic tail attached to their much shorter head, these lures are not necessarily portraying a squid or octopus. The shredded tail simply gives the lure a supple flexibility and exposure to the enclosed hook. When towed through the water the tail gathers together and forms the profile of a fish or a swimming squid.

Small versions can be used wherever predators are chasing baitfish at the surface, but they are most commonly used for trolling bays and coastal waters when requiring a lure that won't spin or tangle and can be towed quickly. They can be used at almost any speed but are typically towed between 4–10 knots, which appeals to the speed-feeding pelagics and also allows the angler to cover a lot of ground in the search for fish.

The bigger gamefishing versions of these lures have a tough job to perform. It's a big blue sea out there and finding a fish will often involve searching over many kilometres. Speed is important as it enables an angler to cover ground quickly. These lures must appeal to huge fish, get noticed in a vast ocean, act like a vulnerable baitfish while towing massive hooks and a stiff thick trace, and then, when they finally get eaten, must detach from the hooks and slide away. A good one will do it all!

The mere size and shape of a big lure may appeal to a large fish, but what is even more alluring is the sight of its diving, splashing and fast head-shaking action while being towed at speeds of 5–8 knots, or faster behind a boat.

Many of these lures are designed to create a long 'smoking' trail of bubbles that stream out from the rear and add to the terror routine.

The bubble trail also gives the lure visibility. If you look into the sky on a clear blue day, you might not notice a tiny silver speck. But if on that same day you saw a long thin white vapour-trail, you may well find yourself following it until you noticed the speck of the jet at the far end that was causing it. A bluewater trolling lure works in much the same way: before it can be eaten it must be seen.

The bubble created by the lure as it rips through the surface is valuable for another reason: the initial envelope of air that peels back from the nose gives the lure a long

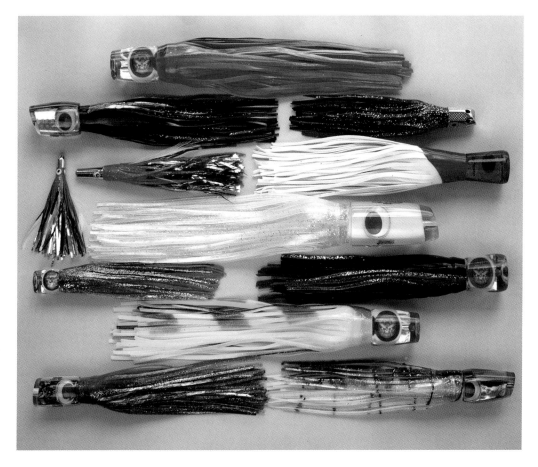

Skirted trolling lures come to life at high speed. Their bubbling, splashing routine gives the impression of a desperate, terrified baitfish that thinks it has seconds to live

elliptical tapered profile of shimmering silver that not only helps it get noticed, but also gives it a larger fish-shaped outline until the bubble fragments.

One of the predators that bluewater anglers most want to catch are the billfish like marlin and sailfish. These are powerful fish that require strong heavy-duty hardware to hold them. This is a major problem for most lures, but skirted trolling lures have been designed not only to swim with the weight and drag of heavy hooks and leader, but also to slide up the trace when a fish is hooked so the weight of the lure is not swung about when the fish is jumping and used to tear the hooks loose. Skirted trolling lures come in many different shapes and key features give each its own individual action. The functions assigned to different designs may include:

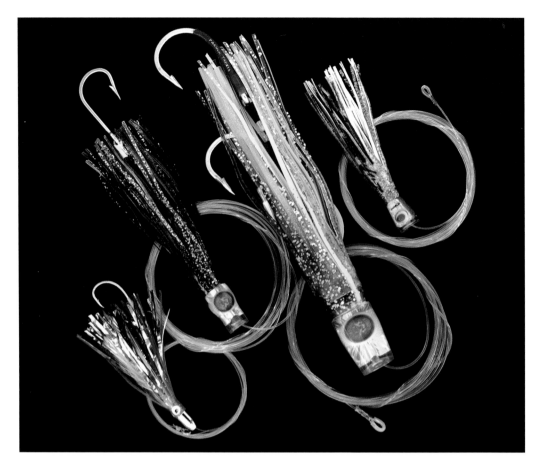

Skirted trolling lures are used offshore to attract large gamefish with an
action that looks like a terrified baitfish. They look simple enough but the subtleties
involved in design and application make them a specialist's tool

- A weaving action.
- A vibrating action that transmits a pulse through the water.
- A diving action. When diving beneath the surface chop, a lure is more visible from
  the sides and is also easier to attack and connect with.
- Sound: splashing, popping, 'tearing water' and perhaps rattles or whizzes.
- Periodically breaking the surface and splashing, without leaping out of the water.
  This gives the appearance of a terrified fish which has spotted its attacker and is
  trying desperately to get away. If the prey is terrified it's usually because it's good to
  eat. A detached baitfish in this situation is a key trigger for a predator's assault. If the

lure leaps from the surface it may still look realistic, but it will be much harder to connect with and is likely to tumble and tangle the hooks and leader, badly affecting its action and appearance.

- Holding a bubble of air in the vortex drag (vacuum) at the back of the head and then releasing it slowly as a fragmented bubble trail.
- Skimming beneath the surface without breaking it.

Anatomy of a skirted trolling lure

PUSHERS

- These are basically a cylinder-shaped head with a flat 90-degree angle on the face. They 'push' water, creating a pressure wave around them with a bubble in the vacuum behind the head.
- The shorter the head, the more it can pivot in the water pressure and shake. This adds to the action but reduces its ability to handle speed or choppy conditions.
- These lures often feature an offset tow-point (leader hole) which also gives them more action.
- Overall, the design is simple, uncomplicated and easy to run. They track straight, have a good action and a reasonable grip on the water.

CUP-FACED CHUGGERS

- These lures are similar in many ways to the pushers, but feature a concave cup on the face and usually taper in at the front and back of the head. The length and angle of these tapers and the shape and depth of the cup are crucial design elements that make a significant difference to the lure's action.
- The lures are symmetrical, with no top or bottom, and so are very easy to rig and require little expertise to trim for maximum efficiency in the water. They track in a straight line but may include a slight side-to-side weave in their action.
- The cup sucks the lure beneath the surface and gives it excellent grip on the water (without weight). This is very helpful on rough windy days and at high speed.
- Some cup-faced chuggers will dive much deeper than other head shapes. This makes them more visible and easier for the fish to connect with.
- Diving depth is influenced by the forward taper on the head. A steep angle gives extra depth. Short heads generally dive deeper than long heads.

These pusher heads have a flat face that creates a pressure wave around
the body which causes it to sway and shake

Cup-faced chuggers create strong bubble trails, grip the water at even very fast speeds and
are easy to position. They are a great choice for experts and beginners alike

✤ The length of the head relative to the size of the cup will either stabilise the lure or make it more erratic. A large cup on a shortish head will give a very strong head-shaking vibrating action and a short-spaced regularly breathing bubble trail. A longer head with a smaller face and cup will be more sedate and have a tighter action.

✤ A long head works well at high speed due to its stability. Because it has more planing surface it will perform better on the lower towing angles, such as when set long, either as a flat line or from an outrigger.

✤ The cup tears a substantial splash at the surface and the rear taper holds a large envelope of air, leading to a long thick smoking trail.

✤ Their symmetrical design and great traction mean these lures require no additional weight in manufacture and so are able to swim attractively at low speeds as well as higher ones. They are an excellent, easy and versatile lure.

BULLETS/BULLET JETS

✤ As their name implies, these lures are usually a short cylinder with a rounded nose. They are often made from metal as the weight helps to keep them in or on the surface at speed without tumbling out.

✤ They appear to have no action, but in fact the tapered nose will cause the lure to weave slightly at speed (unless this action is smothered by weight or drag).

RON CALCUTT

Each of these different cup-faced chugger shapes has a different action. The width compared to the length of the head makes a difference as does the forward or reverse tapers and the depth of the cup on the face. Even the sharpness of the leading edges on the face will crisp or dull the swimming action

LEFT Bullets and bullet-jet heads track just below the surface with only slight movements and bubble trail. This more subtle action often appeals to timid species that are balked by some of the more aggressive lures

RIGHT Konaheads were a favourite a few decades ago but recently have been superseded by more advanced styles

- The symmetrical bullet nose keeps them skimming just under the surface where they track in a straight line, generally without a bubble trail.
- Once seen, bullets make a steady sub-surface target which leads to a clean strike. Despite negligible action and bubbles they are often successful, especially on timid fish that may be daunted by more aggressive lures. They are very popular for tuna.
- Bullet jets are a bullet with a series of holes drilled from front to back in the head of the lure. These scoop or create a burst of bubbles that extends from the skirt as a thick bubble trail. Because the jet holes create a wash-through, there is no vacuum behind the head and so the bubbles come out in a burst rather than a long stream, then are absent until the lure next breaks the surface.
- Both styles are simple to rig as there is virtually no action to try to preserve. They are also simple to use in a wide range of sea conditions.

- Their sleek profile and low water-drag makes them a popular choice for use at high trolling speeds.

KONAHEAD

- This was one of the first big game lure designs. Konaheads have an elongated and tapered cylindrical head with a scooped and angled face. The leader hole is offset towards the back of the slant.
- The intentionally unstable design causes the lure to weave erratically from left to right, then break through the surface where it splashes and grabs a bubble of air before diving and starting over.
- The konahead has caught many fish in the past, however its action is susceptible to the dampening effects of heavy leader and hooks.
- Its unpredictable surface movements make it harder for a gamefish to catch and therefore its hook-up rate is less consistent than the newer designs.
- Konaheads are also more difficult to tune to ensure they track correctly in the water.

ANGLED (FLAT) SLICED HEADS

- These are a successful and commonly used design. They come in a wide range of variations, from long straight cylinders with a face the same diameter as the body to multi-tapered rounded bodies with a face smaller than the width of the body. All have a flat angled face which, along with the tapers, gives them their action.
- These lures can be weighted or designed to run with their face angled forwards or backwards. Sometimes they alternate between both. A big angle will induce the lure to rise or dive and some will weave from side to side.
- The angle of this bevel varies from 15–25 degrees. If the angle is excessive, the lure will slide up over the surface or skip out and tangle. A small angle (nearly vertical) will cause the lure to plough through the water, but with less surface commotion and less sideways movement. One rule of thumb says that the rougher it gets, the less slant you should have on your lures.
- These lures usually rely on the head being oriented with its face angled forwards. If the face is angled back, the lure will dive but swim lazily and for long periods without a bubble trail.
- Angled sliced heads are often oval in profile, with a smaller diameter side to side than from top to bottom. This helps them to orient either up or down and reduces an unbalanced lure's tendency to roll and weave in a slow spiral from side to side.

Angled sliced heads are a diverse, widespread and very popular style of skirted lure. The combination of angle at the face, overall head shape and the sharpness of the leading edge will determine which of a wide range of swimming actions will be delivered

- To ensure correct orientation they often have lead inserts moulded into the head to keel it.
- How the hooks sit in the tail can also affect how the head is oriented. The hooks will want to orient themselves with their shank at the bottom. The shank is longer than the point and so has more weight and acts as a keel. Some anglers will pin the hook into the desired head attitude by jamming a toothpick into the back of the leader hole alongside the leader. This temporarily locks the hook angle (and leader) to the head until a fish is hooked.
- Sliced heads require a little tuning of factors such as rigging, towing angle, positioning and speed to get optimum performance.

HARD OR SOFT HEADS
- Many manufacturers are now making skirted trolling lures with soft heads instead of the older-style hard resin heads. The reasoning is that a hard head will feel unnatural to a fish, whereas a fish missing the hook on a soft head will not be put

off and will return until it is hooked. In our experience, however, this is not the case. Many times we have watched billfish repeatedly strike a hard head and keep returning for more. Just as often we have watched a fish crash a soft head, miss the hook and never return. This claim may be more marketing talk than reality.

🐟 Both styles have their advantages. When a billfish bites down on a hard head, its mouth is more likely to slip down the head to the hooks when pressure is applied; this isn't as likely on a softer head that it can grip securely. Conversely, the soft heads are usually made of a lighter material, giving the lure a more vibrant action. (*See Buoyancy* below, *page 192*.)

ANGLES

🐟 There are often several angles on a lure head that influence its action. Besides the face, there is usually a forward taper (a bevel sloping down towards the face) and a rear taper. These may be separated by a parallel section.

🐟 A forward taper will induce the lure to dive. A rearward taper will give the head a shaking action and form an initial attachment point for an enveloping bubble of air.

🐟 The difference in the length and degree of each taper creates many different lure actions – some great, some duds.

🐟 The length, diameter and angle of the collar where the skirt is attached will also affect the water flow over the skirt and hence the lure's action.

🐟 Another factor that is surprisingly influential on the lure's performance is the sharpness of the edges around the face. A sharp angular edge will accentuate the action, giving quick crisp movements, while a smoothed-over rounded edge will muffle the action. On a rough day the surface commotion may allow a slow-moving lure enough action to attract fish; but on a calm day the lure with sharp edges will have a noticeable advantage.

WEIGHT

🐟 Weight – sometimes a substantial amount of lead or brass tubing – is often added to these lure heads. However, the design must ensure that the water-flow pressures that give the lure its action are strong enough to overcome this weight or the lure will not move much in the water.

🐟 Weight is used in some lure heads as a keel to orient the lure the right way up.

🐟 Extra weight gives the lure some resistance to wind and helps it to stay in the water rather than being pulled through the surface chop, which can cause it to tumble

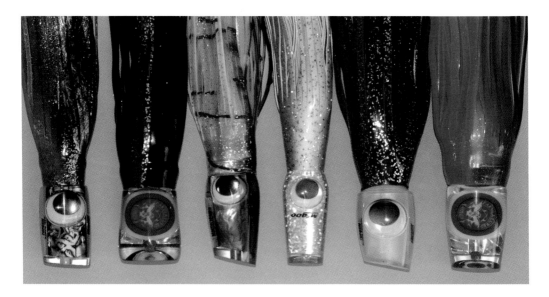

The many different angles of a skirted lure's head all contribute to its overall action. Forward tapers, rearward tapers, angled faces, scooped faces, narrow heads, fat heads, long heads and short heads — all make a difference. And that's just the head end!

through the air. However, surface traction can often be achieved through design rather than with extra weight. After all, a solid 1-kilogram lump of lead will skip all over the surface at 10 knots, while a lightweight plastic lure can suck down and stay put at 12 knots if it has the right design for the job.

- Brass tubing, often used for jet holes, will add noticeable weight to the head.
- The size and number of hooks will also contribute to the overall weight the lure's head has to tow around. If too large they will certainly affect or deaden the lure's action.

SKIRT

- The shredded skirt tail completes the body profile and gives the lure moving colour as the action of water and bubbles causes it to shuffle behind the head. The skirt acts similarly to the tail of a kite in that it stabilises the head. If the skirt has too little drag in the water, the head will seem uncontrollable and wild. Too much drag and the lure's action will be overwhelmed and suppressed.
- Besides length and bulk, water-drag is also determined by the skirt's texture and stiffness. A slick skirt material will have much less drag than a ribbed or heavily textured skirt and the difference it makes on a lure can be significant.

Skirts provide the lure with body and colour. They also act in the same way as the tail of a kite, to stabilise the lure. Skirts usually start life with a cone at the top of the shredded tail. This is cut off before the skirt is glued to the collar at the rear of the lure's head

- A supple skirt will allow the head to pivot at the collar with less restriction than a stiffer material. This can also be achieved by using a skirt with tapered thickness; i.e. thinner (and more flexible) just behind the head rather than at the tail end. This freedom will result in a livelier action.

- Skirts are usually formed with a cone at the top of the shredded strands. Some are actually shaped as an octopus. The top of the cone, or head, is cut off and the remainder, with its shredded skirt, is attached to the shaped collar at the rear of the lure's head. If the attached cone spreads outwards from the collar, like a flared dress, it adds a lot of resistance to the water flow and will seriously reduce the action of the lure.

- If any part of the skirt's (stiffer) cone section extends back past the end of the head collar, this will effectively lengthen the lure's head. The head will pivot at the start of the supple shredded strands, instead of at the end of the lure head's collar. As mentioned above, a long head will have a tighter action and more sedate motion than a similar face with a short head. To attain the greatest movement from the lure, the shredded strands should start from immediately behind the collar. A previously skirted lure can be tuned to achieve this by continuing the splits to the collar with a pair of scissors.

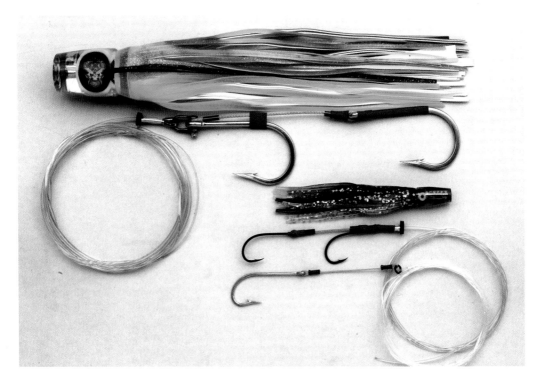

Rigging skirted lures has become an art within an art. Short cuts and inferior components are out of the question if a high percentage of strikes are to be converted into landed fish

≺ A lure can also be tuned for greater action by cutting back the overall length of the skirts with scissors (reducing the stabilising drag) and by trimming the outer skirt so that it is 1 centimetre shorter than the inner skirt.

≺ The placement of any glitter chips in the skirt and the size and type of glitter used can make a big difference to the appearance and sparkle of the finished lure. Large chips lying close to the surface of the skirt material will give a noticeable reflection of light, while small chips buried in coloured vinyl will add little to the fish attraction. Some skirts use holographic chips for extra sparkle.

≺ The use of chrome-like reflective strips as skirts or as inserts in skirts will assist as flash panels and help get a lure noticed from a distance. These have tended to be short-lived, however, as the reflective finish was found to rub off or become tattered. Other, stronger materials were tried but their stiffness detracted from the lure's action. This is an area that may be developed over the coming years.

See also Bibbed lures, Flash, page 94.

CENTRE TUBE

☙ The tube that the leader runs through is usually made of brass or plastic.

☙ It should be large enough to allow the lure to slide freely along the leader so that a jumping fish is denied the weight of the lure to tear the hooks free.

☙ It should not be so large that it allows water to flow through and wash out the vacuum and bubble at the rear of the head.

☙ A metallic tube should be checked for sharp edges that may cut or damage a nylon leader.

HOOKS

☙ For a trolling lure, the hook or hooks should be straight and not kirbed. A kirbed (offset) hook will cause the rig to spin when towed through the water, leading to significant line twist.

☙ The hook's size and strength (gauge) should be selected with the job it must perform in mind. If it is looking for a hold in a large mouth and the leader will be pulled with intense force and the tackle is capable of setting it, then the hook should be big and strong. If it is being used on light tackle for a fish that will not require extreme handling, a thin gauge in a smallish size will be much easier to set and so result in a higher hook-up rate.

☙ The weight of the hooks and rig should not exceed the lure's capacity to move with them. Excessive weight will destroy the lure's action.

☙ All large hooks (other than light-gauge 'chemically sharpened' models) should be

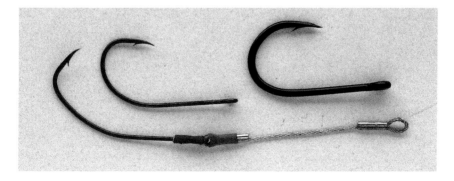

Hook shape and strength are critical issues when rigging lures. Too large and heavy and it may bog the lure down. Also, if it's too weak it may straighten yet if it's too thick you may not bury the barb before it's thrown out. It's a carefully considered balance

regularly sharpened with a Mill Saw Bastard file to reduce the size of the barb and to shape a needle-sharp point.

⚓ High-carbon steel 'chemically sharpened' hooks should have self-adhesive zinc anode strips attached to their shanks so they don't corrode and so the points stay sharp longer.

⚓ A single hook, or the trailing hook of a twin-hook rig, should be positioned at the rear of the skirts. If a second hook is used, it can be positioned just behind the lure's head. To space the rear hook, a short piece of cable is usually used with a crimped loop on the other end. This is attached to the leader via a protective thimble or shackle. This rig gives reasonable protection from teeth and enables a set angle between the hooks if two are used.

⚓ Some lures (many of the slant heads) work well with a rigid hook rig that keels the head, while others (especially the cup-faced chuggers) perform much better with a loose and supple hook system.

⚓ If a lure is to be aimed at large fish, and they will be released, a single hook will make the procedure simpler and safer.

⚓ The metal used on most 'chemically sharpened' hooks and stainless-steel hooks is brittle and not as strong as the steel used in regular hooks (which you need to sharpen yourself).

TOWING ANGLE

⚓ The angle at which the leader approaches the face of the lure determines the direction in which the lure is pulled. This makes an enormous difference to the lure's ability to move. If the lure is being directed upwards, it is freed to weave across the surface, splash and then dive when it wants to. If the angle is low and pulling the lure across the water or into a wave, it will plough along beneath the surface with less movement, less splashing, more leader visible and fewer bubbles.

⚓ There are several ways a steep towing angle can be achieved. Be wary of a long and heavy leader and swivel. Their weight can pull the towing angle down and let the leader slap against the surface where it will be visible and may alert approaching fish.

⚓ The height of most rod tips will give an effective angle to lures set close behind a boat. Bent-butt rods, having less height, will give a much lower angle. These and other lures set further behind the boat will need the additional height of outriggers to maintain the same towing angle. If a lure is set way back it may require the use of a high centre-rigger to lift the line high enough to achieve a similar direction of pull.

✄ Following behind a boat are a staggered series of pressure waves that vary from negligible to substantial according to the length and shape of the boat's hull. A steep angle can be achieved by adjusting the lures' positions until they are 'surfing' down the bottom third of the face of these pressure waves.

JET HOLES

✄ These are a series of tubes or holes extending from the face to the rear or sides of the lure's head (similar to the leader hole).

✄ The purpose of these holes is to enlarge the bubble trail. If they accomplish this, it is probably in a short-lived burst when the lure breaks through the surface. Front to back holes allow water to flow through and so negate the vortex-drag that holds the main bubble at the rear of the head. In other lures, the bubble in this vacuum at the back of the head slowly fragments and forms a long and steady bubble trail.

✄ Lure action is achieved by creating water pressures that move the lure. If jet holes allow some of that pressure to escape from the face through the holes then the action will be reduced.

✄ If the holes are metal tubes, the added weight may also reduce the lure's ability to move in the water.

LEADER

✄ The weight, stiffness and diameter (drag) of the leader can all significantly affect the swimming ability of the lure.

✄ The weight of the leader will pull it down towards the surface and so reduce the towing angle. The longer the leader, the more this is accentuated due to the leverage as well as the additional weight.

✄ Stiffness will reduce the lure's ability to pivot on the leader and move.

✄ The leader's diameter will determine how much drag it takes to move it through the water. For the lure to move down or sideways it must be able to overcome this drag.

✄ The leader's diameter and texture will also affect the bubble envelope cut into the surface by the leader in front of the lure when the lure is dragged down under tension. This envelope of air is highly visible and may cause a fish to turn away or misjudge the beginning of the lure's body. It can cause the lure to appear longer than intended and may lead to strikes on the leader in front of the lure.

✄ Visibility of the leader material itself is also an important consideration if a low towing angle allows the leader to enter or pull beneath the surface in front of the lure.

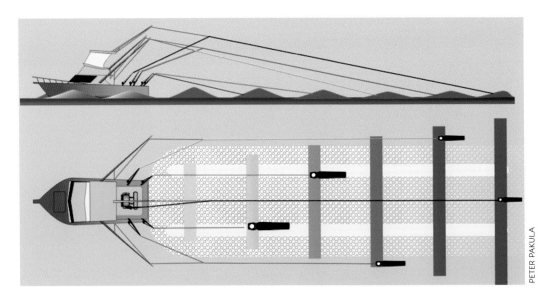

PETER PAKULA

Lures are staggered behind the boat so that a large area is covered and so they don't tangle each other. If the boat develops pressure waves behind, the lures are positioned to 'surf' down the bottom third of these waves. The towing angle off the face of the lure should be maintained by raising the line higher, the further back the lure is positioned. Outriggers and even a high centre-rigger with 'tag lines' are used for this purpose

- The ribbing on multi-stranded wire will hum and vibrate when pulled diagonally down through the water in front of a lure. It will also accentuate the bubble envelope around the leader. Running the lure with a very steep towing angle will help to keep most of the wire out of the water.
- Choosing a lighter lead will usually result in more lure action and increased strikes. This often more than compensates for the extra risk of breakage once a fish is hooked.

BUOYANCY

- This design factor is rarely considered with skirted trolling lures. However, to give a lure action, the forces of water pressure must have enough push to overcome the lure's resistance and weight. A lure with positive or neutral buoyancy is significantly easier to move through the water and so will have considerably more action than an identical shape that is weighted.
- Perhaps in the future we will see designs of heads and skirts that take buoyancy into consideration.

Blue-water teasers

Teasers (or attractors) come in a wide variety of shapes, sizes and styles but are commonly used to perform two functions.

In the first instance, a teaser is presented to a fish as something it really wants to eat, then, right as it's about to pounce, the offering is repeatedly taken away. The purpose of this exercise is to stir the fish up into a heightened state of frustrated rage and increase its desire to kill and eat the prey. When this state is achieved, the fish can be drawn away from cover, presented with a switched offering, or at least sized up and given the appropriate strength tackle. Once the fish has been teased and excited it's also more likely to aggressively slam the real offering without hesitation or wariness, resulting in hook-ups from fish that otherwise might have been too cautious or lethargic to catch.

For example, you might be targeting kingfish, cobia, giant trevally or any other structure-oriented species at a reef edge or bommie. Given the chance, such fish will wrap you around the reef and break free. But by teasing with a skipping or chugger popper with the hooks removed, you can get the fish to eat or at least follow the lure, only to rip it away or back out of their mouths. This will stir up an individual fish, and if there's a school the competition will excite them even more. By continuing to work the lure, you can lead them away from the structure and then offer a lure with hooks on another outfit cast beside the advancing fish.

Another example is the increasingly popular technique of 'tease and switch' when chasing billfish and other game species. In this instance, a hookless teaser is trolled until a fish is seen to approach, then it is ripped away and an appropriate live or dead bait is substituted. By trolling a teaser first, a bigger, more visible attractor can be used, and the boat can be driven at a higher speed which allows it to cover more territory than if a bait had been trolled. By switching to a real bait when the fish is finally allowed to eat, the offering tastes and feels more genuine and so is eagerly swallowed. The process drives the fish crazy and, once again, results in a more aggressive strike and a more secure hook-up when the switch is made. It's also an incredibly exciting form of fishing as it all happens right at the back of the boat in full view of everyone on board.

Until recently, the switched offering, and sometimes the teaser as well, were real baitfish. This was because the billfish were more likely to proceed if they were allowed to feel and taste the bait. Nowadays, there are soft plastic representations of common bait species that not only look realistic but feel, smell and taste realistic. This makes the

TIM SIMPSON

LEFT A range of aggressive teasers are available to the offshore angler. Some are designed to dive and shimmy their mirrored panels at the sun while others simply splash across the surface. If their exaggerated actions can draw a fish in or up towards the boat, it will have a much better chance of noticing the smaller lures following not far behind

RIGHT Here a daisy-chain of imitation squid splash along behind each of the four arms on a crossed spreader bar. A whole school is much more visible than a single and is likely to attract a predator. The lone member of the school – which is slightly separated from the others, is the likely target. This should be the lure with the hook in it that is run close behind the teaser

whole process a lot more versatile and convenient.

The second function for a teaser is simply to gain attention. These attractors work on the principle of creating such a fuss that they are hard to miss, at the same time giving the impression that there is some action going on that is definitely worth investigating. When the fish comes in to investigate further, it sees the range of smaller baits or lures that it may otherwise have missed.

Teasers are usually much larger than the items offered on the end of a line: their purpose is to be noticed and investigated, not eaten. Sometimes a teaser identical to the offering on the end of the line is used, or a similar-sized alternative. In these cases, they are usually used in a bunch to resemble a school and are more visible and attractive simply because of the increased numbers. Using teasers of this type requires careful placement and constant vigilance by the angler to ensure that the right items get eaten!

Teasers are usually towed a little closer to the boat than the closest lure or bait. It's important that the thick visible tow line doesn't prevent fish from approaching other offerings; it needs to be watched and removed quickly if necessary. On the other hand, at least one lure or bait should be fished close behind the teaser as this is where the fish's attention is likely to be centred.

It should be noted that the biggest, noisiest and most visible teaser of all is the boat itself! The throb of engines (deep-pitched diesels, in particular), the pulse of the boat as it rises and falls while pushing its way through the waves, and the sound and appearance of crashing bow waves are impossible to miss. A fish will almost certainly look in the boat's direction to see what is making such a racket. The trick is to grab its attention with something that looks edible or worthy of further investigation before it looks away again. We have often spotted marlin working around bait schools or over structure with our echo sounder. On many occasions we have successfully lured them up from depths of at least 40 metres.

Anatomy of a blue-water teaser

Blue-water gamefishing teasers can be divided into splashers and swimmers.

SPLASHERS

- These stir up a surface commotion and are usually designed to appear as something crashing through the waves, desperately trying to escape from being eaten. The predator knows that prey doesn't do this unless it is good to eat. The appearance of a feeding mêlée in progress or of prey items in flight will almost certainly appeal to a hungry predator.
- The teaser will often take the form of a string of lures (or baits) – either squid or baitfish – or a particularly large and active lure. They work in a similar fashion to a skirted trolling lure except on a larger scale.
- A spreader bar is sometimes employed to tow an ordered school of lures or natural baits. This is a bar or frame (sometimes an X shape) that is towed from the centre and to which strings of attractors are attached. The attractors splash along, following each other in a daisy chain on top of or just under the surface.
- Some splashers bear little resemblance to anything natural. They generate a lot of splash and rely on the non-distinct shower of spray and bubbles to attract attention.

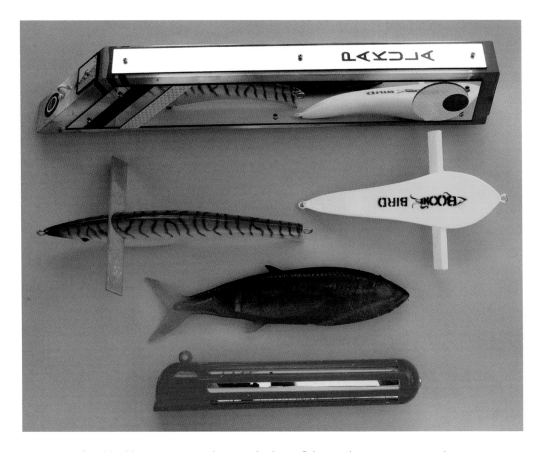

It's a big, blue ocean out there and a large fish may be many metres down. These teasers are used to attract its attention and excite it to feed with their exaggerated flash or splash. When the fish has been drawn closer it will then spot the (smaller) lures and switch its attention to them

SWIMMERS

✤ These spend most of their time sub-surface. Because they are beneath the masking effect of the surface sheen (and prop-wash) and the corrugations of the chop and waves, they are much more visible, especially from side on.

✤ They often have a wobbling, spinning or swimming action, sometimes similar to that of a giant bibless minnow. This produces a pulse in the water which, in spite of the engine nearby, may also attract fish.

✤ Flash panels are often incorporated. Some are polished metal; others use sheets of reflective tape; the most noticeable utilise sections of mirrored plastic or glass and often give the appearance of an underwater disco! On a sunny day the intermittent beams of flashing light they produce are visible for many metres underwater. The teaser should be designed so that it rolls sufficiently to reflect the sun into the water and not just back up to the surface where the angler (but not the fish) can see it.

➴ Swimmers' shaking action often provides an excellent platform for a rattle or a deeper-pitched thudding noisemaker device.

➴ The towing cord's diameter will affect how deep the teaser will dive. A thick tow rope makes it easier to pull in (especially under pressure and at speed); however, an increase in diameter will cause an increase in water-drag pushing against the rope and so a decrease in diving depth.

See also Bibbed lures, Rattles/sound, pages 90–2; and Bibless minnows, pages 98–104.

Freshwater teasers/attractors

The use of teasers (or attractors) while trolling is a highly successful method of attracting the attention of fish and drawing them in to the small lures that they might otherwise miss. Teasers do not have hooks and are intentionally large so that they can be seen, or at least felt, from a distance. They may be run on the line ahead of the lure or trolled on their own tow line or off a downrigger cable.

Various devices are used to grab the fish's attention, but the best teasers not only make them aware of something but actually draw them in with flash and vibrations that feel like a feeding opportunity. Most are marketed to troll for trout and salmon so are designed to work with a strong and erratic action at very slow speeds. Many are rigged slightly ahead of the lure on the same line and, besides the attractive pulse, their physical movements impart a wild action to the lure or bait being towed a short distance behind.

The downside to many attractors is the water-drag they add to the line. This not only makes it difficult to achieve much depth with the lures (unless used with a paravane or downrigger) but also requires the use of heavier line. When a fish is hooked, the whole mess must be towed around by the fish and the angler must fight both on the way back to the boat, taking a lot of the fun out of landing the catch.

Commonly used teaser devices include:

• A string of two or more large hookless blades, like those found on blade spinners.

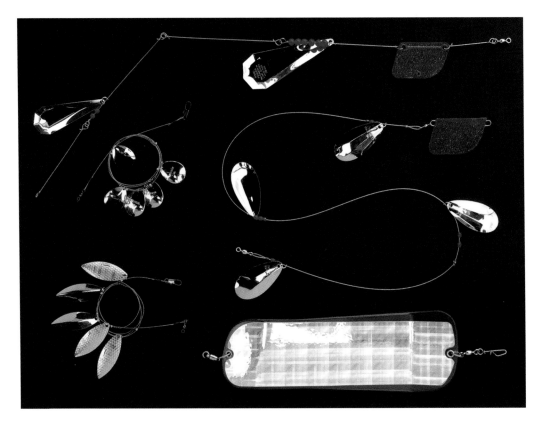

The action and vibration of a multi-bladed attractor is determined by the shape of the blades in just the same way as the blade spinners. Some of the popular versions are shown here: ford fender (top), a string of Colorado blades which have a strong pulse (middle left), below that is a string of willow leaf blades which will allow faster speed, a set of cowbell blades (middle right) and a flasher which spins and gives off a huge amount of flash (bottom right). A dodger is similarly shaped but without the twist it wobbles instead of spinning

- A dodger – a flat oblong sheet (usually metal) with one end cupped and turned up and the other end turned down, which acts similarly to a giant spoon and has a strong side-to-side swaying action.
- A flasher – shaped like a dodger but the ends are twisted so they spin and constantly flash.

These devices are usually very productive when trolling for trout, but there is no reason why the same principle can't be used to attract the attention of any other predator of low-speed lures.

Anatomy of a freshwater teaser

PULSE

✤ The beat or pulse of the teaser is what attracts the attention of a fish and draws it closer for investigation. A strong pulse can be detected by a fish's lateral line from up to 15 metres away.

✤ The beat of the teaser must be attractive to the fish or it will be felt but ignored.

✤ Different types of teasers have different pulses. A string of spinning blades has a pulse dependent on the shape of the blades. (*See Blade spinners, pages 159–61*.) A dodger has a throbbing weaving action while a spinning flasher has an erratic action and creates a strong push of water.

✤ Besides the pulse of the teaser itself, the lure being towed behind also has an enhanced erratic action because it is being flipped around on its leash. This is particularly good for lures that otherwise would have a very subtle action or no action at all (e.g. a fly or squid).

✤ When used at depth on a downrigger, the denser water and increased pressure will dampen the action of lure and teaser. This can be counteracted by a combination that is very active on the surface or by an increase in trolling speed.

✤ A string of blades will also create a lot of audible noise that is detectable at an even greater distance than the pulse.

FLASH

✤ The large and often flat surface of a teaser offers a huge opportunity for flash. Flash can be seen from a further distance than a lure itself and so may draw fish that would otherwise ignore a tiny lure.

✤ Lures are usually run quite close behind a teaser so the amount of flash needs to be matched to the clarity of the water and the mood and sensitivity of the fish.

✤ Fish that come into contact with a lot of anglers and boat traffic are often much more wary than usual. A subtle, softer flash may be required.

See also Anatomy of a long-range casting slug, Flash, pages 128–9.

LEADER LENGTH

✤ The distance between the teaser and lure will greatly affect the action not only of the towed lure but also the teaser itself. The shorter the distance, the faster and greater the action.

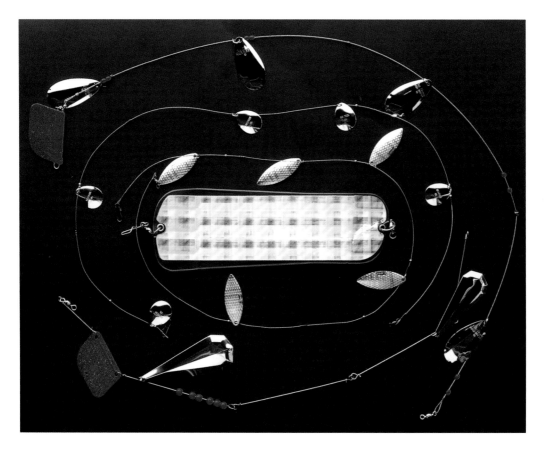

Freshwater teasers (or attractors) draw fish in to investigate the strong flashes and vibrations. The fish then find the smaller lures that they might otherwise have missed. Dodgers and flashers are often attached in front of the lure and their wild gyrations add a particularly appealing action to the lure close behind

- Lures are commonly run between 20–40 centimetres behind the teaser, but with very wary fish this may be extended to 2 metres.
- If a depth device such as a downrigger, diving planer or sinker is used, the distance between it and the teaser is critical. The longer the gap between the teaser and the device, the more action the teaser will have. A distance of at least 1.5 metres should be allowed for a sinker or planer and 2 metres from a downrigger. For maximum action, a length of up to 20 metres can be used.

SIZE

- The water-drag from a teaser can be significant. Not only will this drag dictate the use of heavier tackle, it will also restrict the depth of the lure (because it pulls a lure back up to the surface) unless a depth device is used.
- The water-drag from the lure itself will also pull on the rear of the teaser and reduce the teaser's action. For this reason, the size of the teaser should be related to the size and drag of the lure behind it. A big lure needs a big teaser.
- Dodgers for trout are commonly used in sizes from 5–15 centimetres.

SPEED

- The speed at which a teaser is used will affect its pulse and the amount of drag it causes. Higher speed causes more drag, which in turn lifts the whole rig towards the surface.
- A flasher will generally work at a slightly higher speed than a dodger and with less drag. A flasher is usually trolled at between 3.5–5.5 kilometres per hour. A dodger is usually trolled at between 2.5–3.5 kilometres per hour.
- The suitable speed for a string of spinning blades (and resulting water-drag) will depend on the shape of the blades. (*See Blade spinners, pages 159–61.*)
- The dampening effect of deep water may require a faster speed for downrigger combinations.

Squid jigs

Australian anglers first started using the Japanese Oita or Egi type squid jigs in the 1980s. Before then, squid were lured with a simple coloured blob of plastic and hooks bobbed along just above the weed beds. These caught squid, and still will, but the phenomenal success of the newer 'prawn' type saw anglers quickly switch to the new style.

These jigs are designed to be hopped along slowly or jigged with a sharp lift then an extended settling drop just above the weed beds or squid hunting grounds. They give a great imitation of a prawn, one of the squid's favourite prey. The most important factor though is the way they sink: very slowly and remaining horizontal. This gives the squid ample opportunity to see the prey, line it up and pounce.

The lures can be fished during the day or at night. Many have luminous parts or

TIM SIMPSON

Using specialised jigs to catch squid is fun and is also the first step towards
enjoying a wonderful meal or a sensational fresh bait

belly sections that glow and make the jig stand out in the darkness. They are simply
sunk to the depth at which squid seem to be hunting then slowly retrieved while giving
the lure tiny hops or a slow rise-and-fall action, in the same way a prawn might swim.
Squid usually sit low and close to the weeds or bottom during the day and rise up –
even to the surface – to hunt actively at night. By fishing your jig at the appropriate
level you can catch squid day or night.

Anglers have also found success off the ocean rocks and even in bays with these
lures, fished or even set and drifted under a float – especially if there is some wave or
chop action on the surface to jig the lure sufficiently.

Squid jigs are usually used as they come out of the pack, but you can sometimes
increase their success by binding a strip of natural bait to the back of the lure to give
it extra smell and taste. Some versions come with a series of small points down the back
and a soft wire on the nose to bind and hold the tiny fillet in place.

A variation that has not caught on to any great extent in Australia yet is a floating
version. A bunch of these are attached to short branches of a paternoster rig with a
suitably large sinker at the bottom, then jigged from a boat at the appropriate depth. As
squid often travel in schools, with this rig there is the chance of catching several at once.

Whether the motivation is a feed of calamari or a supply of excellent fresh bait, lure

Squid jigs are a more complex creation than they first appear to be

fishing for squid is not only productive, it is great fun. Every saltwater angler, especially in the southern states, should keep a squid jig in the tackle box.

Anatomy of a squid jig

BALANCE

✧ A significant factor in a squid jig's success is how it sits in the water. It should lie horizontal, balanced between the weight of its lead at the front, its hooks at the rear and the flotation of its body.

✧ Having the lure settle horizontally is critical: Japanese experts say that if the jig dips down at either the head or tail end by more than 10 degrees off horizontal, the squid will become wary or lose interest.

WEIGHT

✧ It is equally important that the lure sinks slowly, with only slightly less than neutral buoyancy. It should appear as a settling prawn which the squid can easily line up and pounce upon.

BODY

✎ The body material or texture of the lure's covering will influence how it feels to the squid. This may affect whether the squid holds on to the jig or rejects it.

✎ When a squid pounces on the lure it will bite it on the back of its 'neck' with a powerful beak. The quality of a cloth coating may affect the lure's ability to resist damage from these attacks.

✎ Some jigs have a flattened back section, sometimes with tiny spikes, to which a real prawn or fillet of fish is attached with a soft binding wire. For some squid the scent and flavour of the real product enhances the action and allure of the imitation.

HOOKS

✎ A crown of angled barbless spikes at the tail of the lure forms the hook. Often there is a pair of crowns. A squid hooked by the tentacles will only pull back against the spikes and not shake or flap around, so the barbless points are adequate to hold it as long as tension is maintained on the line. They also make it easy to remove the squid once it is landed.

✎ It is crucial that the spikes are extremely sharp or the squid may have the opportunity to reject the jig before they find their mark.

✎ A secondary set of spikes may be set in a cluster on the body of the lure in an attempt to snag tentacles holding the front of the jig. It is important that the weight of these additional spikes does not upset the balance of the lure. Also, the squid may become alarmed before it has fully grasped the jig if its first touch comes into contact with a row of spikes.

LUMINOSITY

✎ Many jigs feature luminous paint, a bead or eyes on the lure. This aids in getting the jig spotted, especially as these lures are often used at night. The quality of the luminous material will determine the brightness of the glow and how long it keeps its charge.

✎ Some jigs have a slot that accepts a small Cyalume chemical light stick. This certainly adds a bright glow to the lure but the subtle glow of a luminous product is often more effective.

TOW-POINT

✎ The two popular attachments at the nose of the lure are a swivel (or fixed loop) or a short length of string. The swivel produces a rigid connection and gives the lure a sharp darting action while the string provides a flexible coupling to allow the lure a flowing natural movement.

FEATHERS

Feathers can represent feelers, pectoral fins or legs and give the appearance of motion as they waft in even the slightest water movement. They need to be supple enough to move in a gentle flow.

Selecting the right lure

There are many different species of fish and they live in different habitats, hunt differently, eat different foods and swim at different depths and speeds – and different lures appeal to each one. When choosing the right lure for the job, use this checklist to narrow the selection process down to one or two lure families and sizes.

- Does the lure need to be cast? If so, how far and on what tackle?
- Are there size or weight requirements? Does the lure need to be small and heavy (to sink or cast a distance) or light but bulky (for a sizable offering on light tackle perhaps)?
- What speed is attractive to the particular types of fish you are after? What speed does their usual prey move at?
- Will the lure have to cover a wide area in the hunt for fish, or do you know exactly where they will be?
- What depth will the lure have to be presented at? And how much time will each lure option give you in the strike zone?
- What are the attack triggers that work on the target species? (These might include speed, swimming action, flash, a crippled appearance, smell, splash or profile.)
- What does the usual prey for the target species look like? Is the predator locked on to one particular size and shape of prey?
- Is the angler prepared to work at crafting a life-like action for the lure with rod work, or is a manufactured 'out of the box' action required?

Fishing lines may seem similar but in fact they are often vastly different in their properties. New developments, like the various gel-spun Polyethylene types, can add a degree of feel and control not possible with nylon lines. In some lure-fishing styles it will make an enormous difference to your results

CHAPTER FOUR

Lines and leaders for lure fishing

Lines

A fishing line is no longer just a fishing line. We got by with extruded plastic monofilament lines for a long time, but the relentless advance of fishing technology across the board has introduced new kinds of lines to the market, including nylon copolymers, braided gel-spun polyethylene, fused gel-spun polyethylene (gel-spun polyethylene (GSP) is the same as Spectra). Of the newcomers, braided gel-spun polyethylene and fused gel-spun polyethylene have had the greatest impact on the way we fish.

Braided GSP is the most expensive line you can buy; fused GSP falls somewhere between the braid and advanced nylon monofilament lines. These lines are expensive because the manufacturing methods are slow and intricate. The braided version is made by braiding extremely delicate micro fibres of GSP into a continuous strand, like a woven rope. The fused line is easier to manufacture as it is created by placing a bundle of parallel GSP fibres together and encapsulating them in a plastic coating.

The three unique characteristics of both gel-spun styles are:

- They don't stretch. This gives unprecedented sensitivity to the angler and allows monitoring of the lure's swimming action, bottom contact and bumps from fish.
- They are extremely limp.
- They deliver their breaking strain in a much finer diameter of line than even the best nylon monofilaments. This enables greater lure action and depth and significantly improved casting distance.

A quality braided line is around a quarter of the diameter of a comparable strength nylon mono and a fused line is about half the diameter of nylon. This can make a considerable difference in many forms of fishing.

On the downside is low knot strength. Some of the latest quality brands have achieved reliable high-strength connections with conventional knots by impregnating their braid with a tough resin, but in most brands, even with the best new GSP knots, expect at least a 20 per cent loss in strength. One way to fix this is to start your rigging with a 50-turn Bimini double (*see pages 280–3*), as this is one of the very few knots that forms a full-strength connection. A mono leader can then be tied on, starting with 200 per cent strength in the GSP.

For reasons of knot strength and unpredictability of breaking strain, GSP cannot be used effectively for line-class fishing as you are always giving too much away to be competitive.

A mono leader is nearly always tied in front of a GSP line. All subsequent rigging and knots are then done with the mono, which is a much easier way to go about things. It also creates a clear spacer between the lure and the quite visible GSP line.

The importance of stretch factor

In some forms of fishing you can let a hooked fish run all over the place, but in other forms control is the key element. When the rod is soft and whippy, and the line stretches, you more or less have the fish on a very flexible shock absorber and don't have a lot of direct contact or control. Messages between the fish and the angler are muted, with delays between the bite and the strike making it harder to hook the fish.

A line with no stretch transmits messages to the angler instantly; by the same token, the angler's reactions are instantly transmitted back to the fish. This makes it easier to hook a fish with a line that has little or no stretch.

The transmission of vibrations without any spongy stretch to absorb and dull them makes a no-stretch line extremely sensitive. Many anglers are amazed at how much more they can feel when they first switch to GSP lines. Besides feeling what is going on at the lure end – which for some techniques is critical – you also get a greatly magnified feel of the fish you eventually hook, which makes it even more enjoyable. The information that can be felt through a GSP line has prompted some anglers to describe these new tools as like having an echo sounder on the end of the line.

In a case where a large fish actually inhales the lure back towards it, along with a lot of water, the lack of give can result in the lure resisting that inhalation and the strike being missed. This sometimes happens with 'boofing' or inhaling feeders like barramundi and giant trevally. In this instance, the angler can create short lengths of slack in the retrieve by jerking the lure. These short pauses and small lengths of slack allow the fish to suck the lure back on a strike.

The importance of a fine diameter

Apart from the significant advantages of delivering longer casting range and allowing the angler to cast much lighter lures, a fine line diameter has other important benefits.

The most obvious is that you will be able to fit more line on the reel than is possible with a thicker line and use lines of heavier breaking strain.

In some fishing situations where fast fish may take out a lot of line, an increased spool capacity can be an advantage, allowing you to make long casts or sacrifice a lot of line to a hard-running fish without reducing the diameter of the line load on the reel as much as you would have to using thicker line. On a threadline reel, a thin GSP line will cast a great deal further because a lot more line will travel out before the decreasing line level on the spool creates a step up over the lip of the reel. The extra friction as the line pulls up over this step will quickly kill the distance of the cast on any type of reel with a fixed spool.

The larger the diameter of the line load on the reel, the faster you can retrieve line and the better the drag will perform.

Many fishermen using these new lines tend to half-fill the reel with cheap

---

NYLON AND GSP LINE COMPARISONS (OF EQUAL STRENGTH)

Nylon line

━━━━━━━━━━━━━━━━━━━━━━━━━━━━━━━━━━━━

Fused gel-spun 50% of nylon diameter

━━━━━━━━━━━━━━━━━━━━━━━━━━━━━━━━━━━━

Braided gel-spun 25% of nylon diameter

━━━━━━━━━━━━━━━━━━━━━━━━━━━━━━━━━━━━

---

monofilament then top up with the expensive line. This means you do all of the casting and hooking with the quality line, and there are not too many situations where anglers find themselves subject to the dreaded 'knot-out-in-the-breeze' syndrome.

Another important aspect of using fine-diameter lines is that they are less prone to wind and water pressures. In strong wind or current, a big belly can form in the line which puts the angler out of touch with the lure, making it difficult to hook a fish. The finer the line, the less effect these factors will have, which delivers more control to the angler. With a heavy-diameter line this friction factor reduces the lure's ability to dive to maximum depths. Switching to a fine-diameter line will increase the ability of any lure to achieve greater depth.

Disadvantages of gel-spun lines

With all these advantages, you would think that gel-spun lines would have taken over the market, but that has not happened for a number of reasons. Price is a major consideration for a majority of fishermen, but there are other disadvantages.

Because gel-spun lines are so thin, it is possible (and common) to put a very strong line on a small lightweight reel. Keep in mind what sort of strain the reel is designed to handle or you may find you have over-strained it and done some serious damage.

Most gel-spun lines under tension are vulnerable to abrasion. Nylon monofilament line, and large-diameter lines in particular, can handle a lot of wear and tear before breaking, but most gel-spuns do not like abrasion at all. The better-quality new GSP braids are now being produced impregnated with a tough resin. This results in higher abrasion resistance, greatly improved knot strength and keeps a round profile which casts and handles much better than a flattened out hollow braided line, which is how they used to be.

The very fine-diameter gel-spun lines are prone to developing wind knots when used on a threadline and, if not kept under constant pressure when retrieving, have a habit of collecting loops on threadline spools which result in bird's-nest tangles on subsequent casts. When retrieving, and especially when spooling up, add to the tension by running the line through tightly pinched fingertips. The majority are difficult lines to knot and to maintain most of the line's strength it is necessary to learn a new range of knots and tie them with care.

The gel-spuns are normally dark grey to green in colour, or you can choose them in frighteningly bright colours. The standard colours are clearly visible underwater and the bright colours are highly visible both above and below water. Since these lines are almost always fished with a mono leader of some kind, the colour doesn't matter all that much as far as the fish are concerned. We suggest using a longer trace with brightly coloured main lines.

From the angler's point of view – especially those of us who have already enjoyed the best years of our eyesight – these fine-diameter lines are almost impossible to see in anything other than the best light conditions. That makes it hard to follow a cast to stop the lure with great accuracy, and makes it difficult to see where your line is in relation to snags and obstructions. That's where the bright colours come in: with these coloured lines you can keep track of even the finest line in low light conditions.

When researching this book we read dozens of articles and reviews of these lines and found one common factor: everyone seemed to have a different view of the super lines, as they are called. Some hated them, others were indifferent, while many would never go back to any other kind of line.

Bright-coloured fishing lines help the angler to keep track of exactly where the lure is, especially those of us with failing eyesight. It is vital though that bright line is kept well out of the fish's sight by adding an appropriate length of clear leader

We suggest you at least try some of the cheaper fused gel-spun lines to see how they work with your style of fishing. If you don't like it, go back to nylon; but if you think it improves your fishing, spend some more money and try the braided gel-spun.

TRICKS AND TIPS

❧ Be aware that the breaking strain and reliability of any type of fishing line will be greatly reduced if you do not use the correct knots or if you don't tie them well. When a knot is pulled down tight after being formed, friction created by a lack of lubrication or an incorrect method of tightening can virtually melt nylon monofilament, greatly reducing the breaking strain of the line. Make a point of studying the knot section in

Double or nothing?

There is much talk these days recommending the use of a doubled line at the terminal end of a sportfishing rig. These are tied with a double plait, a Bimini twist or a spider hitch. Tying a double can be a time-consuming and fiddly business in the heat of a fishing situation. In most cases we feel it is an unnecessary complication. Let's look at the benefits of a double and how they can be achieved more easily.

The first two 'knots' will give a 100 per cent strength transition from a single line to a doubled line – if tied carefully and very tightly. The spider hitch will not. The doubled line will then give a 200 per cent starting point from which we tie on our leader, swivel and so on. As all regular knots will lose some strength (usually between 5 and 20 per cent), it makes great sense to go to all the trouble of a double if we are going to push the line to near breaking point. A Bimini double is especially helpful when using gel-spun polyethylene lines as most of these have appalling knot strength when tied with regular knots. For the fishing that many anglers do, however, it is unnecessary and simply tying a leader straight to a nylon mono line with an appropriate knot will be just fine.

The other benefit of a double is having abrasion resistance and twice the strength to pull on a fish once the double is within the angler's reach. For most situations this can be achieved better with a tougher, thinner, less visible length of leader than through the use of two fragile strands of the main line.

this book and practise tying those knots until you get them perfect every time. This is especially important for all connections to the gel-spun lines.

🐟 These fine-diameter lines tend to bed down with coils getting under coils so when you load a gel-spun line onto your reel, make sure you load it under considerable pressure, far greater pressure than you would use to load nylon line.

🐟 For maximum casting, retrieve speed and drag performance, the spool of all reels should always remain filled to within 2 millimetres of the lip of the spool.

Leaders/Traces

In order to stay connected to a fish once it's hooked up, there is often a need for a length of tougher or stronger material at the terminal end of the line: a leader (or trace, as it's often called). The length of a leader, its strength and the material it's made from will vary according to the requirements of the situation.

As in all types of angling, when lure fishing we are trying to entice a fish to bite an offering tethered to the end of our line and at times that quarry can be an extremely sensitive and wary customer. It would be naive to imagine that in clear water a fish does not see almost every aspect of our rig – including connections like rings, swivels, knots, crimps, snaps and, in many cases, the line and leader. Many times we've had fish snap at connections, and watched marlin swim up past a lure to inspect the snap-swivel at the top of a leader before dropping back and eating the lure.

If you doubt how small or indistinct an item fish can see, consider the micro sizes of prey they occasionally feed on. Australian salmon will often gorge on tiny transparent baitfish that we sometimes refer to as 'eyes' because that's all you can see of them. Trout feed on insect larvae the size of a match-head and even marlin over 200 kilograms have been known to eat individual pelagic crab larvae the size of your little fingernail.

The reason we are able to catch fish even though their eyesight is so good is that they are simple creatures and the things they see have no relevance to them. They don't know what a hook or swivel or leader or line means, so if the thing on the end can convince them it's good food they will usually eat it. At least, that's what we hope will happen. However, when they are wary for some reason, the game of deception can get a whole lot more difficult. Perhaps a fish has been hooked before; perhaps it has seen other fish take a line and watched the struggle that resulted; perhaps it is super-sensitive and cautious at that particular time due to predators, noises, environment or some other real or perceived threat. At such times, the more obvious and unnatural an appendage, the more likely it is to be rejected.

The degree of wariness varies greatly between different species, but one factor often overlooked is that even within a single species there are times when the fish are bold and will recklessly attack almost anything and other times when they are impossibly cautious and sensitive. The difficult part for the angler is knowing, or guessing, what is going on at the fish's end – beneath the veil of the water's surface.

In most fishing situations we don't get the luxury of seeing the fish before it strikes. If we get a strike, we know our rig worked and was acceptable at the time; if we don't get a strike, we can only guess whether the fish were attracted to the lure but balked away from the rig or whether there were simply no fish in the vicinity of our presentation. When we can see fish, or know they must be there (and feeding), we can tailor our rig to suit the conditions, but in most situations it pays to fish with the lightest, smallest and least visible hardware the circumstances allow. If you rig for stealth you won't just catch fish when they are bold, but also when they are shy.

A recent graphic demonstration made us acutely aware of how many fish we may miss catching without even knowing the opportunity was there. We were drifting out in clear blue ocean water at the time, with a berley trail to attract yellowfin tuna and mako sharks. For the yellowfin we had live baits and unweighted gently falling pilchards on what are generally regarded as light (and usually successful) traces of 35-kilogram clear monofilament. A few hours later, a whole school of tuna burst into view at the back of the boat and scooped up every piece of berley we threw in. They had swum past the baits, and even when the baits were repositioned amongst the school at the back of the boat they were ignored. I quickly tied on a new leader of 24-kilogram mono and tried again – it was refused. Then I tried a 24-kilogram leader with a 4/0 hook instead of the previous 6/0 – again it was refused. The fish were ravenous and continued to feed on every scrap of food that entered the water – every scrap that didn't have a hook or fishing line attached to it, that is. Luckily they stayed in the berley long enough for me to try many different combinations in the frantic quest to get a bite. I was using a 10-kilogram line with a double, so one of the trials was to remove the trace, remove the double and present the bait on the end of the straight-through 10-kilogram nylon. That was also refused. Finally, in desperation, I tried a 6-kilogram outfit with no trace, no double and a tiny 2/0 hook concealed inside a piece of pilchard. A fish took it immediately and I was hooked up! Two hours later, with the

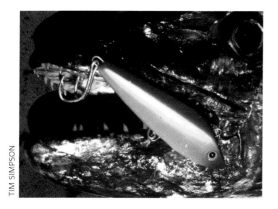

TIM SIMPSON

LEFT Powerful jaws, abrasive bodies and sharp teeth such as those at the business end of dogtooth tuna call for tough traces

RIGHT A leader of sufficient length, strength and toughness is required for powerful fish like this yellowfin tuna. There are often times, however, when fish become extremely wary and line shy. At these times the finest and most stealthy leaders are essential

tuna circling just out of gaff range at the back of the boat, the line chaffed through and broke – because I didn't have a leader to protect it.

Yellowfin can be tricky at times but will usually take a bait on nylon leaders up to 60 kilograms or more. We've even had them take a bait set for small sharks on light wire, so the example above was certainly an extreme case. It must be pretty rare for fish to be so hypersensitive compared to their usual range, but the fact is: in most cases we just wouldn't know; we would simply think there weren't many fish around that day.

Abrasion resistance to the quarry's teeth, body and tail is probably the most usual requirement for a leader, but there are several other functions it can be called on to perform. In tough country like stumps or reef, the leader may have to take the brunt of being dragged through and around such obstructions by the fish and then (hopefully) be dragged out again by the angler.

A leader of sufficient strength and length to allow a snagged lure to be pulled off by hand is also a handy feature, particularly in situations like tropical mangrove creeks where you are constantly throwing your lures as close as possible to the snags and roots. In crocodile country, stepping out of the boat to retrieve a lure from the branch of a tree is not a wise decision.

The additional strength a leader gives is useful to control a fish at the end of a fight. It can be held and used to steer the fish to the net, gaff or bank and is especially helpful when the fish is putting in a last-ditch effort to escape. If the hooks and leader are strong enough, the leader can also be used to lift the fish out of the water, although if the fish is to be released it should be cradled under the belly at the same time to prevent damage to the jaw and throat ligaments.

In the extreme case of big-gamefishing, the leader may be of substantial strength and up to 9 metres long. This is necessary to protect against body damage from a long fish that may get a wrap or two of the leader around its body, and also to allow a crew member to grab hold and try to control the fish alongside the boat. In this instance, the crew will often need to wrap the leader around gloved hands and physically restrain and drag the struggling fish the final metres to the boat, where it is tagged and released or secured.

Casting requirements also dictate the choice of a leader. If heavy lures or extremely powerful casting techniques are to be used, a shock-absorbing leader, preferably one that can be wound onto the reel, will save you from breaking a more delicate line from the strain of the cast itself. (See Chapter 6 for the appropriate knots.)

Besides the cutting effect of sharp teeth and body parts like some gill plates and tail scutes, the amount of abrasion a leader has to withstand will depend on the tension of the line. For example, if you rub a fine line gently across a file it may not break as easily as a heavier line rubbed under extreme tension. The same rule applies when fishing, as far as abrasion resistance to snags, body rubs and non-cutting teeth is concerned. If you're chasing powerful fish with heavy tackle you will need a stronger leader than if you are chasing the same fish with much lighter tackle. Then again, if using nylon line for most round-toothed lightweight fish, or with species that don't put up much of a fight, you will often find that no leader is required at all.

When a leader is required, there are several choices of material. Let's go through some of the options and the pros and cons of each.

Nylon monofilament

The nylon monofilament that leaders are made from is the same as the mono you may use on your reel as a main line, but although nylon fishing lines seem similar (except for the colour) they can in actual fact be very different in their structure and characteristics. Selecting the best type of mono for your requirements as a leader, or fishing line, can make a big difference to your success.

In the manufacturing process, the line designer can select from many additives and

Leaders can be made from various grades of nylon or fluorocarbon. There is usually a compromise between toughness and suppleness. Wind-on leaders are pre-made with a looped end. They are then tied on or looped to a double when required and make a slim, neat connection

different formulas to make the nylon, as well as manipulate the line in different ways by stretching, extruding and so on to achieve various outcomes that appeal to the market. These may include abrasion resistance, knot strength, suppleness, low stretch, high stretch, fine diameter, etc. What most people don't realise is that it's not possible to incorporate all the desirable characteristics into one line. There is always a compromise: to get one you often have to pass up another.

Nylon is used to make the bristles of toothbrushes and brooms. This formula would make an extremely abrasion-resistant leader but is so stiff it's completely unusable for fishing. When selecting a nylon mono for use as a leader, you have to decide which characteristics you want – or need – the most. Fine diameter and suppleness usually have to be traded for toughness.

In our opinion, a leader is usually used to guard against abrasion so the main requirement is toughness. A hard mono is often stiff, but in the lighter gauges this shouldn't present too much of a handicap. In heavier breaking strains a small amount of that toughness may have to be traded for a little flexibility in order to achieve lure action and knotability. We find we achieve greater success with this type of mono in a size just strong enough to get the job done rather than with a thinner, softer and more supple brand that may fracture or wear through during a fight.

The stiff tough lines often have a fair degree of memory, which means they come off their bobbin in coils that match the size of the spool they were stored on. This is unsuitable for a leader but you can easily remove the coils by stretching the line. Even in heavy sizes, simply tie the line to a secure point and give it a good pull. It should then lie straight and be usable.

Some manufacturers have created copolymer leader material that is hard and tough on the outside while soft, thin and supple on the inside. This gives it a much finer diameter for the same breaking strength and makes it more flexible. In extremely heavy sizes this is a good option, as without this compromise a tough leader would be so stiff it would be restrictive and unmanageable and so thick it might limit lure action and depth and be too visible to the fish.

These types of mono do not like the stress of knotting and require a crimp (or swage) to make a secure connection. Even then, unless the crimping tool is adjusted to the correct pressure and the aluminium crimp is correctly sized (snug-fitting), the connection risks losing a considerable amount of strength. Over-crimping – where the alloy crimp can fracture and the mono is crushed too tightly – is probably a more common risk than under-crimping.

Another risk with these super-thin types of mono is that if a fish is able to wear or cut through the tough outer skin, the softer weaker core is likely to split and break. On the other hand, with a solid hard mono, if a nick cuts 10 per cent into the diameter of the leader there is still almost 90 per cent of the strength left.

Referring back to earlier discussion about the wariness of fish, remember to keep the visibility of a mono as low as possible. A clear or lightly tinted transparent line in a shade similar to the water colour will probably be the least visible. We have also had great success with a clear pink tint, which appears a subtle grey when viewed more than a few metres underwater.

The advertising hype about a brand's line being visible to the angler while being invisible to the fish should be treated with scepticism. In every case that we know of, if a line is highly visible to the angler, it's just as visible to the fish – and you won't catch as many fish while using it.

Perhaps the perfect trace line would have a matt finish (we haven't seen one yet). Even if a manufacturer can make a nylon that is completely clear, the shine reflecting off the round polished exterior is more than enough to alert a wary fish – which is why many anglers use fluorocarbon.

Fluorocarbon

This is a product that looks almost identical to clear nylon monofilament. The difference is that it is not made from nylon; it's made from fluorocarbon. Fluorocarbon is the generic name for a plastic resin called polyvinylidene fluoride (PVDF) that was invented in 1970 by Kureha Chemical (Seaguar) in Japan. It's a little stiffer than nylon, has low stretch and is twice as dense so it's tough and sinks quicker. However, the main reason most people rave about it and pay up to ten times the price of nylon is because its refractive index is closer to the refractive index of water than that of regular mono.

The refractive index of an object is a measure of how much light will bend and reflect off the object rather than passing straight through it. A high proportion of light passes through clear nylon monofilament, but the small amount that doesn't is reflected off and we see it as shine. The fish also see it, and this – along with the faint shadow that forms where the bent light deviates off the straight path – is often what spooks the fish when it approaches our offering. The refractive index of fluorocarbon is roughly halfway between that of nylon and that of water. This means that more light will pass straight through the fluorocarbon and it will shine less. Of course, any blending or additives in the line affect the refractive index and make it less effective.

The verdict on the success of fluorocarbon is still being debated. Many experienced anglers around the world have been using it for years now and swear they are catching fish that would have been impossible when using nylon mono. At the same time, others say they have tried it and found little benefit. Perhaps they have used it in unsuitable conditions? If the line is not pure fluorocarbon, or if water clarity isn't good and the sun isn't shining, it probably won't make a lot of difference.

Wire

Fish with sharp teeth usually require the use of wire as a trace, to protect the lure from being bitten off. Because wire is solid in colour and therefore very visible, fewer fish are likely to take a chance and have a bite. In some cases it may be worth sticking with a nylon leader and risking a bite-off rather than going for the security of wire but getting fewer strikes.

Some toothy fish consistently feed by snapping the tails off their prey to immobilise them. Tailor are a good example. You can often get away with nylon for these fish, as if hooked on the rear of a solid-bodied lure the remaining front section of the lure acts as a protecting spacer between the teeth and the fragile line. The only risk is that a really big fish will swallow the entire lure and bite the line in front.

There are several choices of wire available.

7-STRAND WIRE

This is a cable made from seven strands of wire (usually stainless steel) twisted together in a spiral, like rope. Because of the seven individual strands it is quite flexible and resistant to kinking. This wire is available in strengths from 8 kilograms to 114 kilograms and is also available plastic-coated. It is not flexible enough to tie a neat knot and so must be crimped with a snug-fitting (brass) crimp and swaging tool.

A plastic coating makes the wire feel softer and insulates against the minute electrical field created by electrolysis. This is a largely unexplored subject, but anecdotal evidence suggests that, as well as sharks, some other species may be alerted at very close range by the current coming off metal in water. The downside to plastic coating is that it makes the wire significantly thicker and therefore more visible. A bonus is that a secure connection can be made by melting and fusing the plastic coating on a short twisted portion of the wire, using a match or lighter.

49-STRAND WIRE

This is a cable made from seven lots of 7-strand wire spiralled together into a wire rope. It is more flexible and kink resistant than 7-strand and so will give a lure a better action, but is thicker and more expensive. It is not as tough as 7-strand (in the same breaking strain) as each of its strands is only one-seventh as thick. Under pressure, a fish's teeth may gradually fray through some of the 49 fine strands.

Both 7-strand and 49-strand wire have a corrugated spiralling exterior which can be a problem with any fast-moving diving lure. When this type of wire is pulled through the water at an angle – such as when attached to a diving lure – the water flowing over the corrugations will cause the wire to vibrate and hum. The faster the speed or the steeper the angle, the more of a problem this becomes. When a blue-water diving lure is trolled at 7 knots the noise can be really noticeable and will certainly reduce the number of fish willing to make a strike. The next type of wire will usually offer the solution.

SINGLE-STRAND WIRE

This type of wire is just that – a single strand. It is sometimes referred to as piano wire and comes in a camouflaged brown colour in sizes from 10 kilograms to 80 kilograms. This wire has many of the characteristics we want in a leader: it is very tough, very thin for its strength and it won't vibrate or hum when pulled sideways through the water.

The downside is that it has very limited flexibility and is quite easy to kink. If it becomes kinked at an extreme angle its strength is reduced to a small fraction of its

TIM SIMPSON

LEFT When fish are expected with sharp, cutting teeth; some form of wire is usually required. The more strands it has, the more supple it usually is. Single strand (piano) wire is very stiff but because it is so much finer and tougher than multi-strand wire, for short traces it is often the best choice

RIGHT Tim Simpson rigged this giant bibless minnow with a 30-centimetre trace of fine single strand wire joined via a tiny blackened brass ring to a 3-metre nylon leader. It was enough to deceive the wary eyes of this big mackerel

original rate. It cannot be tied or crimped and so to make connections you need to learn the 'haywire twist' and the 'barrel roll' finish. These are worth mastering if you want to retain full strength in your wire. (See Chapter 6 for instructions.)

In many cases we've found that single-strand is the most successful trace when wire is required. Its super-thin diameter is far less visible than the alternatives, especially if you keep the connections short and neat. The stiff loop where it attaches to the lure gives the lure freedom to move without the need for a snap connector.

To minimise the risk of kinking we usually limit the length of the wire to less than 30 centimetres and connect it to a small blackened (stealthy) solid brass ring or crane swivel. The short wire trace is then extended to the full required length of the leader with a suitable strength nylon. The mono extension can end in another ring or swivel, or be knotted straight to the main line and wound onto the reel.

KNOTTABLE WIRE

This is a blend of gel-spun polyethylene and wire strands woven together and particularly suits small and subtle-actioned lures. It is not as tough as pure wire but for lightweight work it offers good protection and great flexibility. As the name says, it can be connected with usual fishing line knots. It comes in breaking strains from 4 kilograms to 40 kilograms.

CHAPTER FIVE

Lures for locations

This section of the book is intended as a start-up guide for Australia's most common fishing environments. We have tried to establish a fundamental lure package for each that will ensure you have the basics in your tackle box when you go to a new place. These are simply a representative range to give you a feel for the styles you should consider. There are many other excellent choices that will work in the same situations, so don't limit yourself to only the lures and colours depicted here. Each year a whole new crop of innovations and variations are added to the market and newly developed fishing techniques may require a totally different style of lure.

When fishing a new area and you are unsure of the lures to take, it is worth checking with a knowledgeable local tackle store or guides of the area for clues about the local scene. Alternatively, contact us at the Lure Insight website and we will advise you more specifically. (Log on at www.lureinsight.com for more information.)

With each fishing environment we have offered advice on what to expect, where to look and how to go about it. This of course will be a brief generalisation and many areas will have local peculiarities and perhaps a different mix of species and prey items. Even so, the leads we give you here will provide a fine starting point and show you some of the lures we would take and why.

Spinning from ocean rocks

Spinning from the ocean rocks is practised on the east coast from southern Queensland all the way down to Victorian waters, with the most activity concentrated in New South Wales. The west coast offers a similar pattern although the availability of suitable rock platforms tends to extend farther north in Western Australia. (There is also an offshoot in the tropical north which is different enough to have its own section.)

Taking high speed light game first, the species include yellowtail kingfish, cobia, black marlin (rare but possible), yellowfin tuna, southern bluefin tuna, northern bluefin (long tail) tuna, mackerel tuna, striped tuna, bonito and Spanish mackerel. Other incidental catches will be made from time to time, but the group listed above will account for the great majority of catches.

Keeping in mind our dictum regarding working the law of averages hard by keeping lures in the strike zone for the maximum length of time possible, you will need to make cast after cast over the longest possible distance when working with high speed lures if you want to maintain a high batting average. This section of the angler's art is all about hard physical work and endurance.

A point in favour of this style of fishing is the fact that you are just as likely to strike fish in the middle of the day as you are at any other time. Fishing can be particularly good in rainy weather, and the style of lures commonly used can be cast into the teeth of a gale when most other forms of fishing are becoming impossible.

It is important to remember that every lure will have its own retrieve speed at which it will do its best work. The simpler the lure's body profile, the harder you will be able to crank it.

Whenever, and wherever, it is safe to work off a low level platform the lure will be retrieved at a flatter angle and thus stay down in the strike zone longer. The higher you have to go the shorter the working time of your lure on each cast because you will be retrieving at a steeper angle.

The possibilities are expanded for users of threadline reels that will cast lighter weights.

Traditional spoons, stickbaits, shallow and deep running minnows may all be used for smaller fish, such as bonito, tailor, trevally, salmon, etc.

There is a rapidly developing offshoot of lure fishing for large fish involving the use of big soft plastics fished at slow retrieves.

PHIL ATKINSON

These are all heavy, long-range casting slugs selected for maximum distance
and high to very high retrieve speeds. **FROM TOP** Gillies 'Pilchard' 85 gm,
Spanyid 'Raider' 85 gm, Blue Fox 'Reflect Pirk' 100 gm, (generic) 'Flat Bar' 80 gm,
River2Sea 'Sea Rock' 90 gm

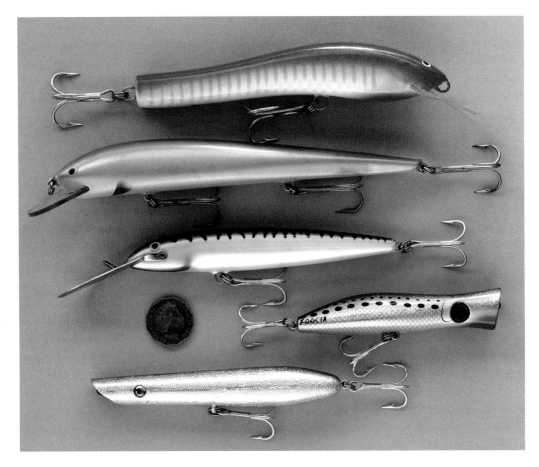

FROM TOP Bills Bugs 'Jew Bug', Nilsmaster 25-cm 'Invincible', Rapala 'Magnum CD18', Halco 'Roosta', Cotton Cordell 'Pencil Popper C67' 2 oz. The top two minnows were selected for predators of large baitfish – such as kingfish, mulloway or cobia. The Rapala is a sinking lure with enough weight to cast and will handle very fast retrieves. The chugging and skipping poppers are great for turning-on lethargic kingfish

Big mulloway have been successfully targeted by anglers fishing big soft plastics as well as oversized bibbed minnows.

On the open ocean rocks and near training walls, mulloway can be found in deep holes and under dense white water. In these situations the big soft plastics are an ideal lure with their ability to stay down deep and produce all the right moves at slow speeds.

Lures with built-in weights come to the fore as do many deep-water jig-style lures. Squid bodies with built-in scents are particularly useful. With a weight inset into the

Large soft plastics capable of being cast on heavy tackle. Used for deep mulloway, kingfish, cobia, etc. **FROM TOP** Storm 'Wild Eye Swim Shad' 15 cm, Storm 'Wild Eye Swim Shad' 23 cm, Kokoda 'Big Eye Buff' 20 cm

body they remind us of the chook feathers with a weighted head used by old timers. It's just possible that the scent of the chook feathers was a vital ingredient.

Finding a suitable location for this style of fishing recognises the following criteria. Big pelagics are often found in locations where a distinct depth contour turns in to the coastline, as is the case with rocks north and south of Jervis Bay. You can look for spots like this by paying careful attention to marine charts which clearly show depth contours. A concentration of white foam over deep water can be a real hot spot. The other option is to look for long headlands that protrude well beyond the regular coastline. When currents, particularly strong currents, come inshore these headlands can be real hot spots. The up-current side of the structure will normally produce a pressure eddy that will hold bait and attract the predators. Depth is not so much of an issue in these locations.

On very quiet days work your lures deep and even try some bibbed lures if you can cast them. On wild and windy days expect fish closer to the surface.

Spinning from the rocks was once the exclusive territory of quality overhead casting reels with excellent drag systems. These days both their strength and greatly improved drag systems make threadline reels a viable alternative for those who prefer them. A good approach is to carry both, using the overhead outfit for long-range casting of heavier metal lures and the threadline outfit for the lighter, more wind-resistant lures. In either case, the reels need to be of very high quality, have high-speed gearing with a ratio of 5 or 6 to 1 and line capacities of 300 to 600 metres. Good quality GSP line will give the angler greater distance and a high breaking strain in a line without the bulk that can cause a lot of handling problems in high winds and rough seas. The shift to shorter, lighter, fast taper rods has also made life a lot easier.

As you stand mesmerised on the rocks belting out one long cast after another, the casting becomes an end in itself. Then the reel stops dead and you're jarred back into the real world as line begins to peel off the reel at warp speed. It's a great feeling!

Light rock spinning

Spinning from open ocean and foreshore rocks around the entrance to larger bays can provide some of sport fishing's most exciting moments. The bigger, ocean front speedsters may have it all over the lighter rock species in terms of power, but this is offset by the fact that many of these fish can turn up in huge schools providing red hot fishing when they come within reach of a reasonable cast.

Species include many of the trevally family, striped and mackerel tuna, salmon, tailor, kingfish, bonito, frigate mackerel and spotted mackerel. Bottom fish can also be targeted and flathead are commonly found at river mouths.

Two distinct approaches are available here depending on the species and nature of the water being fished. The first is dominated by the use of small, high-speed metal lures capable of being cast over a long distance. Lighter spoon styles with body contours creating a great deal of flash and action on retrieve are also very effective when distance is not critical. The second approach includes surface lures, jigs and soft plastics. Bibbed and bibless minnows can also be used. These are good when access to deeper water allows them to be worked at close range and under white water.

PHIL ATKINSON

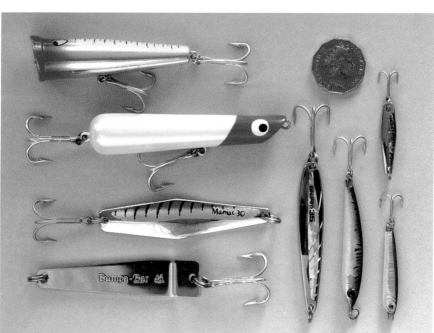

This selection contains a Chugger and a Skipping Popper, for raising or turning-on deep or lethargic predators; medium-speed, high flash spoons for slower species and high-speed, long-range casting slugs in micro bait to pilchard sizes for distance and very fast retrieves.

LEFT COLUMN, FROM TOP Killalure 'Cone Popper', Lively Lures 'Kingfisher Fat R's', Spanyid 'Maniac' 30 gm, 'Bumpa-Bar' 45 gm. **RIGHT COLUMN, FROM TOP** Spanyid 'Raider' 10 gm, Spanyid 'Sniper' 35 gm, Kokoda 'Raptor' 40 gm, River2Sea 'Sea Rock' 14 gm

This selection allows the whole range of the water column to be fished. Soft plastic jerkbaits can be twitched near the surface or allowed to sink. The lead-head jigs can be flicked along the bottom or mid-depth. FROM TOP Blue Fox 'Squidgy Fish' 100 mm with McCubbin lumo jig head, Lunker City 'Slug-Go' 6 in with Mustad Power Lock Plus hook, Ecogear 'Power Shad' 13 cm with Mustad Power Lock Plus hook, Kokoda 'Living Soft Squid' 9 cm with internal jig head, Prestige Jigs 'Bucktail Jig' 30 gm

Choice of tackle will vary according to the dominant species in the area at the time. If tailor, salmon and small trevally are dominant you could use 3–6-kilogram line, but where tuna or kingfish are prevalent you may need 6–10 kilograms. Medium to large baitcasters or threadlines are ideal with 2–4-metre fast taper rods. Outstanding drags and high speed gear ratios are a must.

When fishing relatively calm waters, it is helpful to work as low and close to the water as you can with the tip of the rod held down to maximise the amount of time the lure will be working on the retrieve.

If you are prospecting unknown waters, not seeing fish working at the surface does not automatically mean there are no fish there. Fish may be congregating over bottom structure or weed you can't see, and of course you will never see flathead.

While minnows and surface lures are very effective, it's probably a good idea to stick with metal lures as long as they are working. You get longer casts and you have fewer hooks to remove per fish.

If you start picking off fish with a long cast, try closer casts the next time. A lot of fish will come in with a hooked fish and a long cast could well send them back out again.

Keep your lines as light as is practical to minimise wind and water friction for depth, and to maximise casts in any conditions.

Boat traffic can put an end to your activities in populated areas so make a point of being there to greet the sunrise, or be around when the others have gone home.

Tropical land-based fishing

Very few people would think of our tropical waters when talking about spinning from the rocks, but the fact of the matter is that quite a lot of land-based fishing is done in the tropics. Major differences are that the majority of the species are true tropical fish and that most of the fishing is done in relatively calm water.

TIM SIMPSON

Target species include barramundi, queenfish, threadfin, barracuda, mackerel and big trevally, with giant trevally and golden trevally being the main contenders. In some areas tropical reef fish such as golden snapper, cobia, coral trout, mangrove jack, cod, etc. may be present. Some of these fish are speedsters that race through, snapping at schools of bait or stragglers. A high-speed long-distance lure is great for these. Others slowly prowl the bottom contours and structure and are best targeted with bibbed and bibless minnows, jigs and soft plastics. These fish come in such a variety of sizes, and are often taken in such shallow water that it is usual for very heavy line to be required.

A variety of surface and mid-depth lures. **LEFT COLUMN, FROM TOP** Cotton Cordell 'Pencil Popper C66' 1 oz, Bills Bugs 'Fizz Bug' 14 cm, Rapala 'Skitter Pop' 12 cm, Reidy's 'B52' (jerkbait). **RIGHT COLUMN, FROM TOP** Leads 'Shallow Barra', Nilsmaster 'Spearhead' 8 cm, Tilsan 'Barra', L&S Bait Co. 'Mirrolure 52M' (jerkbait)

GSP line becomes the popular choice simply because you can go way up in breaking strains while still maintaining castability and the length of line you are going to need when a really big fish nails your lure.

A quality, large baitcaster would be appropriate for this sort of work, with line breaking strains of 6–15 kilograms and trace materials up to 30 kilograms in some cases. When mackerel or barracuda are expected it would be prudent to use a short length of wire trace.

It is sometimes possible to fish open water productively, but you will also find yourself working around rocks and coral a lot because that's where the fish are going to be. Rocks and coral will also mean jacks, cod and other species that will bury you in the stones faster than you can blink.

With all of this in mind it would be prudent to think in terms of needing two outfits. A fast one holding a lot of lighter line when hard-running surface speedsters are around, and a second 'stump puller' outfit based on a rod with a lot of backbone with heavy main line and the heaviest practical leader material. Single-handed bait

This group includes fast and medium-speed metals for casting distance to pelagics, a soft plastic 'jerkbait' and swimming shad for slower mid-water species, and a lead-head jig for snag-resistant flicking along the bottom. **FROM TOP** Luhr Jensen 'Krocodile' 42 gm, 'Bumpa-Bar' 45 gm, Spanyid 'Raider' 40 gm, Halco 'Twisty' 55 gm, River2Sea 'Sea Rock' 40 gm, Lunker City 'Slug-Go' 6 in with Mustad Power Lock Plus hook, (generic) Bucktail Jig, Blue Fox 'Squidgy Shad' 150 mm with 'Squidgy Resin Head'

casters are used, but this is generally an area calling for the casting range and fighting power of longer double-handed rods. On odd occasions the presence of bait along beaches will mean that big fish can be taken along open sandy stretches.

Bay and estuary fishing

Boat fishing the bays

Large, sheltered bays, especially those at the entrances to river systems, form a food rich nursery and a refuge for large migrations of baitfish as they move up and down the coast. Expansive weed beds, rocky edges and other structure form a perfect home for other prey, such as prawns and squid. Predators of many types are naturally drawn to this abundant food supply.

At the entrances to the southern bays of eastern Australia there are seasonal influxes of micro baitfish. These are eagerly pursued by Australian salmon, tailor, bonito and juvenile kingfish. The salmon and kingfish can be enormously selective in this situation and demand a cast, near perfect micro presentation to have any hope of a hook-up.

When not obsessed with the massive schools of micro bait, trolling the rocky edges and headlands of the bays will usually provide consistent action from the same species on bibbed minnows. Casting various lures including poppers at any deepwater features like a channel marker is also very effective. In these locations the fish are usually feeding on larger pilchards, whitebait, yellowtail, squid and so on. Casting metal lures at the rock edges and to breaking schools of fish is a delightful way to spend the early (pre-boat traffic) hours.

The tackle used for this is usually spin outfits or baitcasters from 2–6 kilograms, sometimes with mono leaders up to 10 kilograms.

Further into the bays there is also a congregation of bait and predators around other substantial structures in the deeper water, such as bridge pylons, wharfs, channel markers, dropoffs and reefs. A good sounder is a great help. Here a soft plastic or lead-head jig can also be cast and worked along the bottom for flathead, mulloway and others.

Weed beds and wharfs are a great place to cast for squid as they shelter many baitfish, prawns and shrimp.

In the tropics the scene is similar except the species will change to include barramundi, blue and threadfin salmon, tarpon, queenfish, trevally, fingermark, mackerel and others. Some of these species will actively chase bait schools on the surface while others are best worked with bottom jigs or minnows and metal lures cast around the edges and surface structures.

ALISTAIR McGLASHAN

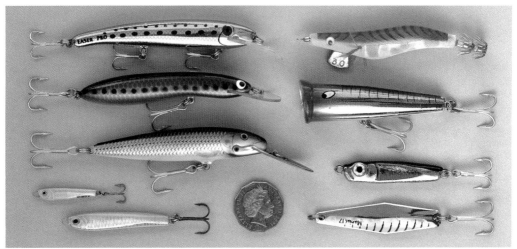

This selection includes minnows of various diving depths and actions, small casting slugs for when pelagics are targeting micro baitfish, a squid jig, a popper for deep or lethargic predators and a flashy mid-speed spoon that can be trolled or cast.

LEFT COLUMN, FROM TOP Halco 'Laser Pro 120DD', Peter Newell original Scorpion 'M3', Rapala 'Magnum CD11', River2Sea 'Sea Rock' 7 gm, River2Sea 'Sea Rock' 25 gm.

RIGHT COLUMN, FROM TOP Yamashita Egi 3.0 squid jig, Killalure 'Cone Popper', Gorilla 'Big Eye' 40 gm (a weighty, compact lure for heavier tackle), Spanyid 'Maniac' 17 gm

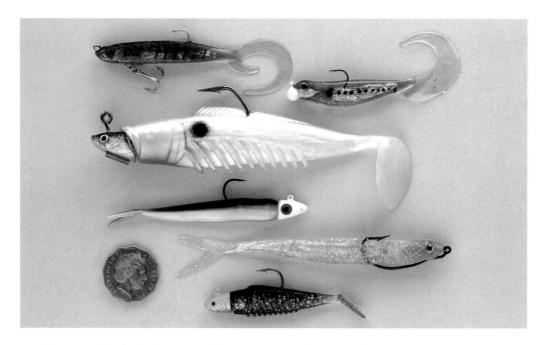

This group of soft plastics covers the water column between the surface and the bottom. There are swimming and flicking or jerkbait styles. **FROM TOP** Storm 'Wild Eye Rippin' Minnow' 15 cm, Kokoda 'Deano single tail' with McCubbin football jig head, Blue Fox 'Squidgy Fish' 150 mm with Squidgy resin jig head (for mulloway), Lunker City 'Fin S fish' 10 cm with McCubbin lumo jig head, Kokoda 'Livin' Bam Bam' 15 cm with TruTurn hook, Blue Fox 'Squidgy Fish' 80 mm plus Squidgy jig head

Boat fishing the estuaries

Moving up into protected estuary waters involves a major shift in terms of species and fishing environment.

In the larger rivers pelagics may school well upstream, but they are more likely to be encountered in the lower reaches. When they are present, bay fishing tackle and tactics will apply.

Structure in areas where a strong tidal run takes place, such as bridge pylons and channel markers, will alter the shape of the bottom and effect water flow in the immediate vicinity. Pressure waves ahead of the structure and eddies behind attract both bait and predators. Sometimes deep holes are scoured out providing shelter from the tidal run and are used to effect by ambushing predators. There is always the possibility that artificial structures may have resulted in debris being left on the bottom creating an artificial reef environment near the main structure. This can all be sussed out with a good echo sounder.

The rapid growth of canal developments with jetties and pontoons galore, along with an increase in the number of large marinas, has created a whole new environment that bream have taken to with gusto. The shade provided by these structures is every bit as important as the structure itself. Oyster racks are another environment that provides shade, and for the bream, a built-in food source. Casting and slowly working tiny soft plastics and micro bibbed minnows in these shaded locations has revolutionised bream fishing.

The rivers are the natural environment of dusky flathead which will be found along the edges of sand flats, in the mouths of gutters and in channels up or downstream from structure. They are also particularly fond of weed beds and areas where weed patches are scattered through a sandy bottom.

In the southern half of the country, flathead, bream, trevally, estuary perch and mulloway will dominate catches in the rivers. In the mid to subtropical zones mangrove jack and some bass add to the mix. True tropical species will be dealt with separately.

A deep rock bar anywhere in a river will be occupied by ambushers of some kind.

Bream, flathead, jacks, trevally and mulloway are all found close to rocks, especially those with deep undercuts.

Soft plastics really come into their own in the estuaries. Fished with a rapid rip and drop action with the rod tip they are lethal on flathead. If you do the rip then stay in touch with the lure on the drop you will catch a lot of fish that swallow the plastic on the way back down. It can pay off to pause between lifts as well, with fish commonly scooping the stationary lure off the bottom. Fishing this style of action for flathead, you will simply be amazed at the range of other species that will jump onto the lure.

It is worth noting that prior to the soft

RON CALCUTT

This selection of bibbed lures covers applications from mid-water bream spinning to scraping bottom while trolling for species like flathead. They can all be cast or trolled.
LEFT COLUMN, FROM TOP Rebel 'Deep Wee Crawfish', Predatec 'Spoonbill', Lively Lures 'Micro Mullet', Rapala 'Shad Rap deep' 7 cm, Manns 'Stretch 12+'. Middle: Attack Lures 'Attack minnow'. **RIGHT COLUMN, FROM TOP** Knols 'Native – small', Manns 'Stretch 5+', Tilsan 'Minnow', 'C' Lures 'Jack Snack', Peter Newell original Scorpion '½'

plastic revolution, advanced anglers were taking a lot of flathead on trolled lures. They used echo sounders to fish dropoffs, sticking to contours around the 3–4-metre mark where the deep diving bibbed lures would be scraping along the bottom. This method is still very productive.

Sand flats and their dropoffs can be a productive zone for bream and flathead, and in some areas of clear water, sight casting is a possibility. Whiting will sometimes take small soft plastics and sight casting to these fish is a special treat.

The natural cover provided by downed trees in the backwaters provides perfect habitat for bream, jacks and bass, and big old bream will be found right alongside bass or estuary perch in the brackish to fresh upper reaches.

Some of the most isolated and beautiful fishing environments are to be found in the

These soft plastics will take a wide range of species but the main targets for the left row are flathead and the right hand row are for bream.

LEFT COLUMN, FROM TOP Blue Fox 'Squidgy Fish' 80 mm with Squidgy fish head, Assault 'Single Tail Spyder Grub' 5 in with ball jig head, DOA '¼ oz Shrimp', Blue Fox 'Squidgy Fish' 100 mm with Squidgy fish head. **RIGHT COLUMN, FROM TOP** Atomic 'Fat Grub' 2 in with ball jig head, Berkley 'Bass Minnow' 3 in with ball jig head, Berkley 'Micro Craw' 1 in with Aberdeen hook and split shot, Berkley 'Micro Power Nymph' with ball jig head, Ecogear 'Grass Minnow' 1¾ in with ball jig head

upper reaches of our rivers. This is often estuary perch or bass country where the fish will always be around cover and often difficult to get lures to. All of the rules governing keeping the lure in the strike zone for as long as possible apply here. Lures that dig in and dive steeply to reach fish before leaving the critical zone come in for a lot of use when fishing snags, as do models that can do a lot without moving far.

In the lower reaches where fish will be associated with more open water, casting accuracy does not have a very high priority, but as soon as you start to pursue fish associated with structures, accurate lure placement can become critical. Fish hiding up

The two metal lures give the option of distance – useful in open stretches for tailor, tarpon, trevally, etc. Spinnerbaits and surface lures are great for estuary perch and bass in the brackish backwaters and the jigs are useful on many fish from bass to flathead.

LEFT COLUMN, FROM TOP Spanyid 'Maniac' 7 gm, (generic) Toby spoon 14 gm, Bill Lewis 'Rat-L-Trap' ¼ oz, AusSpin 'Mini Spin Tandem' ⅛ oz, Rio's 'Prawn' 13 gm.

MIDDLE COLUMN AusSpin 'Mini Grub Spin' ⅛ oz. **RIGHT COLUMN, FROM TOP** Arbogast 'Jitterbug' ¼ oz, Heddon 'Tiny Torpedo', River2Sea 'Bubble Pop 45', (generic) Marabou jig 5 gm

in deep cover and shade do not generally like to leave that cover, so if you want to get strikes, you have to get lures right back in where the fish are. Casting ultra light lures or sensing subtle strikes often demands more sophisticated tackle. Quality reels and graphite rods coupled with fine GSP lines make a tricky job much easier.

Getting lures into some of these very difficult places may involve real casting ingenuity as well as accuracy. Bow and arrow casts, where the rear hook is held in the fingertips and drawn back to load the rod then released to fly away in a dead straight trajectory, are part and parcel of some estuary lure fishing.

Coastal sportfishing

Coastal sportfishing is an interesting small-boat category that explores inshore coastal waters where shallow and deep reefs, headlands and rocky islands are all prime fish holding territory. The big white water washes associated with the rocks in the southern half of this country are natural cover for bait, and therefore prime hunting grounds for bigger fish. Many migrating species also hug the shoreline as they travel. In the tropics rock and coral outcrops will be hot spots.

The washes are normally worked with powerful double-handed threadline or large, high-speed baitcaster outfits capable of casting big lures over a distance. A good casting range makes this form of fishing much safer as the boat is often parked on the seaward side of the wash. Trolling can be done with anything from light baitcasters to heavy overheads.

Minnows are often ideal for this work. Shallow runners can be used when the foam is not too deep and hunters will be working close to the surface where bait schools often congregate in whatever foam there is.

It is always worth while to try deeper lures if you have the depth of water under the

foam, as big snapper and other bottom prowlers are fond of these washes and make a pleasant surprise now and then when they grab a lure.

Surface lures and soft plastics are always worth a try in these waters too. A chugger is often the answer to stir up lethargic kingfish that otherwise will only follow lures.

Metal lures are also well worth having on hand, both for their long range casting ability and their fast sink rate. Don't forget that there will be considerable water movement in these washes and you will sometimes be able to work lures way below the normal crank rate, allowing water movement to assist you.

The element of surprise is a big part of wash fishing where a wide range of species

TIM SIMPSON

241

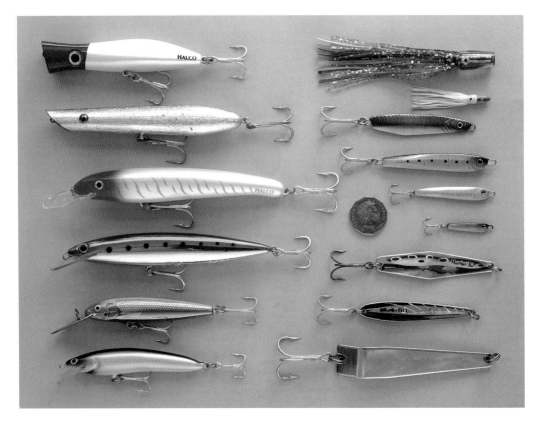

A variety of lure actions and sizes for trolling at different depths, casting to pelagics
locked-on to micro baitfish and casting to washes or fish schools, as well as shallow jigging.
LEFT COLUMN, FROM TOP Halco 'Roosta' chugger popper, Cotton Cordell 'Pencil Popper C67',
Halco 'Laser Pro 190 XDD', Lively Lures 'Blue Pilly – shallow runner', Rapala 'Magnum CD11',
Leads 'Shallow Barra'. **RIGHT COLUMN, FROM TOP** Pakula 'Uzi', Yamashita pearl head squid,
Blue Fox 'Reflect Pirk' 70 gm, River2Sea 'Sea Rock' sizes 75 gm, 25 gm, 7 gm, Spanyid
'Maniac' 30 gm, Spanyid 'Sniper' 50 gm, Bumpa-Bar 75 gm

and fish sizes may be encountered. In more southern waters huge kingfish may be
feeding on the tailor you set out to catch. Further north monster cobia, narrow barred
Spanish mackerel and long tail tuna may put in an appearance. In the tropics huge
trevally, barracuda, a variety of mackerel, and queenfish make a regular appearance.

In a new area always do a sounder search in the vicinity of high reef or islands. It's
often the case that deep reef and bait schools will be close by. Areas of scattered rock
and reef will often fire with jigs when fish move away from the shallows.

A selection of soft plastics to appeal to a wide range of surface, mid-water and bottom species. The group includes two jerkbaits, two swimmers and a jerking squid. FROM TOP Ecogear 'Power Shad' 13 cm with Mustad Power Lock Plus hook, Storm 'Wild Eye Swim Shad' 13 cm, Ecogear 'Power Squid' 14 cm with jointed jig head, Blue Fox 'Squidgy Fish' 150 mm with McCubbin lumo shad jig head, Lunker City 'Slug-Go' 6 in with split shot on Gamakatsu G-Lock worm hook

Tropical estuary and creek fishing

In Australia the estuary and creek systems of the north are the embodiment of tropical sportfishing. Although offering a rich variety of species, it is the glamour of the barramundi that raises our temperature when we think of the tropical north.

If someone sat down to design the perfect sportfish it would look just like a barramundi. A fish with considerable growth potential, an extremely aggressive hunter and a fish that will jump and run until it has used the last drop of fuel in its tank. Cap it off with its spectacular coat of silver to bronze scales and you have an outstanding fish. As a bonus, the barramundi comes with a great supporting cast of lure-munching enthusiasts. In the lower reaches of the system, salmon, mangrove jack, grunter, fingermark, cod and groper, queenfish and a variety of big trevally will all get into the act. In the brackish to fresh upper reaches the spectacular saratoga and tarpon will make an appearance.

The majority of the fishing is done by casting to structure in the form of bank-side snags. The mouths of feeder creeks and any point of tidal runoff from sand and mud banks are hot spots, as is runoff from tidal plains after the wet. When water entering a larger body of water from a feeder is heavily coloured, the line of colour demarcation is also a potential hot spot.

It's worthwhile running a sounder as you go along as trees washed down in floods and now on the bottom in deep water are sure to hold fish. Rock bars and weed beds are also potentially fertile ground.

Traditional fishing methods involved putting medium to deep-diving minnows close to structure, but surface lures, stickbaits, soft plastics and bibless rattling lures that are sometimes used as vertical jigs have also become popular in more recent times.

The area that is probably least exploited is structure and reef in deep water as well as deep channels. The focus is on the creeks and bank-side snags as a rule, but some quite spectacular fishing is available on deep jigs when the right sort of territory is located.

On a trip we attended where a few people with no idea how to cast went along, a guide put them over a rock bottom in deep water and let them bait fish the bottom. They took a haul of arm-stretching fingermark and were repeatedly creamed by large fish that behaved like express trains on the other end of the line. Any of those fish could have been taken on jigs and big soft plastics. This makes the point that the traditional view of the north does not automatically cover all of the available options.

Trolled deep-diving minnows can be used to work deep structure. The lure should run occasionally touching bottom and if free spooled as soon as snagged most will float free. Shallower running lures are often trolled along the edge of weed beds and stands of reeds. Lily pads can be worked with cast soft plastics, spinnerbaits and buzz baits.

The thing that adds enormously to the range and variety of barramundi fishing is that they have a passion for working the tides and using the massive runoff from the wet to their advantage.

Barra are very smart about working the tides. They use the run up tide to access areas denied to them on the ebb, and they use the very bottom of the tide to ambush bait that is waiting for the run up to get back into cover.

Southerners having their first barramundi trip often pass up excellent water because it looks too dirty or shallow to have fish in it. The run off from a mud flat can

DAVID GREEN

RON CALCUTT

This selection covers the options of casting or trolling for a range of species varying in size from small mangrove jacks to large barramundi. Many have deep-diving bibs, but even these can be effectively twitched in shallow water. **LEFT COLUMN, FROM TOP** Lively Lures 'Mad Mullet 3 in – Deep', Jonesy 'Nifty', Nilsmaster 'Spearhead', Leads 'Deep Jack', Predatec 'Spoonbill'. **RIGHT COLUMN, FROM TOP** Reidy's 'B52' (jerkbait), Halco 'Scorpion 150DD', Halco 'Scorpion 125DD', Manns 'Stretch 12+'

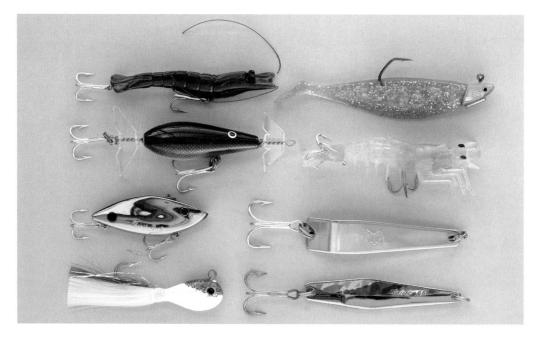

This set opens up some options like jigging rock bars, channels and deep tree stumps.
The fizzer is fun at twilight and the metals offer casting range for fast pelagics in the open
stretches or for vertical jigging over deeper reef.
LEFT COLUMN, FROM TOP Rio's 'Prawn' 20 gm, Bills Bugs 'Mouse' 75 mm, Cotton Cordell
'Super Spot C25', Perfection Jigs 'Bucktail' Jig 60 gm. **RIGHT COLUMN, FROM TOP** Blue Fox
'Squidgy Shad' 125 mm with Squidgy 12 gm Resin head, Prawnstar 25 gm,
Bumpa-Bar 45 gm, Spanyid 'Raider' 65 gm

be the colour of strong white coffee with the consistency of custard, but barra will still be in there feeding on the bait waiting at the entrance to a little gutter for the rising tide. Lateral line detection and the scent of bait are quite important in this environment, so it is best fished with lures like shallow stickbaits that can be jerked around in the strike zone for as long as possible. Some of these productive drains may be little less than a slight indentation in the mud, channelling a small amount of water off the flat. It doesn't take much to attract the barra.

When casting at snags, accuracy is vital so a single handed baitcaster is the popular choice. Trolling tackle is less demanding. Nylon lines over 6 kilograms or GSP line of 10–15 kilograms extended with a mono leader up to 30 kilograms is typical. Hooked fish often need to be hauled clear of the snags so a strong drag is also required.

The blue water

Once you head out away from the shoreline, the features that indicate where fish might be become a lot more subtle. Instead of obvious features like a headland, breaking reef or a river mouth, the signposts are in the form of current edges, feeding birds, water temperature changes, roaming bait schools and significant bottom formations. In fact, many of the other indicators occur through the influence of a major bottom structure. Reefs, drop-offs, wrecks and the edge of the continental shelf will all affect current flow and accumulate baitfish and large predators above them.

The lures you use to catch these fish can be broken into two groups – surface lures and deep jigs. In most cases the lures will need to work at high speeds. There are two reasons for this. One is that the fish we are chasing are highly active pelagic species that expect their prey to move extremely quickly. The other is that you often need to search over a large stretch of ocean to find the small pockets of fish within it. Travelling at speeds of six knots or more allows you to find them more quickly.

Species targeted with high speed jigs include kingfish and Samson-fish in the south with cobia, giant trevally, dog-tooth tuna and others being added in the north. Moderate speed jigs yo-yoed from the bottom to mid-water will catch a wide range of reef-oriented species from snapper to coral trout. The deep lures must be heavy enough to sink vertically and quickly into depths sometimes 80 metres or more.

The surface lures range from metal slugs cast to schools of small tuna feeding at the surface through to substantial trolled skirted lures designed for use with large hooks and leaders for ocean giants like massive tuna, marlin, sailfish, dolphin fish and others. High-speed bibbed and bibless minnows are also great for mid-sized fish that prefer a more subtle, sub-surface lure.

Splashing or flashing teasers help to attract the fish's attention and draw it to the boat where it can spot the smaller lures that may otherwise have been missed. As the quarry's attention will temporarily be fixed on the loud boat and teasers above, the lures are spread in a staggered pattern from close behind the boat, where the white water wake just starts to clear, to perhaps 100 metres back if a lure is run from a high 'rigger for tuna.

The best positions are often close to the boat just where the wake clears enough for the fish to get an unobstructed view of the offering. This distance will vary with the boat's design and speed. Lures in varying sizes and colour schemes are set at staggered

TIM SIMPSON

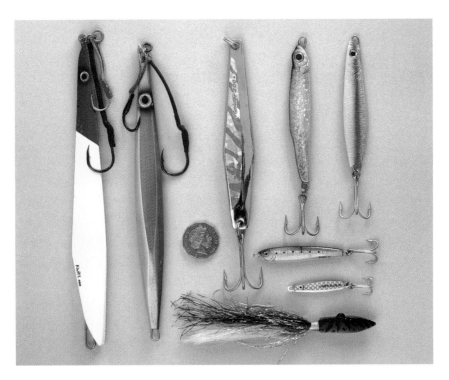

This selection covers lures for casting to surface fish and jigs to fish the offshore reefs.
TOP ROW, LEFT TO RIGHT River2Sea 'Knife' 400 gm, McLaughlin 'Zest' 300 gm, Spanyid 'Raider'
200 gm, Kokoda 'JigKing' 150 gm, Blue Fox 'Reflect Pirk' 130 gm.
LOWER GROUP, FROM TOP River2Sea 'Sea Rock' 40 gm, Javelin 'Lazer Slug' 20 gm,
(generic) Diamond head bucktail and tinsel jig 100 gm

A set of high-speed trolling lures, including a small 'Xmas tree' to catch little tuna for bait or sport and a selection of serious offshore big fish lures covering a variety of different actions and sizes. The high-speed bibless is great for species that prefer a sub-surface lure. **LEFT COLUMN, FROM TOP** Wilson 'XTS Bullet #1', Leads 'Bibless Minnow' 18 cm, Pakula 'Rat', Pakula 'Medium Sprocket', Joey Yee 'Apollo' 30 cm. **RIGHT COLUMN, FROM TOP** Pakula 'Uzi', Pakula 'Vamp'

positions so that they overlap without tangling when the boat makes a wide turn.

Most of these species are ocean wanderers that travel the world on the currents that carry them. They are temperature sensitive and will only be found where the warm tropical currents reach. In summer these clear, blue currents flow from north Queensland all the way to the bottom of New South Wales and sometimes even to the top of Tasmania – hopefully close to the coast so anglers can reach them. In the west they can extend down beyond Perth.

Tackle to chase blue water speedsters will vary enormously depending on the size of the quarry and also how much of a challenge the angler wants to make of the encounter. This will range from a high performance 3-kilogram baitcaster for the small fish to a massive outfit holding 1000 metres of 60-kilogram line for a 500-kilogram marlin. A fish weight-to-line-strength ratio of 5:1 is considered challenging and a 10:1 ratio or better is outstanding. These fish are some of the fastest and most powerful on earth so in all cases the tackle will need to hold 300 to 1000 metres of line and have first class strength and performance.

Trolling tactics

We have said a lot in this book about the way various cast lures can and should be worked, but have simply referred to trolling as trolling, and not gone into the skills and subtleties of this area of fishing.

Trolling can simply be a matter of dragging lures around behind a boat trying to locate scattered fish. More often it is something of an art used with great skill by practitioners who can place lures in the critical strike zone with great accuracy.

The first lesson that needs to be absorbed to successfully troll multiple lures is that you have to select compatible lures. Compatibility is usually based on the effective trolling speed of the lures in question. If you put out a bibbed lure that is highly effective at one knot, then toss out a skirted lure that likes to be run at seven knots, you have big trouble on your hands. Run at the right speed for the bibbed lure and the skirted lure will have all the attraction of a block of concrete dragged through the water. Pick the speed up for the skirted lure and the bibbed lure will spin madly, fly out of the water and probably tangle with the skirted lure. Pick a speed in between and neither lure will catch a fish. So you have to think in terms of compatible lure styles, and selection here is often made on the basis of making a presentation to a particular fish, or group of fish, and where you expect those fish to be in the water column.

In a bass lake you will probably choose deep divers that will work at a very slow speed, and you might choose to fish them off downriggers to get them down deeper than the lure will swim unaided.

Offshore you might choose skirted lures that will work at speed in, and just below, the surface layers. A true high-speed minnow or bibless lure might be safely added to the mix to increase the vertical deployment of the spread.

Fishing a wash you might go to shallow running minnows that will do the best work at medium speeds and run just under the foam.

Vertical deployment usually dictates lure speed and style. If you think the fish are going to be near enough to the surface to see a shallow running lure, speed can be used. If you need to get down deeper, you will be fishing slowly with a bibbed lure or using some aid to depth such as a downrigger.

Horizontal deployment is important in every form of trolling. If you put six compatible lures out and run them 15 metres behind the boat, odds are they will all tangle the first time you make a turn. So the first issue is to stagger the lures so this won't happen.

The length of the drop back is also important in that there are fish that won't come near a boat and will only hit a lure if it is a long way back. Other fish will come up to explore the prop wash and they will take a lure placed close to the propeller. Some fish may swim up the wake or come into it from the side, spotting a lure between the long and short drops. So we vary the drop back of lures to avoid tangles and to cater to fish that may come in from different angles.

There is another angle to consider here, and that is the height and breadth of the spread when considered from the rod tip. Most boats used for trolling will have side rod holders that are angled out, then stern holders that are facing dead astern at either side of the transom. To that you might add a couple more rods set in the centre of the transom. All of this spreads the rods across the boat and increases the width of the spread, but the lines will still be close to one another in vertical terms.

One thing we can do about this is to stagger the towing angle by leaving some lines coming off the rod tip and others taken down from the tip and attached to the reel frame with a rubber band. You could even take a couple of lines all the way down to tow eyes set low on the transom of the boat.

The idea here is that when a fish strikes, the band will break and release the line. This works well for sub-surface lures as the towing angle is kept low. It is also useful for skirted lures on windy days as it stops them being blown around. Be very careful of the band's strength, though! They are surprisingly strong and may cause the line to break if the band is stronger than the line. Check them with a weighing scale.

So now we have the lines set apart in terms of height and width. Boats fitted with rocket launchers commonly troll one rod, usually with the longest drop, from the launcher and others deploy outriggers to really get the lines apart.

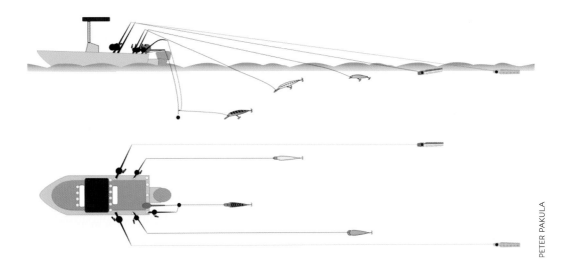

Obviously, the bigger the boat the more spread you can get on the lines and the more lines you can have out at any given time. Smaller boats can use fewer lines, and for slower trolling it can be an advantage to get rod tips down as close as possible to the surface of the water. Adjustable rod holders that clamp to side rails or sit in rowlocks can be set up to have rods at all angles.

The situation then is one where the lateral and vertical deployment of lures is dictated by the selection of lures initially, then the spread of the rods, and finally by the way the lines are presented from the rod tips. If you don't take care about all of these things, trolling multiple lures may get to be a miserable experience.

Even when you do everything right a rogue bibbed lure can create a terrible mess. A rogue lure is one that will not tow straight, tearing off to either side or going from one side to another when used at a speed where it should be working well. It might simply be out of its speed range or a dud lure, but it is more often the case that the tow-point is not in correct alignment. (*See page 80* for tuning instructions).

The casual observer may see trolling as a fairly lazy, even boring approach to fishing, but it is far from that. At sea, experienced anglers will have their eyes glued to the lures trailing behind, making adjustments to get the very best possible presentation back there. Even on a still lake the skipper will be glued to the echo sounder, trying to keep those lures as close as possible to the strike zone. This is a situation where the skipper, more than the individual anglers may well be responsible for the fishing outcome for the day.

The freshwater

In the saltwater we consider the moon, the state and time of the tides, barometric pressure, and wind strength and direction when we think about chasing fish. Big water temperature shifts can also play a major role.

In the freshwater a similar set of rules apply, without of course the role played by the tides. Even without tides, you will find yourself working around the moon, which is the factor influencing tides anyway.

Trying to isolate significant factors in the freshwater you would have as a priority water temperature and the state of the barometer.

If you consider the southern-most end of the barramundi's range, which is represented in stocked impoundments, you will find that the fish simply shut down in water temperatures under 26°C, then get very active from 27°C. Like all freshwater natives they will be at their best on a rising to high barometer and switched off by a low or falling barometer, which often coincides with strong winds.

It pays to study the comfort zones of various native fish, and to use an echo sounder with a surface temperature feature to learn about these. The fish, of course, can adjust temperature to a degree by moving from shallow to deep water, but there will be times when water that is too warm will keep them out of the shallows, or conversely too cool in the depths, which will push them up towards shallower water warmed by the sun.

Given ideal water temperatures and good barometric pressure, impoundment fish will normally work the shallows at night and retire into the depths during the day. They all use cover and ambush tactics to a degree, and all like deep shade.

If shoreline snags or rocks are adjacent to deeper water you will find them along the shoreline at any time. Given extensive shallows with reed beds, drowned trees or bushes or grass, they will be up there from night into early morning. Fish will also stick to the shoreline when heavy rain has the water level rising and they have access to what was shoreline grass and shrub.

Throughout this book we have stressed the importance placed on the time the lure spends in the strike zone. It is worth noting then that this critical strike zone will vary according to water temperature. Fish will move to and from the shoreline, and from top to bottom away from the shore. Lure choice varies to accommodate a variable strike zone.

In freshwater where the quality and colour of the water can vary enormously, choosing a lure that can be seen might take priority over a popular clear-water colour

RON CALCUTT

scheme for the fish in question.

In dirty water go for high contrast colours and patterns and look for hard edges in simple colour schemes. Flash also comes to the fore in dirty conditions where there is still enough light to make it possible.

As water quality improves try softer more subtle colour schemes. In very clear water, natural colours and partly transparent bodies come into play.

Some of the freshwater fish have eyes set towards the top of the head, so you can expect them to be monitoring the water ahead and above. Although they will never top the popular colours hit parade with most anglers, black to purple are excellent colours with high visibility when viewed from below silhouetted against the light.

Be cautious in your selection of lures that produce noise. The freshwater can be a much quieter place than much of the saltwater. Noise is a relative factor, and while the right kind of noise will work in your favour, the wrong kind could work against you. Pulsing vibration from a lure with a strong swimming action is a great attractor, as is the subtle noise created by a spinnerbait. Lures with built-in rattles can vary in effectiveness, although on their day they can be the deadliest lures around.

In low light to dark conditions surface lures can work a treat. Once again be aware that different styles of surface lure will create a wide range of noises. The most subtle would be the fizzer, which can be kept in one place for a long period of time making a low-level noise. The waddlers are fairly noisy, but the noise they make is very natural. Poppers vary according to the skill of the angler using them. A loud pop, then the lure left sitting on the surface for ages is probably the most effective way to use them. The drawback with surface lures is that you will always get a percentage of missed strikes, although some believe that this is compensated for by the adrenaline rush associated with surface strikes.

So, choosing lures is largely a matter of matching the lure to the habitat the fish in question is working at the time. During the heat of the day when bass may well be working deep over structure or weed beds, lures that stay down there are the way to go. Fish holding deep may be targeted with soft plastics that can be worked slow and deep and left in the strike zone. Spinnerbaits cast well out from the boat then slowly worked back just off the bottom can be very effective, as are bibless rattlers.

Cover over deeper water will call for hard diving lures or lures that will sink or suspend. When the fish move up into the shallows it is time to go over to shallow runners, stickbaits and spinnerbaits.

Night feeders may hang along the edge of drop-offs during the day. Deep trenches formed from a long-gone river bed or scoured out along the entrance of a feeder stream may be worked trolling deep divers with or without downriggers. Daytime deep trolling with large lures is a popular technique on those impoundments stocked with barramundi.

Plastics are another deadly way to approach fish working deep. Keep retrieve speeds down to the point where you are nearly falling asleep.

Because our main freshwater species have only a slight overlap in habitat, and the impoundments tend to have one dominant species, we will look at the freshwater by species rather than location.

Bass

A decidedly pugnacious nature makes the bass a priority target for many lure anglers. They are a great looking fish that can be extremely temperamental at times. One morning they can be red hot on just one particular lure, the next they will eat anything that moves. You never can claim to have them 100 per cent wired.

Bass give the angler a great excuse to have the biggest tackle box available

TIM SIMPSON

RON CALCUTT

overflowing with expensive lures. At one time or another, a basic plastic worm or the most expensive Japanese lure will be just the thing to have on the day.

You won't catch a lot of bass just dragging lures around behind a boat hoping for a fish. Sadly, a lot of people only fish this way, catching fish occasionally, but missing out more often than not.

In impoundments, where most bass are caught these days, you have to find out where the fish are before you start thinking about lures. If the water is rising they will be in the shallows, but they could all be on just one side of the dam. They will take surface lures early then go onto shallow runners as the sun rises.

Another time they could be hanging deep on a weed bed or over the original river bed. They could be among drowned trees or working suspended bait schools at a particular depth anywhere in the dam. The first job is to locate the fish and then select lures to work the environment they have chosen.

Without a boat, walking the bank at first and last light, or well into the night, casting surface lures or shallow runners can be very productive. If you are working from a boat a decent echo sounder is a must. On one of the dams we fish we repeatedly see the old adage proven that 10 per cent of the fishermen catch 90 per cent of the fish.

These spinnerbaits and jigs open up the deeper regions of a lake.
LEFT COLUMN, FROM TOP AusSpin 'ProSpin tandem' ½ oz, Fina 'Tandem Willow' ½ oz,
Persuader 'Assassinator – Clacker Blade' ³/₈ oz. **RIGHT COLUMN, FROM TOP** (generic) Marabou
jig, (generic) Bucktail jig, Nilsmaster 'Jigging Shad', Nilsmaster 'Jigger-3', Rio's 'Prawn' 5 gm,
Brett Thomson tailspinner

A selection of bibbed lures for around the edges and two bibless rattlers to probe deeper structure or suspended schools. **LEFT COLUMN, FROM TOP** Rapala 'Husky Jerk' (suspending) 8 cm, Predatec 'Boomerang B65', Rapala 'Shad Rap SR05 Deep', Deception 'Shrimp'. **RIGHT COLUMN, FROM TOP** Lake Police 'Jackall TN60', Cotton Cordell 'Super Spot C21' 2 in, Halco 'Poltergeist 50', Custom Crafted 'Fish Stick', Knolls 'Native – small'

Nine out of ten anglers are going home from a dam full of fish having caught two or three fish, while the remaining one in ten has caught and released dozens of bass.

If the fish aren't working around the shoreline, then a good sounder is a must to find fish. Once you find them and determine what depth they are working at, you can then go on to select appropriate lures to tempt them.

The other secret to successful bass fishing is to be prepared to try different lures and different presentations with those lures if one doesn't work. It doesn't matter how well it worked yesterday, if you know where they are and you're not catching them, start working your way through the tackle box.

Bass must be the fussiest fish around at times. Lures that have proven themselves over and over again will suddenly drop dead in their tracks, and a lure that always works in one place may not work in another.

Surface lures. **LEFT COLUMN, FROM TOP** Bills Bugs 'Mouse' 40 mm, Heddon 'Dying Flutter', Arbogast 'Jitterbug' ³⁄₈ oz, Halco 'Night Walker'. **RIGHT COLUMN, FROM TOP** Yamashita 'Pop Queen' 5 cm, Heddon 'Tiny Torpedo', Bills Bugs 'Flutter Bug – small'

Wild bass can be another matter altogether, and are more likely to be associated with bank-side cover. That's not an absolute rule, but it is normally the first thing you would try on strange water. Lures that will crash dive right alongside a log get high priority along with slow sinking soft plastic presentations.

On larger bodies of water it will pay to keep an eye on the bottom, looking for any kind of structure or deep weed beds that may be holding fish. Vertical rock faces and any kind of overhang are also favoured by bass.

It is this unpredictability that makes the bass so attractive to anglers. You have to keep thinking about what you are doing and always be prepared for the bass to suddenly change the rules of engagement.

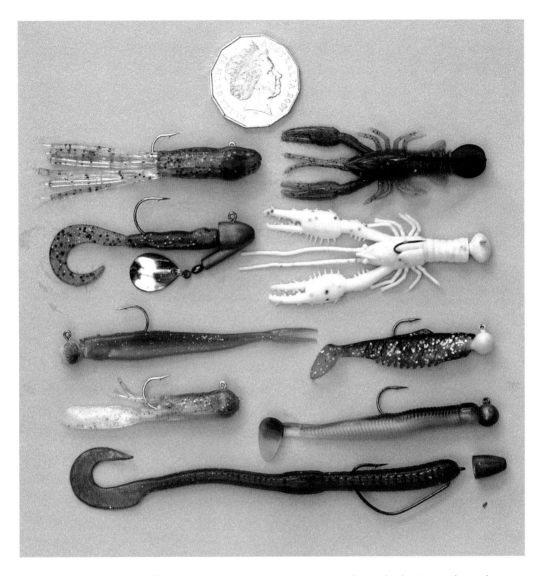

This selection of soft plastics allows slow presentations along the bottom, through snaggy structure or among suspended schools in mid-water. **LEFT COLUMN, FROM TOP** Wilson 'Tube' 75 mm with internal ball jig head, Ecogear 'Para Max' 3 in on a TT Lures 'Rev Head' jig head, Berkley 'Bass Minnow' 3 in on a ball jig head, Ecogear 'Pad Tue' with internal ball jig head, Wilson '6-in Curly Tail Worm' on a Gamakatsu G-Lock hook with sliding worm weight. **RIGHT COLUMN, FROM TOP** Atomic Craw 3 in (trimmed) on a Gamakatsu Arky 26 stand-up jig head, Mad Man 'Crawfish Worm' 3 in on a McCubbin lumo football jig head, Blue Fox 'Squidgy Fish' 50 mm on a McCubbin lumo football jig head, Ecogear 'Grass Minnow L' on a ball jig head

Impoundment barramundi

We have already discussed barramundi in the previous tropical fishing scenarios, but a lot of things change when barra are introduced into impoundments. The major change is the size of the fish. With no natural predators other than anglers making it hard for fish to achieve maximum growth potential, impoundment barra are re-defining our expectations with regard to potential catch sizes. Instead of being a highly prized rarity, fish in excess of 15 kilograms are getting to be a relatively common sight.

When you see the number of mega impoundment barra appearing in the pages of Queensland fishing papers these days, you can't help but entertain thoughts of fish in excess of 45 kilograms setting the benchmark for a trophy specimen. Even the common captures are big enough to make you consider not just the species when tooling up, but the size potential of the fish you are going to seek. For example, your lures will need to retain their action when fitted up with larger, heavy duty rings and the strongest treble hooks.

It could be that the largest fish will only be landed when deep trolling in open water where you will have time to play the fish out. The best braids will give you line strength in low diameter lines which will attain maximum trolling depth with big lures.

Although we are not hearing much about it at this stage, there is great potential to be explored in the field of deep water jigs that are being used offshore with great success.

When the fish are in the shallows and through the trees in periods of low or no light, head-on confrontations will call for lines of at least 15 kilograms breaking strain. An alternative to going head to head is to put the pressure on when you can, then free-spool the reel and follow fish that go around timber.

Barra will be half hearted about feeding in water temperatures under 27°C, and pretty much shut down under 25°C. Above 27°C they switch on and become quite aggressive in their feeding.

TIM SIMPSON

261

This group of casting or trolling bibbed lures offers various diving depths from shallow to very deep. **FROM TOP** Halco 'Laser Pro 190 XDD', (left) Rapala 'Shad Rap' 9 cm, (right) Halco 'Scorpion 125', Lively Lures 'Mad Mullet 6 in – deep', Predatec 'Viper', Tilsan 'Big Barra'

Barra tackle needs to be suited to accurate casting and hard fighting. Drag systems need to be smooth but capable of delivering a lot of braking power. Two-handed baitcasters are a popular choice here.

Allowing for the fact that there will be a lot of pressure applied to the line, and that these fish will charge around tree trunks or barge right through drowned scrub and bush, traces and knots are a most important part of the exercise.

A main line of 10–15 kilograms is a popular option, as is the inclusion of a double at the end of your line. Opinion varies enormously with regard to the length and breaking strain of the leader, with 15 kilograms the minimum and 30 kilograms a realistic maximum. You will need at least 1.5 metres of leader and could go up to 4 metres.

A selection for the surface and the depths. The two near-surface bibbed jerkbaits work over shallow weed beds or amongst timber and the fizzer is great for night-time. The bibless rattlers and the spinnerbait put out strong vibrations and together with the soft plastic can be used at any depth. **LEFT COLUMN, FROM TOP** Luhr Jensen 'Amazon Ripper' 6.5 in, Storm 'Wild Eye Rattle Shrimp', Halco 'Trembler 110', Blue Fox 'Squidgy Fish' 150 mm with Squidgy 10/0 Resin head. **RIGHT COLUMN, FROM TOP** Rapala 'Long Cast Minnow LC12', Reidy's 'B52', Cotton Cordell 'Super Spot C25', AusSpin 'Big Native Shad Spin' spinnerbait

Golden perch

Another species absolutely thriving in the impoundment environment is the golden perch or yellowbelly. Once considered a sluggish fish caught on bait in muddy inland rivers, the golden perch has emerged as a prime sportfishing target since extensive stocking has taken place. Primarily a summer fish, the yellowbelly is happiest in waters around 24°C. The fish have a definite preference for quiet, balmy weather. They can be found in the shallows and margins of the shore when the water is warm and can be polaroided and cast to in the right conditions. When the weather heats up they move back into deeper water.

In terms of preferred habitat, the yellowbelly has much in common with the bass. Those who understand bass generally don't have much trouble coming to terms with yellowbelly. They will work the margins where they slip through reeds and deep grass and scrub. Drowned timber, bankside snags, rocks and deep weed beds are all happy hunting grounds. Golden perch are particularly fond of shrimp which goes a long way towards explaining their interest in the weedy margins. Lures that imitate shrimp will always be a popular item with these fish.

They are not a fish that tears around chasing prey; slow erratic retrieves with small lures are generally the way to go. When the fish are in the shallows, suspending and shallow running bibbed lures are an excellent choice, as are shrimps, worms and other soft plastics.

When they move off the shallows, bibbed divers that will get down in 2–4 metres of water along with bibless rattlers, spinnerbaits and soft plastics including worms, large insects or crayfish imitations will be a good choice.

Going beyond 4 metres, trolled deep divers are a proposition as are weighted lures like spinnerbaits, jigs and soft plastics. The deeper and darker the water, the more important a contrasting colour and strong action may become to get noticed.

Always keep the leader in mind if things are slow and be prepared to go to a lighter leader if you are not seeing any action. The lighter leader will also add some depth to diving lures and improve the action of all bibbed lures.

Another handy thing to know is that these fish can be made to strike at times when they are listless and simply follow lures without striking. The trick is to retrieve a suspending or slightly buoyant lure for a while then pause in a dead stop. The fish will be confronted by the lure right in its face and when forced to make a decision will often pounce on the lure. This is, in fact, a tactic that will work with shy, lethargic or curious fish in many waters.

TIM SIMPSON

A selection of deep-diving bibbed lures, jigs, spinnerbaits, soft plastics and
a sinking rattling bibless minnow, all of which allow you to explore the various
surroundings and depths that these fish frequent.

LEFT COLUMN, FROM TOP Tilsan 'Bass', Atomic 'Craw' 3 in (trimmed) on a stand-up jig head,
JJ's Lures 'Stumpjumper 3A', Blue Fox 'Squidgy Fish' 80 mm on a McCubbin lumo shad jig
head, Atomic '3-in Fat Grub' on a Gamakatsu G-Lock hook with a free-running cone weight.

MIDDLE COLUMN, FROM TOP (generic) Bucktail jig, Custom Crafted '65-mm Scud', AusSpin
'Ultra Spin double Colorado' 1/2-oz spinnerbait, AusSpin 'Skirt Tail Jig' 3/8 oz, Ecogear 'Pad Tue'
with internal ball jig head, Blue Fox 'Squidgy Wriggler #5' with McCubbin lumo shad jig
head, Wilson 'Tube' 75 mm with internal ball jig head.

RIGHT COLUMN, FROM TOP Luhr Jensen 'Hot Lips Express' 1/2 oz, Rebel 'Deep Wee Crawfish D76',
Hart 'Backflash' 1/2-oz tailspinner, Charlie Brewer Slider 'Bass Grub' 3 in on a McCubbin lumo
dart jig head, Deception 'Shrimp', Halco 'Trembler 70', Wilson '6-in Curly Tail Worm' on a
McCubbin lumo football jig head

Murray cod

Murray cod are the stuff of legends. Wherever there was water within the range of the Murray cod there was a legend of some monster capable of eating whole dogs and sheep. Some of the captures of the past were nearly big enough to justify such legends, and current reckonings still put the maximum growth potential at 180 centimetres and 113 kilograms. That's a powerful big fish!

The average capture these days is estimated to be between 2 and 5 kilograms, and even that's not a fish to be taken lightly. Their diet is still listed as including crustaceans, frogs, insects, molluscs, fish, water birds, snakes and possums. So, if you have a possum lure you can go and try for a giant cod.

It says a lot about the Murray cod that no further stocking will be permitted outside its natural range due to its predatory nature.

The keys to lure-fishing for cod are its appetite and cosmopolitan diet, plus its territorial nature. Given a good piece of cover and a shut down bite, experienced anglers will keep banging away at the cover with a variety of lures until the cod is sufficiently peeved to come tearing out to destroy the interloper.

BILL CLASSON

Given the power and bulk of the fish, its engine room requires a lot of fuel for sustained effort. Therefore you can think in terms of a quarry that will prefer ambush, where a short burst of speed will take the quarry unawares and use the least possible amount of fuel per kilogram of energy consumed.

They do not like direct sunlight and like to lay up under heavy cover where shade gives them a considerable advantage over fish looking in from an area of bright light. Rocky undercuts and ledges, heavy snags, stands of timber and any area offering cover close to underwater traffic might be occupied by a big cod. Although they like to come out of

A selection of big, very deep, quick diving lures for casting or trolling. They all have a strong, pulsing action and their large bib helps them to flip over logs without snagging. **FROM TOP** Peter Newell 'Kadaitcha' large, Custom Crafted 'Hammerhead' 110 mm, Halco 'Poltergeist 80', Predatec 'Boomerang 80UD', JJ's 'Stumpjumper 1A' 100 mm, Manns 'Depth 20+'

cover and roam about at night and explore weed beds close to their hiding place, they also take advantage of the hard edges between light and shade created when the sun shines straight down onto structures of any kind. Although the area of shade has been reduced, the fish that occupies it has a distinct advantage over everything in the vicinity. The preferred average depth to work will be around 3–6 metres, but they will take surface lures at times, especially at night.

The gloomy waters and light conditions where these fish operate suggest the use of

These lures are big, bulky or put out a strong vibration – sometimes all three!
The two surface lures give some excellent and explosive fishing at night and the others
all sink which allow slow probing around rocks, stumps and ledges.
LEFT COLUMN, FROM TOP Bills Bugs 'Rat' fizzer, Mad Man 'Lizard' on a Mustad Impact hook
with a free running cone sinker, Halco 'Trembler 110', Atomic '5-in Fat Grub' on a fluorescent
jig head. **MIDDLE COLUMN, FROM TOP** AusSpin 'Big Native - tandem' ⅝-oz spinnerbait, Mad
Man '5-in Crawfish Tube' on a Terminator (weedless, rattling) 'Pro's Top Secret Jig' ½ oz.
RIGHT COLUMN, FROM TOP Lunker City 'Water Widow' 125 mm on a Gamakatsu G-Lock hook
with free running cone sinker, Cotton Cordell 'Super Spot C25', Bills Bugs 'Flutter Bug' 10 cm

lures that move at slow speeds and with a strong pulse that can be detected at maximum range. Slow speeds will allow these fish to move into position for an attack once they feel the lure approaching.

Cod of all sizes have a large mouth in relation to overall body size and lures to 15 centimetres are not too big for these fish. The huge mouth and very rough crusher plates call for tough leader materials, and the habitat and size of the fish also determine that the leader be up to 3 metres long and have good abrasion resistance.

A main line of 15 kilograms coupled with tackle capable of applying pressure with this sort of line is a prudent way to go when fishing for these fish.

Saratoga

After the first encounter with a saratoga it is often the angler who is captured. These belligerent fish are a true living fossil and have so much going for them you can't help but fall in love with them. The upshot lower jaw and eyes mounted high on the head tell the story of a fish that hunts prey at the surface. The location of large dorsal and anterior dorsal fins way back towards the tail combine with the tail itself to give this species serious blast off power. It can simply hurl itself clear of the water, and it does this with abandon when hooked. Saratoga are said to have a growth range to 90 centimetres, although they are commonly taken around the 50–60-centimetre mark.

Slow moving shallow runners, surface lures and suspending lures all work on saratoga, as do small spinnerbaits – especially when a stinger hook is added. Much of the time, small baitfish form a major part of the diet for saratoga, but they are partial to any small creature at the surface. Frogs are a favourite prey and surface frog-imitating lures are a fun way to get explosive strikes, although saratoga are sometimes

DAVID GREEN

difficult to hook as the palate of their mouth consists of a smooth bony plate. Even so, the strike and a single jump is often ample reward for an angler.

They are an odd fish in that they will work in a wide range of environments. They like all the usual ambush spots such as snags, lily pads, reeds, drowned trees, rock faces, undercuts and so on, but you will also find them cruising around in open water in some locations. Cania Dam in Queensland, for example, often has big saratoga wandering about way out in the open.

Fishing with top-water lures in the twilight hours for saratoga has to rank along with the very best lure-fishing experiences available.

By sneaking along the shoreline with an electric motor, you can soon cover a lot of territory and find where they are working.

269

This range has been selected to keep the lure on or near the surface. Even the spinnerbait is fitted with two Colorado blades to keep it running high. **LEFT COLUMN, FROM TOP** Rapala 'J-9' jointed minnow, Rio's 'Rubber Lips' 65 mm, Manns 'Stretch, 1 Minus', Atomic '2½-in Paddle Tail' on an AusSpin small 'Jig Spinner', Heddon 'Tiny Torpedo', Panther Martin 'Superior Frog' ⅜ oz, Berkley 'Bass Minnow' 3 in on an Owner 'Weedless Ultra Head' jig head. **RIGHT COLUMN, FROM TOP** AusSpin double Colorado 'Ultra Spin' ⅜ oz, Rapala 'Long Cast Minnow LC10' (jerkbait), AusSpin 'Bass Buzz' ¼ oz.

Trout

Trout are a cold water species and so are limited to areas in the southern reaches of Australia where high altitude or melted snow keeps the water temperatures low. As many of the waterways are unable to maintain a sufficient self-sustaining population, they are often reliant on regular stocking.

For fast growth and large size trout require a waterway that has cool water, sufficient dissolved oxygen, a large food supply, protection (cover) and a suitable pH. Not many streams in Australia have all of these requirements on a regular basis, but finding the right one can make for some extremely enjoyable fishing. The biggest fish and the most prolific trout waters are found in the lakes.

At times trout will chase other fish in a variety of sizes, but often they swim slowly; grazing on adult and larval insects, snails, shrimps, worms, yabbies and small land animals. During spawning they will eat trout eggs and fingerlings washing downstream.

In streams and rivers, trout will patrol slow moving stretches and the bottom of deep pools. Many more will set up station in the sometimes very shallow water of the main current flow, in a vantage point where they can see everything washing down but they themselves are out of the flow in the pressure eddy in front of a rock or the back eddy of a bank or corner. They are even more likely to be there if cover or deep water is nearby.

TIM SIMPSON

The fish will face up-current and selectively pick morsels that the stream brings to them. The lure must approach them coming from upstream and operate at such a slow speed that it is effective while not moving much faster than the current. When spinning the shallow riffles, a lure that is also able to suspend above the bottom is less likely to be snagged. Tackle is usually an ultra light threadline loaded with 2 or 3 kilogram line.

Trout are a notoriously sensitive fish with good vibration detection, great eyesight and a staggering sense of smell. In bright, clear, shallow water they are especially wary and must be stalked with great stealth. Tackle should also

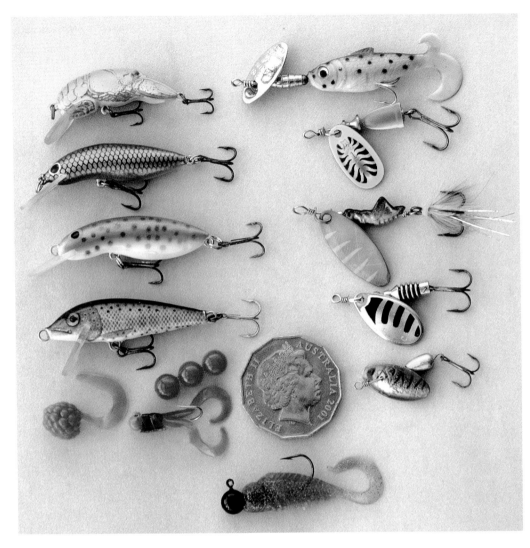

This selection is for streams. The natural prey would at times include fingerling trout.

LEFT COLUMN, FROM TOP Rebel 'Teeny Wee Crawfish F77', Peter Newell original Scorpion '1/2', Attack Lures 'Attack Minnow', Rapala 'Original Floating' 5 cm, Luhr Jensen 'Jenseneggs' and 'Bob Tail' (trout roe imitations), 'Cajun Critter' double tail (trimmed) on a 1/32 oz McCubbin lumo jig head, Blue Fox 'Squidgy Wriggler #2' on a ball jig head.

RIGHT COLUMN, FROM TOP Panther Martin 'Minnow' 1/8 oz, Blue Fox 'Super Vibrax #1', Blue Fox 'Nature', Rublex 'Celta #2', Panther Martin '#2 Holographic'

This set is for the lakes. The lures are a little bigger, heavier and deeper running than the stream group. There's also an ultralight spoon for trolling deep behind a downrigger.

LEFT COLUMN, FROM TOP 3-in curly tail 'Squirmin Grub' on a Gamakatsu 'Arky' jig head, Ecogear 'Grass Minnow – M' on a ball jig head, Atomic 'Craw' 3 in (trimmed) with internal ball jig head, McGrath minnow, Rapala (sinking) 'Countdown CD7', Predatec 'MinMin', Wigston's 'Little Tasmanian Devil', Wigston's 'Tasmanian Devil'.

RIGHT COLUMN, FROM TOP Panther Martin 'Minnow' 1/8 oz, Blue Fox 'Super Vibrax #2', Rublex 'Special Celta #3', Wordens 'Rooster Tail' 1/6 oz, Luhr Jensen 'Canadian Wonder #2', Pegron 'Tiger Minnow', Spanyid 'Maniac' 9 gm

be rigged for stealth with the thinnest line possible and no unnecessary hardware.

Their feeding style and activity varies widely in lakes, depending on the food source and conditions. When water temperatures are suitable they often hunt around the edges in among the rocks, weeds and timber as this is where most of their prey lives.

Trolling is very popular and successful in lakes as it allows lines to be set at different depths through the use of sinkers, downriggers or paravanes. When coupled with a good depth sounder, the lure can be adjusted to the depth where fish or fish-holding structures are found. This is particularly useful on highland lakes as the water will often stratify into dramatically different temperature layers which in turn have different oxygen levels. A thermocline is one of these layers and due to suspended particles it often shows on sounders as a thin horizontal band. In warm conditions, many of the baitfish and trout will be found in and around this level.

In the poor visibility of many lakes, especially when trolling down a few metres, a slow moving lure with a strong, pulsing action will help trout to sense and home in on your offering. The water moving, throbbing action of teasers/attractors can also be used to draw fish that miss the more subtle action of the lure.

Tackle for the lakes ranges from 2 or 3-kilogram line on a threadline spinning outfit to 6 kilograms or heavier on a stronger spin or baitcaster rig when trolling with attractors or paravanes.

In all trout fishing, it is in the angler's interests to cover ground, either by walking (up-current), and probing with cast lures or by trolling the edges of a lake.

CHAPTER SIX

Handy knots to know

Fishing cannot begin until we've connected our lure to the line. This is not always as straightforward as we might hope. Perhaps we will need to add a stronger, tougher leader at the front end – to take the wear of an encounter with a big fish – or the bottom. We often want a loop attachment to give the lure more freedom to move. And one thing we always need is a strong connection: one that won't fail when the real pressure is applied; which is often when the biggest, strongest and most desired fish of all is on the end!

There are many knots known to fishermen, but in reality an angler should only learn a small handful and then practise and become familiar with them until they are perfected.

Here we've listed a selection of knots that should take care of any situation a lure fisherman will need. They've been chosen because they do the required job, remaining neat and castable while retaining as much of the line's strength as possible.

Gel-spun Polyethylene (GSP) 'super' lines are a special case. They are so thin they often cut through themselves when pressure is applied to a regular knot. Most are also

If you take care to tie good knots, when the big one jumps on, you'll be ready!

extremely slippery and when tied with regular knots they may simply slide undone. Because of the resulting poor knot strength, many GSP brands drastically underrate their breaking strains. An un-knotted GSP line labelled as 10 kilograms may actually break at well over 15 kilograms. New GSP lines are being developed and released with improved knot strength, but even so we have included special knots that are particularly useful with these fabulous new lines and which retain most of the lines' original strength.

Uni knot

The uni knot is very useful, strong and easy to tie. It is commonly used to tie a firm connection in nylon or fluorocarbon to a snap clip, lure, ring, hook or swivel. As it is a slip knot, it's also very handy for attaching line to the spool of a reel. It has good knot strength but with light lines the strength can be improved even more by folding the end of the line over and tying the knot with a doubled strand.

The knot is often shown tied with four or more turns through the loop but we find it just as strong with only three and this makes it possible to tie in very heavy nylon leaders up to 100 kilograms or more. When it is firmly tightened just in front of a lure it can even be used as a loop knot.

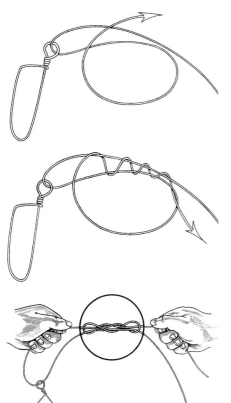

1. Pass the line through the object being secured (snap clip) then back parallel to the main strand before curving away, out and back towards the object again. Then pass the tag end over both strands and you now have a loop alongside the main line.
2. Working inside the loop and away from the snap clip, wrap the tag end three times or more around both parallel strands.
3. Pulling on the tag either side of the knot, snug the knot up so that it gently grips the main line. Then lick to lubricate it.
4. Slide the knot down onto the snap clip and firm the knot by pulling tightly on the tag end and the main strand. Trim the tag and you're done.

Super-improved clinch knot

This knot provides a maximum strength connection when a rigid attachment is required, such as joining on a swivel, snap or the ring of a lure. The diagrams make it look a little complicated and messy but it's actually quite quick and easy.

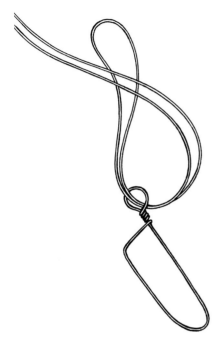 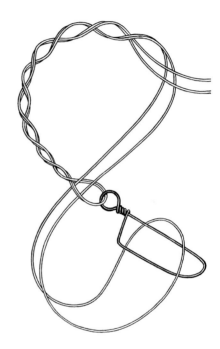

1. The knot is tied with a doubled strand. This can be either the end of a previously tied double such as a Bimini twist or the tag end of the line simply bent back on itself for 30 centimetres or so. Thread the loop through the eye of the ring and then wind it back around both of the doubled strands.

2. Do three to five wraps then poke the tag-end loop back through the gap that has formed immediately in front of the ring. Now pull the tag loop through and pass this loop over the item being connected.

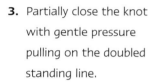

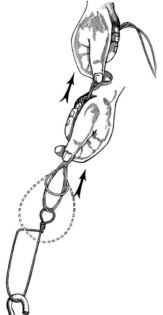

3. Partially close the knot with gentle pressure pulling on the doubled standing line.

4. Now, use your right hand to pull the wraps up the line away from the ring so the tag-end loop pulls up and snugs around the main strands. (This step is made easier if the item is hooked over a secure fitting so that both hands are free.) If you do this correctly the loop will disappear once the knot is tightened.

5. Lick the knot to lubricate it then pull evenly on both strands to draw the knot down tightly. Try to ensure that the strands going through the ring are not crossed. Bunch the wraps up with one hand as you snug the knot tighter with the other – until the wraps form a compact barrel. If you're using a double, the knot is finished. Otherwise, trim the tag end and you're done.

Double uni knot

The double uni knot is strong and very useful for joining two lines or for adding a leader. The tag ends lie parallel to the main strands and so pass through the guides very well when casting. When a leader with a diameter more than twice the thickness of the main line is to be joined it will increase the knot strength if you tie it with a doubled-over strand of the lighter line. If you need a 100 per cent strength connection between an old line and a top-up of new line, first tie a double in each of the lines and then tie the doubled ends together with a double uni knot.

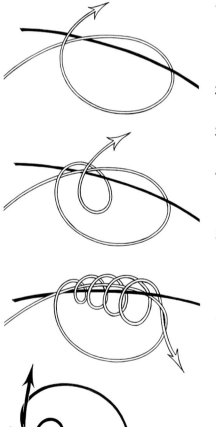

1. Overlap the ends of the lines to be joined. Pass one tag end around the other line before curving it back and over the top of the two parallel strands. You now have a loop on one side.
2. Wrap the tag end around the two parallel strands and up inside the loop.
3. Make four wraps in all. (Three in very heavy lines.) Then snug it down but don't pull it tight just yet.
4. Now make an identical knot with the tag end of the other line. Again, snug it down but don't pull it really tight.
5. At this stage you have two knots snugged up around both of the overlapping strands of line. Lick the knots to lubricate them and then pull on both of the main lines. The knots will slide together.
6. Tighten the knots by pulling firmly on the main lines and the tag ends. The tag ends can be trimmed quite closely.

Bimini twist double

A Bimini twist double is a fairly quick and simple procedure after a little practice. If tied carefully it will transform a single strand of fishing line into two strands with no loss of strength at the connection.

These are particularly useful for maintaining full strength in your main line when joining it to a heavier leader. The knot where the leader and main line join will be weakened but since you are now tying it with a double strand (that is twice as strong) it will still have considerably more strength than the main line. In Gel-spun 'super' lines, where most brands experience a significant loss of strength as soon as a knot is tied, they are an important step in tying on a leader.

The following instructions tell how to tie a short double, which is all you require to achieve the full strength connection to your leader. All subsequent rigging is then done with the nylon leader, which is much easier to tie strong knots in than Gel-spun 'super' line.

1. Take a tag end of around 30 centimetres and pinch it to the main line after creating a loop of around 1 metre in length.

2. While one hand holds the tag end and mainline, the fingers of the other hand hold the end of the loop and then spin it around to create twists. For nylon lines you only need 20 twists, but with GSP lines you are better off to have 30 or more as it is far more slippery.

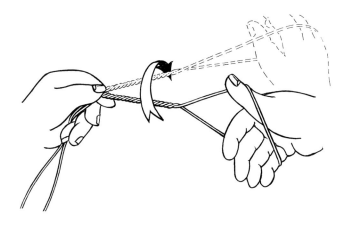

3. Now find a place to sit, or just squat down. With your heels on the ground and your knees together, place the loop under your feet and around your knees. You should now have the 1-metre loop around the outside of your feet and knees. You will be maintaining the twists in the line by holding the main line and tag end in one hand a few centimetres above your knees.

4. Hold the tag end in one hand and the main line in the other. Keep pressure on the lines and hold each of them at an angle (45 degrees off the imaginary centreline) to maintain pressure on the twists. Then gently spread your knees. As the loop widens the twists will get tighter and tighter.

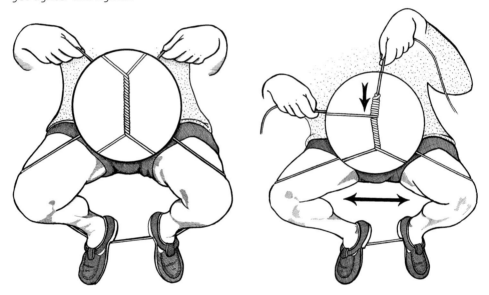

5. Once the twists are tightly packed together, shift the hands holding the tag end and main line so that the angles change. Take the tag end and move it down, so its angle changes from 45 degrees to slightly more than a 90-degree angle. At the same time move the main line up to vertical.

   Then carefully guide the tag end down over the tightly packed twists while you gently spread your knees wider. The increased pressure from your spreading legs will cause the tag end to wrap tightly back down. Keep the binding closely packed over the base twists by guiding it with the hand holding the tag end. Stop spreading your legs when the over binding reaches the end of the twists.

6. While maintaining pressure on the loop with your knees, pinch the end of the bind with the thumb and forefinger of the hand holding the tag end. This locks the wraps so they won't unravel.

Then let go of the mainline with the other hand and use it to take over the finger lock, so the first hand is free again – for the next step.

7. We now make a half hitch with the tag end to lock the binding in place. The best way is with a figure-eight half hitch. Bring the tag end to the centre of the two loop strands, then take it under the far strand, back over the top of it (angled towards the binding) and then through the loop you just created. The tag end will end up in the centre of the two loop strands. Snug it up tight and then relax. The Bimini is now locked and won't unravel.

You need a little more security on the knot before it is ready to fish with. You can do a couple more tight half hitches and then cut the tag end off flush. With nylon this is often sufficient but with GSP lines, because there is no stretch to hold the hitches in place, they will sometimes loosen and back themselves undone while bumping through the rod guides. To stop this we can do an extra little bind to lock the tag end under enough wraps that it can't escape. This is often called the 'Rizzuto Finish'.

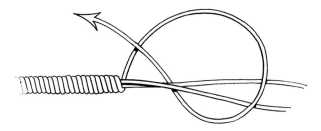

8. Take the loop off one of your feet and both of your knees. It should still be under tension from the hand holding the twisted section and the strands of the loop will be lying fairly close together.

Following on from the half hitch that locked the Bimini, we now make a five-turn hitch around both strands of the double loop.

Take the tag end towards your foot, then over and around both strands of the double five times as you wrap it back towards the knot – all inside the same hitch. When finished you have one half hitch which has five turns around both strands of the double loop. Don't pull it tight just yet.

Now, lay the tag end beside the bottom of the Bimini twist and hold it tight between the thumb and index finger of one hand. With the other hand we are going to bind the loose five-turn hitch over itself so the tag end is buried in its centre. To do this we start folding the knot end of the hitch's loop tightly and closely around the two strands of the double and the tag end strand, which will all be lying parallel. Bind the loop in the opposite direction to the spirals of the five-turn hitch. As each bind goes into place, one of the spirals should disappear. Five turns and you're done.

All the spirals should now have been converted to tight binds hard up against the bottom of the Bimini twist. Now, while holding it all tight between the pinched fingers of one hand, pull the tag end and the remaining loose loop should disappear. It's finished.

When working with GSP lines it's worth coating the tie-off area with a dab of Superglue or Aquaseal as this seals the tag end and stops it from unravelling.

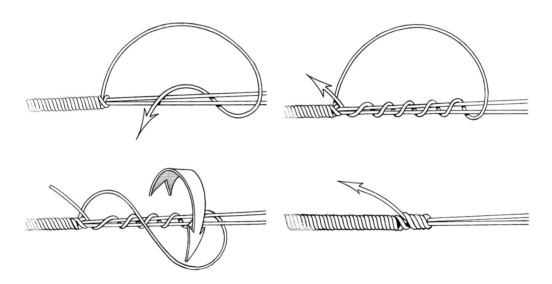

Albright knot

The Albright is a popular knot for connecting heavy leaders to much lighter main lines. One advantage is its slim diameter. Whereas most knots end up with three layers of the thick line within the knot, an Albright has only two parallel strands.

Like most knots it will slightly weaken the line, so to maintain maximum strength we tie it with two strands of the lighter line – after first tying a double such as a Bimini twist. The Albright can also be used to tie a nylon leader directly to the loop of a wire trace made of single-strand wire.

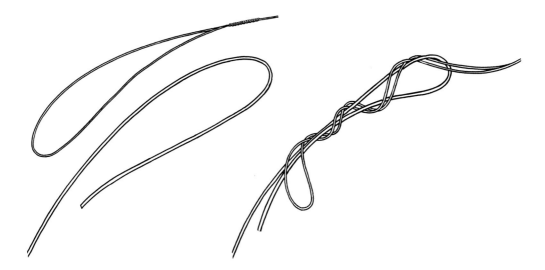

1. The lighter line can be bent over to give a doubled strand with which to tie the knot or for greater strength; a Bimini twist double is tied first. The heavier leader is folded back to form an open loop around 15 centimetres long.

2. Thread the double in the lighter line through the loop in the leader and wind it down and around both strands of the leader.

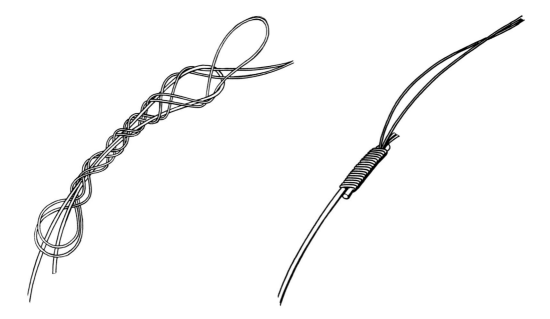

3. Complete several wraps down – four will do for mono but more are required for gel-spun lines – then continue to wrap the lighter line back up and over the down-wraps. Now thread it back through the loop in the leader so that it lies alongside the doubled strand at the point of entry.

4. Lubricate the knot by licking it, then tension it carefully, initially with pressure on all strands, then release the tag ends and tension the double strands firmly against the leader. All the wraps must pack down tightly against the end of the leader loop.

The tag end of the leader can be trimmed very close as it will not pull through. The tag ends of the double can also be trimmed very closely as long as the knot has been tightly snugged-up. As an extra precaution against it bumping loose while casting, it's a good idea to dab a drop of Superglue or Aquaseal on the tag ends.

Albright variation

This version of the Albright knot is for joining a gel-spun main line, in which a double or end loop has been secured, to a heavier nylon monofilament leader. The Rizzuto finish is intended to facilitate a smoother passage through the rod guides.

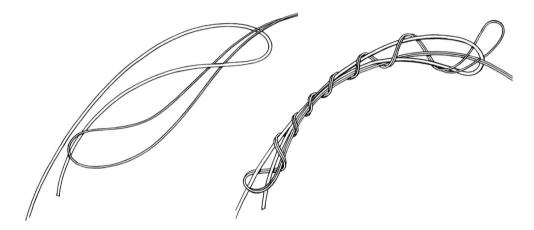

1. Double over the end of your monofilament leader and pass the loop of the gel-spun double through.

2. Pull the tag end of the double out 20 centimetres or so and then hold it in a pinch with the same fingers that are holding the nylon loop. Then wrap the double back over itself towards the end of the nylon loop where it entered. Make at least seven wraps to be secure. Poke the tag end through the nylon loop so that it emerges on the *opposite* side to which it entered.

Lightly pull the gel-spun wraps back along the mono to spread them out, then snug the knot down very firmly by pulling alternately on both sides of the doubled gel-spun. Be careful not to pull a gel-spun loop off the front of the nylon.

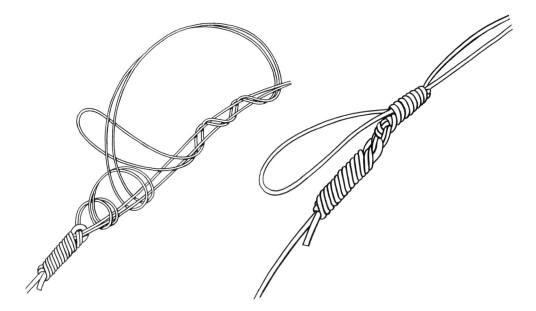

3. Having closed the Albright, half hitch the gel-spun loop tightly a couple of times around the standing part of the double. Finish off with a Rizzuto finish as described in Step 8 for the Bimini twist double on pages 283–4.

4. Close the Rizzuto finish and trim the tag ends. Then add a dab of Superglue or Aquaseal to the tag ends and you're ready to fish.

Slim beauty

The slim beauty is a good alternative to the Albright as a way of joining a heavy monofilament leader to a lighter nylon main line. It is neat, strong and travels well through the guides when casting.

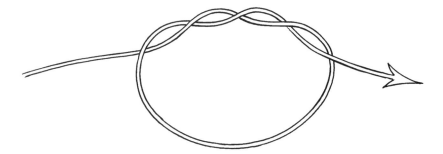

1. Tie a double overhand knot in the heavier line.

2. Pull the loop down until it rolls into a figure-eight shape. (If necessary you can then push the tag ends in the opposite way to open up the figure eight a little.)

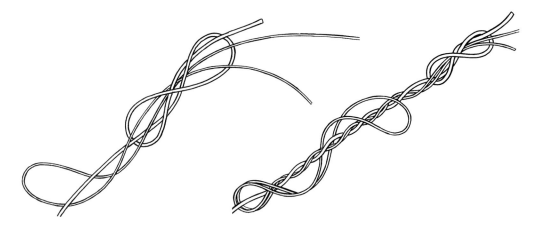

3. The knot is made with two strands of the lighter line. This can be either the end of a pre-tied double or otherwise fold over 30 centimetres at the end of a single line. Thread the double strand of the lighter line through the figure eight. Enter alongside the tag of the heavy line and exit beside the main strand of the heavy line.

4. Now wrap the loop of lighter line around the heavy line four times. Hold in place with a pinch and then wrap another four times back over the top of the previous four.

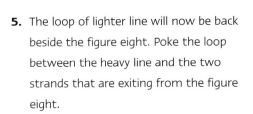

5. The loop of lighter line will now be back beside the figure eight. Poke the loop between the heavy line and the two strands that are exiting from the figure eight.

6. Lick the knot to lubricate it then begin to tighten it. Firstly, snug up the overhand knot in the heavy line. Then pull gently but firmly on both pairs of strands in the lighter line until it butts up and beds down tightly against the figure eight. Fully tighten the knot in the heavy line and then trim all tag ends.

Gel-spun leader knot

This is a neat way of joining a monofilament leader to a gel-spun line that has already had a short Bimini twist double tied on the end of it.

As long as you use as many turns as can be snugged up in the thickness of mono being used, the knot will give good strength.

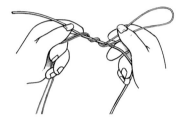

1. Overlap the two ends to be joined then wrap the end of the gel-spun double around the monofilament leader away from its tag end. How many times you do this will depend on the relative diameters of the two lines.

When the leader is of a similar diameter to the GSP line, this would be 20 turns or more. When the leader is much thicker than the GSP line, it may mean 10 turns or less. (If too many turns are made, the knot will not be able to be snugged up tight.)

2. Having completed the wraps, thread the tag end of the mono leader through the end loop in the gel-spun and hold it in place.

Be careful to ensure that the strands of the double are even, otherwise all the strain will be taken by one strand of the double when the knot is finished and this will reduce the knot strength.

3. Holding the leader and its tag end in one hand, use the middle finger to guide the end loop of the double down to the mono as it pulls up.

Tighten the knot by pulling on the GSP line with the other hand. (If you can hold the GSP line above the Bimini knot, the double is more likely to remain even as you pull the knot closed.)

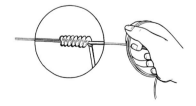

4. As you pull on the gel-spun line, the monofilament will start to spiral around and will eventually end up in a tight barrel around itself and the gel-spun. Simply trim the tag end and it's finished.

Twisted leader knot

This knot is useful for joining a light nylon or fluorocarbon leader to a single strand of gel-spun, such as when fishing for very shy species with light tackle. This knot looks elaborate and complicated but it's really quite easy and it's rare to find a knot like this that gives a strong connection between GSP and a mono leader without first having to tie a double.

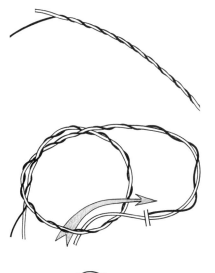

1. Wind the gel-spun line (black) 20 times around one end of the monofilament leader.
2. Form an overhand knot in the twisted lines and pull the entire monofilament leader through.
3. Pull the entire leader through the same overhand knot again so another wrap is added.
4. Do this two more times so four wraps in total are made through the same overhand knot.
5. Then, lick to lubricate and with firm but gentle pressure on all four strands, close the knot. Should any stray loops appear, pull on the gel-spun line to close them.
6. Trim the tags and then the finished knot should look something like this.

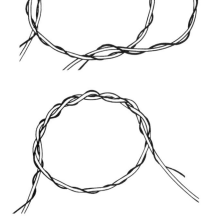

Wind-on leader

A wind-on leader is simply a leader that is connected to the main line in such a way that it can be wound through the guides and onto the reel (or cast off it). They can be made using one of the various knots that join line to leaders, but there is another neater method gaining popularity. Anglers using exceptionally heavy leaders or reels with small level-winds or tip runners will find advantages in the bound-on loop shown here.

This method is used because there is only a single strand of the heavier line in the connection so it is often less than half as thick as any knot. This allows thick nylon as strong as several hundred kilograms to be wound through game rod guides and leaders of 30 kilograms or more to pass easily through baitcaster level-winds. These instructions describe how to make a light to medium tackle leader that can be joined to the main line by looping the top of the leader and the end of a double line inside one another. These leaders are made up at home before fishing and kept ready in small ziplock bags for quick connection when required.

The method uses a length (up to 60 centimetres for heavy leaders) of hollow Dacron or Gudebrod braided nylon (available from tackle shops), loop-spliced at one end and then sleeved over the leader. You will also need:

- A length (up to 1 metre) of fine single-strand wire, doubled over to form a loop-splicing pull-through needle, the ends of which are splayed out to prevent them from accidentally disappearing up the sleeve.
- A length of monofilament for your leader, which should be rated at twice the breaking strain of the Dacron sleeve or more. The braided sleeve must fit snugly over the nylon leader.
- A length of thread suitable for the final binding. This may be waxed thread like dental floss, gel-spun line, or even fine monofilament. (A fly-tiers thread bobbin makes this easy.)
- A rubber band.
- A large paper clip or clothes peg.
- A short piece of dowel or a large diameter pen to act as a loop gauge.
- A pliable, rubber-based sealant, like Pliobond or Aquaseal.
- Superglue (the tiny pots with a brush are excellent).
- Some fine sandpaper to round off the end of the nylon leader.
- A set of nail clippers to trim the final binding.

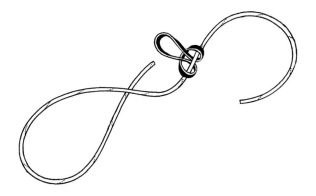

1. Mark the sleeve at one-third of its length with your rubber band.

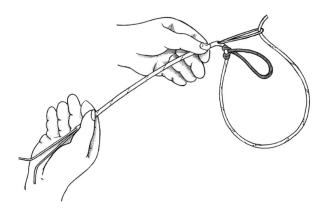

2. Thread the compressed wire loop up the long end of the Dacron. Push it out through the weave just before the rubber band, and then catch the very tip of the short end of the Dacron in the bend of the wire loop.

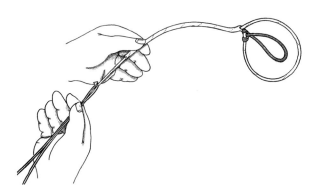

3. Withdraw the wire 'pull-through' needle and with it the short end of the Dacron. As you pull the short end all the way through you will bunch up the longer, outer length of Dacron.

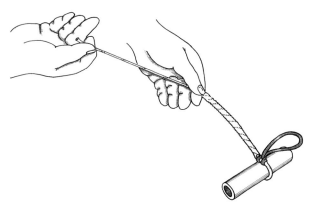

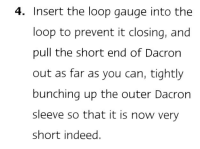

4. Insert the loop gauge into the loop to prevent it closing, and pull the short end of Dacron out as far as you can, tightly bunching up the outer Dacron sleeve so that it is now very short indeed.

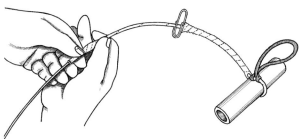

5. Secure the bunched outer sleeve by placing a large paperclip or clothes peg on the inner sleeve to hold the bunched outer sleeve back. Then, work the mono leader – the end of which should be rounded off with fine sandpaper – up inside the inner sleeve.

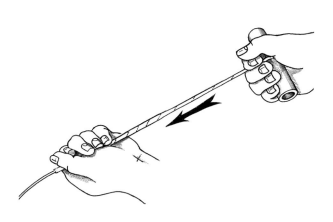

6. Having worked the mono leader right up the inner sleeve to where the outer sleeve is tightly bunched over it, remove your clip and push the outer sleeve all the way back over the inner sleeve and leader. (Now, while you will not be able to pull the leader out of the sleeve, pushing the sleeve back up the leader will dislodge it. This eventuality is prevented by securing the end of the Dacron sleeve to the leader with a sealed binding.)

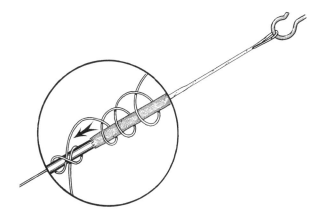

7. Having stretched the leader out fairly tight by whatever means you have available, begin your final binding with a clove hitch on the mono, just short of the Dacron sleeve. (Several additional wraps within the clove hitch may be required to prevent it sliding.) This is followed by a binding or series of half hitches up and onto the Dacron sleeve. Bind over as many of the frayed ends of the Dacron as possible. Any remaining protruding strands of the Dacron may be snipped off later with your nail clippers.

    The finish to this whipping is achieved by five binds over a small pull-through loop. The tag of the binding thread is then poked through this pull-through loop and pulled back under these last wraps.

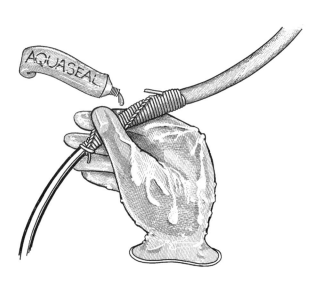

8. For extra security you can put a short dab of Superglue at the end of the outer Dacron sleeve. Then, after trimming, you may like to give the Dacron/mono section a very thin penetrating coat of flexible sealant like Aquaseal (preferably with the aid of a rubber glove to protect your hand).

Non-slip mono loop

Also known as lefty's loop, this is a particularly strong loop knot for attaching a lure to a nylon or fluorocarbon leader. It allows the size of the loop to be adjusted before it is tightened and this is especially handy as a small loop is less visible and maintains a round shape which gives more freedom to the lure.

1. Form an overhand knot in the leader, pass the tag through the towing eye of the lure, then back through the overhand loop.

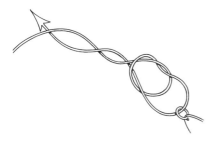

2. Pull up on the main strand to partially reduce the size of the overhand knot. Then gently pull on the tag end, sliding the overhand knot towards the lure eye. This lets you adjust the size of the loop. Now wrap the tag end around the main line.

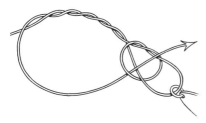

3. Make three wraps in total and then pass the tag back through the overhand knot. Hold the overhand knot at the distance you want the finished loop to form and then pull on the main strand until the overhand knot tightens.

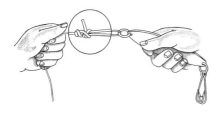

4. Lubricate the knot with a lick and then tighten with pressure on the tag end until the wraps bed down against the overhand knot. Now hold the main strand in one hand and the lure in the other and pull apart to snug the knot up tightly. Trim the tag and you're done.

Perfection loop

The perfection loop is a popular knot for attaching lures with a rigid tow-point onto heavy nylon leaders. Like some other loop knots it is not particularly strong so it is most useful where a leader is needed for abrasion resistance and not pulling strength.

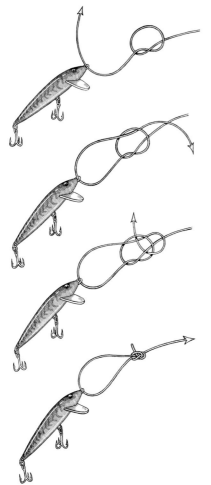

1. Tie an overhand knot in the leader and then thread the tag end through the tow-point of the lure.

2. Thread the tag end back through the overhand knot and then over the standing part of the leader.

3. Pass the tag under the front leg of the overhand knot and then out between the strands on the far side of the overhand knot (as shown in illustration 3).

4. Before tightening the knot, snug the overhand knot down a little by pulling gently on the standing line. Then reduce the size of the loop by feeding the tag end side of the loop back through the overhand knot and then pulling on the tag. When the size is right, secure the knot by pulling firmly on the standing part and tag end of the leader.

Duncan's loop

This loop knot is basically a reversed uni knot. It's easy to tie in leaders over 15 kilograms in strength and maintains good knot strength, although reducing it to an effective size will leave the front portion of the leader a little kinked.

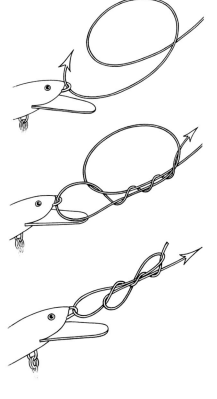

1. Make a small loop in the end of the leader and then thread the tag end through the tow-point of the lure.

2. Keeping as close to the lure as you can, now pass the tag through the loop three or four times to make three barrel wraps around both parallel strands. (The tag will emerge from the loop at the opposite end to the lure.)

3. Snug the knot up by gently pulling on the standing part of the leader, but don't pull it completely tight. Lick the knot to lubricate it and then pull down on the top of the knot with one hand while holding the main strand with the other. This should enable you to slide the loop down to the desired size before it tightens up. Then pull on the tag and main strand firmly to fully tighten the knot.

4. Trim the tag and the attachment is complete.

Rigging with single-strand wire – haywire twist with barrel roll finish

These procedures can be used to connect single-strand wire to a lure or hook, a ring or swivel, or simply to make a loop. They can be done either left-handed or right-handed using these instructions.

1. Make a large loop in the end of the springy wire. Start with the tag end about 30 centimetres long. Then reduce the size of the loop to the desired final size. You do this by lightly holding the crossed-over wires with the tips of the thumb and index finger of one hand while compressing the egg-shaped loop smaller with the other hand.

   The hand doing the compressing will have its thumb pressing on one side of the loop, the index finger pressing on the other side of the loop and the side of the first joint of its middle finger pressing against the end of the loop. As they compress the loop smaller, allow both ends of the wire to slide against the pinched fingertips of the other hand. Be careful to maintain a rounded egg-shaped loop. Don't squeeze the sides and kink it at the top. When the loop is small enough (say 6 x 4 millimetres) the twisting begins.

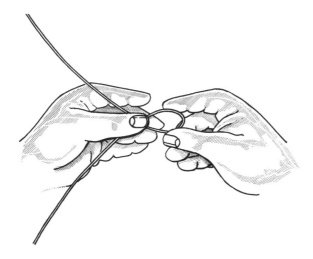

2. Before you can start the barrel roll it is essential that you understand what you must do. To make a strong connection that will not slip, kink and break, the two strands must spiral around each other evenly, each at 45 degrees off the imaginary centreline. What will happen if you are not careful is that one strand will become straight and the other will be wrapped at 90 degrees around it. This is not strong and will allow the wire to slip under pressure, kink and break if there are not enough of the proper barrel rolls to hold it.

The secret to a good barrel roll is holding the wire in a way that makes the wires spiral around each other while maintaining their 45-degree angles from the centre. To do this, the hand holding the crossed-over wire strands becomes a 'push rod' that doesn't really hold the wires – it just keeps the two wires spread and maintains the angle between them. The crossover in the two strands sits hard up against the pinched tips of the thumb and index finger. The tips of these fingers are slightly offset as the top of the thumb-tip is pushing against the upper strand of wire, while the top of the index fingertip is pushing against the lower strand.

To maintain the angle, the top strand will run over the index finger, between the knuckle and the middle joint. The other strand runs down over the tips of the bottom three fingers.

Imagine a line running through the centre of the loop and then keep the two strands at 45 degrees off this line. This sounds quite simple, but to maintain it while twisting the wires together can take some practice. Get this bit mastered and the rest is easy!

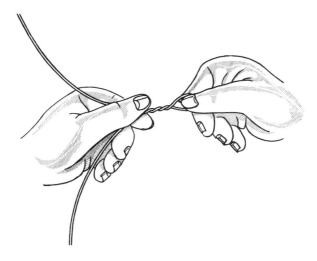

3. Making the twist

Hold the loop firmly and stationary. If you have trouble holding the wires steady you can grasp the loop tightly with a pair of pliers, but as they can scratch and damage the wire it is always best to use bare fingers if you are able. If using bare fingers, squeeze the tips of your thumb and index fingers together through the loop.

Then, rotate the hand holding the wire strands a quarter turn (90 degrees). The twist has begun! Re-position the hand and then do another quarter or full half-turn. Then another and another and another. At all times watch the angles to make sure the strands are spiralling around each other equally. Remember, the hand and fingers doing the twisting are never really holding the wire firmly, they are merely pushing up against the crossed strands and guiding them around.

(As the twist becomes longer you may find it necessary to let go of the loop and hold the twisted section tightly with pliers while you continue with the twists.) When you have six tight, even spirals you're ready for the barrel rolls to finish it off. Now the thing you've been battling to prevent, you intentionally allow to occur!

Make another twist with the wire strands but allow the main strand to straighten and the tag end to wrap around it at 90 degrees. This is achieved by rotating the 'twisting' hand at a slightly different angle. Once again, the squeezed finger tips will guide the wire strands in the direction you want them to go.

Continue wrapping the tag end around until you have five tightly compacted barrel rolls over the straight main wire.

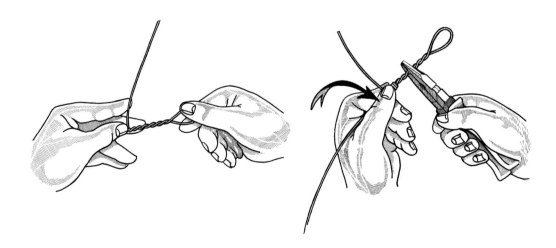

4. The final step is to remove the tag end. If you trim this with cutters there will always be just enough of a stub sticking out to prick you or rip your skin while handling your fish. A much neater way is to use this wire's susceptibility to breaking when kinked to intentionally create a kink and break the tag end off flush, right up against the last barrel roll.

To do this we make a right-angle bend in the tag about 2 centimetres from the barrel rolls. This bent tag gives you a little more grip on the wire for the next step.

Hold the loop in your 'holding' hand with the loop pointing towards you and resting on the tips of the middle and third fingers. The index fingertip rests in the right angle between the tag end and the main strand of wire. Your thumb tip is pushing against the barrel rolls.

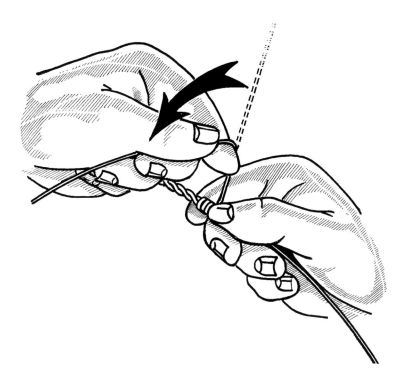

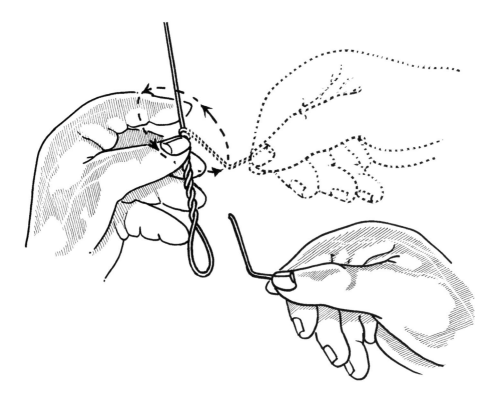

Now that you have the wire loop held securely with one hand, with your other hand grasp the bent area of the tag and bend it down flat against the twists and eye. You are trying to cause an acute kink right where the tag leaves the last barrel roll. If it doesn't break at first, bend the tag up, parallel against the main wire and then bend it down again. If you make sure all the bending is done at only one point, right against the barrel rolls, the wire is sure to break off flush and leave absolutely no stub at all.

Now, if there is a slight curve or dog-leg in your twists you can gently bend it straight. Otherwise, you're finished.

Conclusion

We had to draw a line somewhere and say, 'That's it. That's the book.' In truth, we might have written as much again and still had more to say. This is a subject with its beginnings way before the authors' time and a fluid developing nature that ensures constant change and improvement. That said, the essentials of the business remain constant. By way of signing off, a summary follows of the basics for all lure selection and presentation in any environment.

Strike zone

At the top of the list is a point that we have emphasised throughout the book. Successful lure fishing hinges on your ability to define the strike zone and choose a lure and presentation that will put a suitable lure in the critical strike zone for the maximum amount of time.

The strike zone will vary according to the terrain, the time of day and the nature of the fish itself. You stand more chance of catching a marlin on or near the surface than you do on the bottom in deep water; and in the middle of the day a lure that will dive deep and work slowly will be the best approach to a Murray cod stationed under a log.

Colour

There is no one magic colour. In clear water subtlety is often the message, while in dirty water you might have to use colour and sound to be noticed. The fish has to know the lure is there for you to have any chance of getting a take. Depending on the conditions, different colours will be noticed from the greatest distance. Flash is also a major drawcard for many situations. Even adding a prominent eye can help to get your lure noticed and eaten.

A recent national survey of lure fishermen revealed some interesting facts. They were asked to nominate their favourite species, their favourite lures and their favourite colour. Although some lures turned up more often than others, in every category, every species and every type of environment they nominated hundreds of different makes and styles of lures. The lure that got the most votes would be only a few votes ahead of the next most popular and so on, so there was no one killer lure that everyone should be fishing with. When it came to colours, they offered every colour and every combination the human mind could conceive of. Even so, gold and pink stood out – as has always been the case – as did colours in the darker range: black, purple and so on.

Action

Different species have different triggers that excite them to strike. It can be the feel of the swimming action, the shape and size, surface splashing or simply the speed of something trying desperately to get away. Some fish feed visually, some by sensing motion or smell.

Each lure will have a different motion or action in the water, even those that look similar. This action can signify a prey species, an injury, vulnerability or fright. Even then, speed will alter it. This is often critical, as many fish will evaluate a target in detail by the feel of its motion through their lateral line. The lures that look right *and* give the right message with their action are the ones that catch the most fish.

Smell

The best lure you could choose for a fish and a particular situation might be rendered useless if you peel an orange or have sweaty hands before you tie the lure on, or perhaps fiddle with a fuel tank and get the smell of petrol on your hands. Some species are much more sensitive to smell than others and will be able to smell an offending scent long after your nose has failed to detect it.

Leader

Speaking of tying lures on, a poor connection between you and the lure may render the world's most effective lure invalid. Use brightly coloured main lines by all means if that suits you, but if you are going to use a high-visibility line for sensitive fish, you have to use a low-visibility leader to the lure and that leader might need to be a very long one.

Casting

Once you have your lure selection right, the critical element determining success or failure often comes down to the number of casts the angler makes. The important stuff always comes down to numbers. Twenty per cent more time in the strike zone increases your chance of catching a fish by 20 per cent – it's as simple as that. A 10 per cent increase in casting range covers at least 10 per cent more water. Make 10 per cent more casts than someone else in the boat and you stand a 10 per cent better chance of hooking a fish.

When you consider the extraordinary range of makes, sizes and colours offered as effective lures, the message becomes clear that fish inhabit a wide range of environments, and within those environments they exhibit an equally wide range of behaviours and preferences that might change from day to day, even hour to hour. This inevitably leads us to conclude that you need to acquire a lure collection based on models that will give you the best and longest presentation in the strike zone at a speed that suits the particular predator; a variety of colours allowing you to exploit variations in light and water conditions; and variation in action, size and general profile to match natural food prevailing in the area at the time.

There's a lot you can say about fishing with lures and the learning never stops. The good part is that almost everything about lure fishing is fun. Buying lures is fun. Sorting out your tackle collection is fun. Selecting a lure you think will do the job and getting a hit on that lure is great fun. Making a perfect cast to cover is a real blast.

Fish that jump into the boat chasing a lure to the top can create tremendous excitement. A lively mackerel with razor-sharp teeth has set us to fancy dancing, and a flathead jumping into the boat has stunned us. Nothing will ever cause the adrenaline to pump like the bulging water behind a surface popper as something big closes in on the target, and surface strikes from just about any fish will turn your legs to jelly. A hundred casts into featureless deep water can lull you into a trance, but when the whole thing comes to a jarring halt and line begins to scream off the reel you move into orbit – the feeling really is that good.

If you'd like to let us know any of your interests (such as vintage lure collecting) or questions, log on at www.lureinsight.com and we'll keep you posted with developments. If you have half as much fun as we do fishing with lures, you will be one happy and lucky angler.

Glossary

assist hook Japanese term for a free-swinging hook dangling from the top of a deep-water metal jig. This is often used instead of the traditional treble hook at the tail.

baitcaster A small overhead reel, usually with a level wind, designed for casting distance and accuracy. Only top quality, small versions are able to easily cast less than 7 grams. A baitcaster rod is designed to be used with the guides on top of the rod and usually features a trigger grip for the index finger.

berley Finely chopped animal or vegetable matter used to attract and stimulate fish to feed.

bib A flat projection at the front of a lure, set at an angle, that causes the lure to dive and 'swim' when pulled through the water.

bloop Refers to the action and sound of a chugger popper being pulled to make it 'pop'.

blooper An alternate name for a chugger popper.

boil Usually refers to an up-welling of water behind a lure from a near miss or close inspection by a fish. It can also refer to an up-welling due to water movement over a submerged object like a rock in current.

bommie A rock or small reef in the ocean, usually just submerged. When in current or swell it disturbs the surface or causes waves to break.

boof Describes the sound made by some fish species (like barramundi) when they strike their prey. They suck water into their mouths with such a violent implosion that it can be heard, especially when at the surface.

braid The braided versions of gel-spun polyethylene fishing lines.

breathing The act of a skirted trolling lure coming to the surface, breaking through and then diving with a new trail of bubbles.

bulging A retrieve style used with bladed spinners and spinnerbaits where the lure is retrieved at a constant pace right at the surface, so it bulges the water above it.

bullet weight A conical, usually free-running sinker often used up against the head of soft plastics or above a swivel in front of the lure. Also called a worm weight.

burn and kill A retrieve style usually associated with spinnerbaits where the lure is given a fast retrieve spaced with pauses.

buzz bait A version of a spinnerbait with a propeller blade that raises it to the surface where it causes a splashing surface commotion while retrieved.

buzzing A retrieve style for spinnerbaits or buzzbaits where they are retrieved along the surface to cause a commotion and splash.

Carolina rig A rig for soft plastics where the lure is rigged on a leader of around 30 centimetres to 1.5 metres behind a swivel and sliding sinker. A heavy sinker gives good bottom contact in deep water while the lure drifts around behind on its leader. A bead or two is often used between the sinker and swivel to make sound when jerked.

centre-rigger A vertical centre pole used with a release clip to hold the towing angle up high when trolling skirted lures long distances behind the boat.

counter-shading The colouring of a fish – from dark on its back, blending through side patterning or reflective silver to a light-coloured or silver belly. Designed to make the fish blend into the background and become invisible from whatever angle it is viewed.

cover Bottom structure or vegetation that a fish can use to hide or ambush from.

crankbait An American term for a bibbed lure.

curly tail A curled, flat tail shape used on soft plastics. It folds out like a twisted ribbon and gives a swimming action when moved through the water.

Cyber-flexxx A patented gel-polymer marketed under different brand names but made by Z-Man Fishing Products USA. Used to make soft plastic lures that are far more durable and buoyant than the more common plastisol versions.

daisy-chain A group of lures (often plastic squid or fish) run together in line or on separate droppers to give the impression of a school.

devon A style of freshwater spinning lure popular in past years (and not covered in this book). It consists of a weighted tube body with an angled blade on either side at the head end to make it spin like a propeller.

downrigger A device consisting of a spool of strong line, a boom, a weight and a release clip. Downriggers are used to take lures or baits down to any desired depth.

downrigger slider rig A secondary line and lure attached to a line already set in a downrigger. It is attached via a free-running snap clip around the fishing line and settles in the belly between the rod tip and release clip.

downrigger stacker clip A double-release clip that attaches to a downrigger cable anywhere between the boat and lead weight. It allows more than one outfit to be fished off the one downrigger.

drop shot A Japanese rig for deeper water fishing soft plastics. It consists of a weight attached to the end of the line and a hook or hooks attached 30 centimetres or more above that. The lure body is then hooked through the nose and jigged at the appropriate depth.

Dyneema The registered trademark of DSM High Performance Fibres and Toyobo Company, Japan, for their (Asian-produced) gel-spun polyethylene – as used to make fishing lines.

feather jig A trolling lure consisting of a moulded, conical head with a tail of feathers bound to the back end.

flat line A gamefishing term describing a lure trolled straight from the rod tip without the use of an outrigger.

flipping An American term for accurately placing a lure in heavy cover by dropping it from the end of a long rod or gently casting it under-handed.

fluorocarbon A line made of polyvinylidene fluoride (PVDF) that is often less visible underwater than nylon, due to its refractive index.

gel-spun A term used to describe the various types of line made of gel-spun polyethylene. See also Dyneema; Spectra.

grub A term used to describe many plump-bodied soft plastics.

GSP line A line made from gel-spun polyethylene fibres.

GT A common abbreviation of Giant Trevally.

hard-body A lure with a solid body, typically of timber, polyurethane or hollow, hard plastic.

holographic A three-dimensional effect created by a special photographic technique.

iron An American term for a metal lure used in saltwater for casting or jigging.

jerkbait A lure designed to be used by jerking it with the rod tip to imitate a crippled fish. Typically a soft plastic or bibbed lure with little or no action of its own. Also known as a stickbait.

jerk minnow A bibbed minnow lure designed to be fished by jerking it in the strike zone. An alternate name for a jerkbait or stickbait.

jig This should specifically refer to lures that are fished with a jigging action, such as lead-head jigs, deep-water metal jigs, some soft plastics, squid jigs and sabiki jigs, but some anglers confusingly refer to almost any lure as a jig.

jigging A usually vertical lure-retrieve technique involving repetitive hopping or a rip-pause-rip or rip-sink-rip routine. The lure path would look something like a jagged lightning bolt.

jig head A hook with a weighted head (usually made of lead) moulded to it. The hook normally has a right-angle bend near the eye so the moulded-on head doesn't move and so the line is pulling from the top of the head.

jig-n-pig An American term for a lead-head jig with a flap of pork rind attached to the hook for added attraction.

jigworm An American term for a soft plastic on a jig head.

lateral line A sensory organ that detects low-frequency vibrations and water movement. Indicated by the line (row of pores) along the upper flank on both sides of a fish.

leader A length of nylon, fluorocarbon or wire attached to the end of a line to give extra handling strength and protection against abrasion and teeth. Also known as a trace.

lipless crankbait An American term for a bibless minnow.

lure A man-made device, sometimes constructed from natural materials and usually representing a food item that induces a fish to eat or at least bite it.

lux the scientific unit of measurement for illumination.

minnow The name of a slender species of fish. It is also used to refer to some (slender) bibbed and 'bibless' lures that imitate fish.

mono An abbreviation of monofilament, meaning one strand. Usually refers to nylon fishing lines.

nervous water A choppy or ruffled surface caused by a fish (or school) swimming just underneath.

outriggers Long poles attached to the sides of a boat. Used with release clips to temporarily separate trolled lines and hold them at a high angle to the water.

paddler An alternate name for a waddler. A type of surface lure.

paddle tail A flattened tail shape used in soft plastic lures. Similar in shape to the end of a canoe paddle. The term is often confused with and used to mean a T tail. See T tail.

paravane A diving device attached to a line to take the lure deeper.

paternoster A rig involving short branch lines tied to the main line.

P E line A Japanese term for a gel-spun polyethylene line.

pH The hydrogen ion content or the acidity of the water. Most fish prefer a neutral pH level (7 on the pH scale).

pirk A European term for a slender metal jigging lure.

plastisol A soft polyvinyl chloride thermoplastic. The mouldable material from which most soft plastic lures are made.

plug A non-specific American term for a solid- (hard-) bodied lure with a hook or hooks attached.

release clip A peg or device that holds a line until a set strain is reached.

reverse counter shading Colouring a lure light on top and dark on the bottom so that it stands out against its background and is easily seen by a fish. See also counter-shading.

selective harvest Deciding to release or harvest fish to eat based on species, size and relative abundance.

shad A species of slim but deep-bodied fish. Also a term used to describe lures of a similar shape, especially soft plastics.

shock leader A leader added to take the strain of casting. It is usually long enough to make a couple of turns around the reel's spool when the lure is near the rod's tip.

short strike When a fish strikes short of the lure.

side-surface planer A paravane-type board designed to stay on the surface but plane out at a strong angle to the side of the boat. It is towed on a strong line and can hold and separate fishing lines via an attached release clip until a fish strikes.

sight casting Casting to fish that can be seen.

skirt A section or component of some lures consisting of a tassel of flexible strands (usually finely shredded plastic).

slow rolling A retrieve technique (commonly associated with spinnerbaits) involving a slow, steady and deep retrieve bumping over or through any bottom obstacles.

smoke trail The stream of fine bubbles following a skirted trolling lure.

snag An obstacle on the bottom such as a rock or log that a line or lure can become caught-up on.

snap Various types of clips (with or without swivels) used to attach a lure to a line.

They can improve the movement of some lures and make changes quicker and easier.

soft plastic A type of lure or lure body made from moulded soft plastic, usually plastisol. Soft plastics come in a wide variety of shapes, colours, flavours and scents ranging from the realistic to the fantastical.

Spectra The registered trademark of the American company Honeywell (previously Allied Signal), which licenses the American rights to produce gel-spun polyethylene fibres from the inventors, DSM High Performance Fibres, Holland. (Honeywell then supplies the American manufacturers of GSP lines.)

spinner Originally referred to a lure that spins when retrieved but more commonly now refers to all lures that are cast and retrieved.

spinning The act of casting and retrieving a lure at a pace that gives it an action attractive to fish.

spinning reel Most types of reels can cast and retrieve a lure but this term is used specifically to describe a threadline reel.

spook To scare a fish.

spreader bar A bar or device to which the line is attached in the centre. From either end of the bar a leader with often multiple imitation or real fish or squid is run to form the impression of a school. These are used either with the final, straggling lure having the only hook or as a hookless teaser.

stickbait A lure designed to be used by jerking it with the rod tip to imitate a crippled fish. Typically a soft plastic or bibbed lure with little or no action of its own. Also known as a jerkbait.

stinger hook A secondary hook added to cover the tail end of a lure.

strike The act of a fish biting a lure (or bait).

strike zone The area within which a strike from a fish is likely. This will depend on how far it can clearly detect a lure and how far it is willing to travel to get to it.

structure Bottom formations or objects likely to shelter or influence the location of fish around them.

swirl An eddy around your lure where an attacking fish missed or rejected your offering.

tag line A secondary line with a release mechanism, attached to the top of an outrigger or centre-rigger pole. It allows spread lures to be released with a minimum of drop-back slack.

Texas rig An American term for a soft plastic rig. An unweighted hook is inserted into the body of the soft plastic lure, often in a way to make it 'weedless'. A sliding weight runs on the line ahead of it.

thermocline The transition layer of temperature change between warm surface water and cold, deep water.

thumper tail An alternate American term for a T tail in soft plastics.

topwater lure An alternate American term for a surface lure.

tow-point The loop, ring or entrance to a lure where the line joins it. This becomes the point to which the towing force is directed.

tight action Short, rapid side-to-side movement in a lure.

trace An alternate term for a leader. Usually applied to the use of wire.

trailer hook A secondary hook added to the hook of a spinnerbait. Also called a stinger hook.

transducer A device linked to an echo sounder that changes electrical pulses into sound pulses, and vice versa.

trolling The act of towing a lure (or bait) behind a boat to give it action while searching for a fish.

trolling sinker A lead weight added to a line to take a trolled lure deeper. Often paravane shaped for additional depth.

T tail An action tail shape used in soft plastic lures. The tail ends in a flattened wedge section similar to a 'T' lying horizontally.

tube A style of soft plastic lure with a hollow, conical head followed by a fine-stranded tail section.

twitch A short jerk.

walk-the-dog An American term for a technique with an otherwise actionless surface lure. The floating lure is tweaked first one way and then the other to make it zigzag its way over the surface.

weedless Describes a way of rigging a hook point so that it is shielded from catching on weeds and snags.

wide action Wide, slow, side-to-side movement in a lure.

worm Often used to mean a soft plastic worm, but in America it is used to describe almost any freshwater soft plastic lure body.

worm hook A specially shaped hook with a 'Z' bend near the eye to hold a soft plastic lure body in place.

worm weight A (usually) free-running conically shaped sinker for use with soft plastic lures.

yo-yoing A retrieve technique for vertical jigging where the lure is jerked upwards but then allowed to sink again before repeating.

ACKNOWLEDGMENTS

A special thank you to the following people who helped with valuable information, photography or assistance:

Peter Newell; Steve Kovacs; Bradley Sissins; Dan Trotter; Alan Dolan; Kerstin Fritsches PhD; Professor Justin Marshall; Geoff Wilson; Peter Pakula; Dave Harrigan; Bill Classon; Steve Wilson; Alistair McGlashan; Phil Atkinson; Dave Green; Rod Harrison; Rick Huckstepp; Ross Cusack; Steve Williamson; Perry See Hoe; Chris Baty; Keith Graham; Scott McGowan; Gil Schott.

Thank you to the following companies who assisted with information or product for photography:

Attack Lures; AusSpin lures; Basser Millyard (Pradco); Bills Bugs; Black Pete Marine; Bumpa-Bar Tackle; C Lures; Custom Crafted Lures; Dunphy Sports (Blue Fox/Rapala); Fishing Agencies of Australia (Momoi); Freetime Australia (Storm); Gus Veness Fishing and Sport; Halco; Hex Head Lures; Jarvis Walker (Boone); Javelin Lure Company, J M Gillies; JML Trading (Ecogear); Juro OZ Pro Tackle; Lively Lures; Lowrance Australia; Luhr Jensen – USA; McGoo lures and tackle; Mustad Hooks; Offshore Sports (Gamakatsu/Atomic); Osaka Tackle (Jinkai); OTM Sport Fishing (Kokoda); Pacific Lures; Pakula Tackle; Platypus Lines; Predatek lures; Pro Angler; Pure Fishing Australia (Berkely); Rapala; Reidy's Lures; Rio's Lures; Spanid lures; Sports Imports Australia (River2Sea); Tabata Australia (Nilsmaster); Tackle Master lures; Tacspo; Top End Imports; Top Gun lures.

BIBLIOGRAPHY

BOOKS

Helfman, G. S., Collette, B. B., and Facey, D. E. 1997, *The Diversity of Fishes*, Blackwell Science, USA.

Kageyama, C. J. 1999, *What Fish See*, Frank Amato, USA.

Pepperell, Dr J., 2001, *Fish Tales*, Random House Australia, Sydney.

Ross, D. A., Ph.D. 2000, *The Fisherman's Ocean*, Stackpole Books, USA.

Shelton, Dr P. 1989, 'Science and Artistry in Designing Effective Fly Patterns' in Church, B. with Jardine, C., *Stillwater Trout Tactics*, Crowood Press, UK.

Sosin, M. and Clark, J. 1973, *Through The Fish's Eye*, Harper and Row, USA.

Turner, G. 1989, *Fishing Tackle – A Collector's Guide*, Ward Lock, UK.

MAGAZINES

Fishing World (Aust.)

Freshwater Fishing (Aust.)

In-Fisherman (USA)

Marlin (USA)

Modern Fishing (Aust.)

Sport Fishing (USA)

INDEX

jack barracuda jewfish saratoga wa
rlin kingfish queenfish pike dart c
d trevally scad permit mackerel sa
h salmon saratoga flathead emper
nson fish spearfish amberjack bar
er barramundi herring marlin ki
sh mulloway tuna squid trevally s
er tailor tarpon jewfish salmon sar
ass fingermark samson fish spear
yellowtail snapper barramundi he
l trout tuna spearfish mulloway t
lfish perch rainbow runner tailor
ror bonito bream cobia cod bass fin
cuda jewfish saratoga wahoo yellou
gfish queenfish pike dart coral tr
lly scad permit mackerel sailfish
on saratoga flathead emperor bonit
h spearfish amberjack barracuda j
nundi herring marlin kingfish qu
oway tuna squid trevally scad perm